SPIRITS
& LIQUEURS
COOKBOOK

SPIRITS
& LIQUEURS
COOKBOOK

STUART WALTON AND NORMA MILLER

LORENZ BOOKS
NEW YORK • LONDON • SYDNEY • BATH

This edition published in 1997 by Lorenz Books
27 West 20th Street, New York, NY 10011

Lorenz Books are available for bulk purchase for sales
promotion and for premium use. For details, write or call
the sales director, Lorenz Books, 27 West 20th Street,
New York, NY 10011 (800) 354-9657

Lorenz Books is an imprint of Anness Publishing Limited

ISBN 1-85967- 415-1

Publisher: Joanna Lorenz
Senior Editor: Linda Fraser
Copy Editors: Jane Hughes and Jenni Fleetwood
Indexer: Hilary Bird
Designer: Sara Kidd
Photography: David Jordan
   and Janine Hosegood (cutouts)
Food for Photography and Styling: Judy Williams
Illustrator: Madeleine David

Printed and bound in Spain
D.L.TO: 1172-1997
10 9 8 7 6 5 4 3 2 1

CONTENTS

INTRODUCTION

AT WHAT POINT IN HISTORY alcoholic drinks were first used in cooking, quite apart from fulfilling their time-honored role as intoxicants, is a question that may never be answered. It seems a fair guess, however, to suggest that it was related to the discovery of fermentation.

The ancient Egyptians used fermented grains for making prototype forms of beer. These grains also enabled them to refine the techniques for producing leavened breads. It was found that adding beer sediment—which was still full of live yeast—was the quickest and easiest method of encouraging the start of fermentation in a new batch of dough. This technique was still going strong in the Middle Ages, in England, when dough fermentation was initiated by the addition of froth from the head of the finished beer. Without being fanciful, it could plausibly be argued that this use of beer in bread-making represented the first appearance of alcohol in the culinary arts.

Wine, too, played its part in the foods of classical Greece and, later, Rome, not initially for adding flavor but for its acidity. The action of acids in softening the fibers of tough-textured meats led to the invention of marinating, which is still an indispensable procedure in kitchens all over the world for tenderizing the meat of older animals. As well as making tough meat more supple, marinating would have removed excess salt from meats that had been encrusted with it, or soaked in brine, for preservation. Wine vinegar, its alcohol lost to acetic acid, may have been the first recourse, but wine itself appears in sauce recipes in the historically important late-Roman cookbook of Apicius (third century A.D.). The wine itself was commonly infused with spices

Right: Turning the drying germinated barley in the peat kiln at Glendronach Distillery near Huntly, Banffshire, Scotland.

to mask the rank flavors of oxidation or acetification.

Today, adding wine to a sauce or using beer in casseroles are commonplaces of the domestic kitchen. The drinks featured in this book, however—spirits, liqueurs and fortified wines—are very different from wine or beer. What they have in common is that they all depend to some degree on distillation. Even the fortified wines—sherry, port, Madeira and the others—are made stronger, and in some cases naturally sweeter, than ordinary table wine by the addition of a distillate.

Distillation (from the Latin *destillare*, to drip) is the extraction of higher alcohols from fermented drinks by using the action of heat to vaporize them. Compared to fermentation itself, distillation is a remarkably simple process, largely because it is much more readily subject to external control. Whereas freshly pressed grape juice needs the right ambient temperature to

begin the process of turning into good wine, a spirit can be produced from wine simply by applying heat to it. Alcohol has a lower boiling point than water (about 172°F compared to 212°F), so it vaporizes into steam some time before the water content in the wine starts to boil. When the alcohol-laden steam hits a cool surface, it forms a dripping condensation, and reverts to a liquid of which the alcohol constitutes a much higher proportion than it did in the wine. Boil that liquid again, and the same procedure will yield an even higher alcohol content, and so on.

Much academic debate has been generated in the last 30 years or so as to when and where distillation was first discovered. The Greek philosopher Aristotle, who lived in the fourth century B.C., writes of distillation as a way of purifying seawater to make it drinkable. He comments in passing that the same treatment can be given to wine, which is reduced thereby to a sort of

Right: This bubbling stream provides one of the essential ingredients for whiskey distillation—clear springwater.

"water." He was tantalizingly close to the breakthrough, but the experiment did no more than prove for him that wine is just a form of modified water, and that a liquid can only derive flavor from whatever happens to be mixed with the water that forms its base.

The documented beginnings of systematic and scientifically founded distillation, at least in Europe, come from the celebrated medical school at Salerno around A.D. 1100. Wine itself was held to have a range of medicinal properties (a view that has once again found favor in the 1990s), and the extraction of what was held to be the soul or spirit of the wine, through distillation, is what led to the naming of distillates as "spirits." Alcohol was believed to be the active ingredient in the healing powers of wine. Up to that time, the word "alcohol" was applied as a generic term to any product that had been arrived at by a process of vaporizing and condensation. Its origin from the Arabic word *al-kuhl* refers to the Arab practice of producing a black powder by condensing a vapor of the metal antimony. The powder was then used as eye makeup, which is why eyeliner is still occasionally known as kohl. It was not until the sixteenth century that "alcohol" was used specifically in reference to distilled spirits.

Not only medicine but the ancient practice of alchemy were involved in the European origins of distillation. Alchemy was a respected branch of the physical sciences, and was chiefly concerned with finding a means of transforming ordinary metals into gold. It was wholeheartedly believed that if such a process could be discovered, it might well be possible to apply it to the human body and extract the essential life force from its mortal shell, thus guaranteeing eternal youth. With the realization that alcohol could be repeatedly distilled to a greater and greater purity, it was thought that spirits

could be the Holy Grail.

Although it can't have taken long for the Salerno doctors to ascertain that whatever other remarkable properties distilled spirit had, the power to confer everlasting life wasn't one of them, the medical uses of spirits were to endure for hundreds of years. It was Arnaldo de Villanova, a Catalan physician of the thirteenth century, who first coined the Latin term *aqua vitae*, "water of life," for distilled spirits, indicating that they were still held to be associated with the promotion of vitality and health. (That term lives on in the Scandinavian *aquavit*, the French *eau-de-vie* and other spirit names.)

Undoubtedly, the earliest distillates were of wine, since it had a more salubrious and exalted image than did beer, but grain distillation to produce the first whiskeys and neutral spirits followed later in the Middle Ages.

Many of these prototypes contained herb and spice extracts, or were flavored with fruit, in order to enhance the medicinal properties of the preparation. The additives also conveniently masked what must have been the fairly raw taste and off-putting aroma of the unadulterated liquor. Anybody who has smelled and tasted clear spirit dribbling off the still in a brandy distillery (or, for that matter, has had a brush with illicit Irish poteen or American moonshine) will know how far such untreated spirit is from the welcoming smoothness of five-star cognac or single malt scotch. The infused distillates were the antecedents of many of the traditional aromatic liqueurs and flavored vodkas of today.

That, for centuries, was the official account of the birth of distilled spirits. In 1961, however, an Indian food historian, O. Prakash, argued that there was evidence that distillation of rice and barley beer was practiced in India around 800 B.C. Others have argued that, if so, it probably arrived there from China even earlier. Thus, current theory cautiously credits the Chinese as the discoverers of the art.

It seems unusual that distilled alcohol was not remarked on or even apparently encountered by soldiers engaged in the European invasion of India led by Alexander the Great in 327 B.C. His campaign is reliably credited with having brought back rice itself to Europe, but any rice spirit appears to have been overlooked. Perhaps, if it was drunk at all by the invaders, it was in a diluted form, and was not therefore

Right: An original pot still has become a museum piece at the Jameson Heritage Center, Midleton, County Cork.

Above: The final character, precise color, and the richness and roundness of flavor of both cognac and whiskey are derived from the final maturation period in wood.

Left: Copper pot stills—the original distilla-tion vessel—are widely used in the Cognac region of France as well as by the whiskey distillers of Scotland.

perceived to be any higher in alcohol content than the grape wine with which they were familiar. Then again, it may just have been rejected as smelling or looking unclean. Whatever the explanation, if the Chinese or Indians did

practice distillation as long ago as is claimed, the expertise they had stumbled on centuries before the Europeans remained specific to that part of the world.

The original and still widespread distillation vessel, used in the Cognac region of France, as well as by the whiskey distillers of Scotland, is the pot still. It consists of the only three elements absolutely essential to the process: a pot in which the fermented product (malted grains, wine, cider, etc.) is heated; the alembic, or tube, through which the alcohol vapor driven off is sucked up; and the condenser where the steam is cooled and reliquefied. To obtain a better quality product, spirits are generally distilled at least twice for greater refinement, so the still has to be started up again. Moreover, not all of the condensed vapor is suitable for use in fine liquor. The first and last of it to pass through (known as the heads and tails) are generally discarded for the relatively high level of impurities they contain. The invention of the continuous still in the early nineteenth century, in which the process carries on uninterrupted to a second distillation, made spirit production more economical and easier to control. This is the method used in making France's other classic brandy, Armagnac, and it is now the preferred apparatus for most spirits production worldwide.

Probably the first spirit to be taken seriously as an object of connoisseurship, as distinct from being purely medicinal or just a method of using up surplus grape or grain production, was the brandy of the Cognac region of western France. It was noticed that the superior, mellower spirit produced by the light wines of Cognac responded particularly well to aging in oak casks. The casks were traditionally fashioned out of wood from the Limousin forests of the region. Cask-aged spirits derive every bit of their final character, from the precise shade of tawny in the color to their richness and roundness of flavor, from the maturation period they undergo in wood. They will not continue to develop

in the bottle. The complex classification system in operation today for cognac is based on the length of time the spirit has been aged. It is testimony to a reputation for painstaking quality that dates back to around the end of the 1600s.

Scottish and Irish whiskeys rose to similar prominence soon after. Their differing production processes resulted in quite distinct regional styles, depending on the quantities of peat used in the kilns where the malted grain is dried, on the quality of the springwater used in the mash and, some have claimed, on the shape of the still.

Varieties of whiskey are made all over the world these days, from North America to Japan, but all attempts to replicate the precise taste of great scotch—for all that the ingredients and procedures may be identical—have inexplicably foundered.

At what point a distilled drink stops being a spirit and turns into a liqueur is something of an elusive question. The one constant is that, to be a liqueur, a drink should have some obvious aromatizing element (perhaps even a hundred or more in the case of certain celebrated products). This doesn't mean that all flavored distillates are liqueurs—

flavored vodkas are still vodka—but there are no neutral liqueurs. Some of these products have histories at least as venerable as those of cognac and scotch. The most notable are those produced by the old French monastic orders. Bénédictine, the cognac-based, herb-scented potion that originated at the monastery in Fécamp, in Normandy, can convincingly lay claim to a lineage that rolls back to the beginning of the sixteenth century.

The first and greatest cocktail era, which arrived with the advent of the Jazz Age in the 1920s, rescued a lot of the traditional liqueurs from the niches of obscurity into which popular taste had relegated them. The Benedictine monks may have been a little shocked to hear that their revered creation was being mixed with English gin, American applejack, apricot brandy and maple syrup, shaken to within an inch of its life and then rechristened the Mule's Hind Leg, but at least it was drunk—as were the giggling flappers after knocking back three or four of them.

Gradually, spirits and liqueurs found their way into cooking too, either as enriching ingredients, such as the brandy

Above: The all-important water that flows through an old-fashioned water wheel at a traditional distillery in Northern Ireland.

used in coq au vin, or to boost flavoring, as with the fruit liqueurs used in ice creams and mousses. Certain dishes are constructed entirely around a particular drink: There would be no rum baba without rum, no zabaglione without marsala.

In this book, we shall look first at the histories and compositions of all of the most important spirits, liqueurs and fortified wines, and then at ways in which they may be used classically and creatively in the kitchen. We hope that you will come to see these renowned products not just as drinks in themselves, but as indispensable elements of gastronomy too, so that you may need to clear a passage between the liquor cabinet and the kitchen cupboard. And, unlike other cookbooks that use liquor in their recipes, this one allows you to learn something about the drinks you are using while the casserole is cooking, the mousse is setting or the sorbet is freezing.

May the spirits be with you.

SPIRITS

THE EARLIEST SPIRITS were almost certainly fairly straightforward, rough-and-ready distillations of ordinary wine. For centuries, a form of distillation had been practiced using herbs and flowers infused in water, then cooked and condensed. The resulting essence was used medicinally, in cooking or just as a perfume. As we saw in the Introduction, the discovery in Europe of the art of distilling alcohol arose as a result of alchemical experiments designed to find the "elixir of life." The powerful brew that was arrived at by distilling was thought to contain the "soul" or "spirit" of the wine.

When it was realized that anything that had been fermented to produce alcohol could in turn be distilled into spirit, the process came to be applied to materials that were fermented *specifically* for distillation, rather than being consumable products in themselves. So, mashed malted grains were responsible, in regions that lacked the climate for wine making, for the first drinks definable as whiskeys.

As wine itself was held in high esteem and was imported in great quantity by the cooler countries of northern Europe, such as England and Holland, the spirit produced from wine was the first to receive true acclaim. Traders on ships docking in at La Rochelle and other ports in the Charente region of western France had no particular taste for the acidic, flavorless wines of the area, but the strong spirit the wines could be turned into was considered a lot better than other such distillates found elsewhere. Thus did cognac first come to prominence.

A memory of the alchemical quest to find the magic elixir was preserved in the Latin name first given to the product of distillation: *aqua vitae*, water of life. That phrase has remained inseparable from spirits terminology: The French call their spirit *eau-de-vie*, the Scandinavians *aquavit*, and the Celts *uisge beatha*, which was eventually corrupted by non-Gaelic speakers into "whiskey." In Russian, it became, more humbly, "little water," or vodka. The alternative medieval Latin name was *aqua ardens*, "burning water," for reasons that are not hard to fathom. The association with fieriness, both in the method used to extract the alcohol and in the sensation that drinking it produced, lived on in the naming of distilled wine *Gebranntwein*

Above left: Scotland's smallest distillery, in Pitlochry, was built in 1837.

Below left: Traditionally, whiskey was aged in used oak sherry casks.

Below: The dark berries of the juniper tree contribute the characteristic perfume of gin.

("burned wine") in German, *brandewijn* in Dutch and eventually brandy in English.

Despite being highly prized, these early spirits would not have tasted particularly pleasant to us. They would only have been distilled once and would therefore have contained high concentrations of fusel oil, a group of compounds known in scientific parlance as the "higher alcohols," the "higher" referring to their greater acidity. It was only in 1800 that a physicist discovered the benefits of redistillation, or rectification. This dispensed with a large proportion, though not all, of the raw-tasting higher alcohols and resulted in a purer spirit. It also stripped away a lot of the positive byproducts of distillation that gave the drink its character, and so for a while the infusions of herbs, spices and fruit extracts that had originally been used to disguise the roughness

of the alcohol came back into favor in order to give it flavor.

Eventually, the correct balance was struck. The products that needed some distillation character—brandies and whiskeys—retained it (undergoing a double distillation) and had it enhanced by aging in wooden casks, while those that were intended to be as neutral as possible, such as vodka and gin, were subject to repeated redistillation. (In the case of gin and similar products, a neutral spirit base is created by prolonged rectification, so that the aromatic ingredients that are added can stand out the more boldly.) Most commercial spirits produced today have been thoroughly rectified, which is not necessarily a blessing: One thinks of the relentless blandness of some brands of white rum. The trend owes much to the fact that most of the white spirits are drunk with mixes these days.

Above: This modern distillery produces the neutral spirit base for both gin and vodka.

When tasting a fine spirit—aged cognac, single malt whiskey, sour mash bourbon or old Demerara rum, for example—the procedure that is used for tasting wine clearly won't do. Try rolling a liquid with 40% alcohol around your mouth and you'll soon wish you hadn't. Some tasters judge them on the nose alone; others add a similar quantity of water, which many feel emphasizes their aromatic sub-tleties. I prefer to be brave and taste them undiluted. If you follow this route, the trick is to take in only a very little liquid, keep it at the front of the mouth just behind the lips by lowering the head after sipping, draw some air over it quickly and spit it out before it starts burning. The whole exercise is much brisker than tasting a mouthful of wine.

AQUAVIT

FLAVORINGS
Anise
Fennel seeds
Dill
Cumin seeds
Caraway seeds
Bitter oranges

HOW TO SERVE
Aquavit should
be served like good
vodka—that is, ice-
cold and neat from a
receptacle no bigger
than a shot glass. The
bottle should be kept in
the freezer prior to
serving. It makes a
superb wintertime
aperitif, especially for
guests who have just
come in from the cold.

MIXING
Try substituting aquavit
for the vodka in an
otherwise textbook
Bloody Mary.

MONG THE VARIOUS spirits whose collective
names are derived from the phrase "water
of life," Scandinavian *aquavit* or *akvavit* has a
particularly ancient history. It is known to have
been distilled in northern Europe since
medieval times, and its use as a drink—as
distinct from its purely medical application—
dates back at least to the fifteenth century.
 Production of aquavit is very similar to that of
flavored vodkas. Its base is a neutral grain
and/or potato spirit, which is rectified to a high
degree of purity and then aromatized, usually
with fragrant spices. The Scandinavian
countries and Germany are the production
centers of true aquavit. Its
alternative name, schnapps,
derives from an old Nordic
verb, *snappen*, meaning to
snatch or seize. It denotes the
way in which it is traditionally drunk, snatched down
the throat in a single gulp.

HOW IT IS MADE
Potatoes are boiled in a con-
traption rather like a huge
pressure cooker, and the
resulting starchy mass
is then mixed with
malted grains. After
fermentation with
yeast, it is double-
distilled to obtain
a neutral spirit.
Dilution brings it
down to a drinkable
strength, and contact
with charcoal—as
well as the accepted
flavoring elements—
gives it its final
character.

AALBORG

*A premium high-
strength aquavit from
Denmark*

OTHER NAMES
Germany: Schnapps *Denmark*: schnaps
Sweden/Norway/Netherlands: snaps

TASTES GOOD WITH
Despite its cinematic association with reckless
drinking sessions, aquavit has a genuine gastronomic history. It formed an integral part of the
original Swedish *smörgasbord*, which was a
more modest feast than the lavish spreads of
today. It consisted of just bread,
fish (generally herring) and
perhaps cheese, washed
down with aquavit. The dry
savoriness of the spirit com-
plemented the appetizing role
of the salty food. Divorced
from its edible accompaniments, aquavit lives on
today as an aperitif,
knocked back in one
and followed by a
chaser of local beer.

*PEACH COUNTY
SCHNAPPS
A mild
fruit-flavored
commercial
schnapps*

ARAK

ALTHOUGH THE DISCOVERY of distillation is still hotly disputed, it is just possible that some form of arak, or raki, was the very first spirit. There are claims that it was made in India around 800 B.C., and certainly the production of a fiery, clear spirit on the subcontinent, and down in the South Pacific too, goes back many centuries.

Arak is not really one drink, but a generic name for a group of clear distillates for which the base material and method of production vary according to the region of origin. In Java, Sumatra and Borneo, the fermented juice of sugar cane provides the base, but there are also rice versions. The sap of palm trees, which ferments very readily in sultry temperatures, is popular as a source of arak in India.

The drink came to the Middle East and the Mediterranean with the

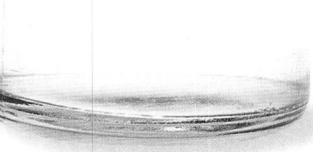

RAKI
Simple Turkish raki
that has not been
cask-aged

OTHER NAMES
Arrack, arraki, racki, raki, rakija

HOW TO SERVE
Like aquavit, arak or raki should be drunk in fairly abstemious measures. Owing to its rough potency, arak is not generally served chilled, and it is safer to sip it appreciatively rather than down it.

FLAVORINGS
Figs, dates, grapes, raisins and plums

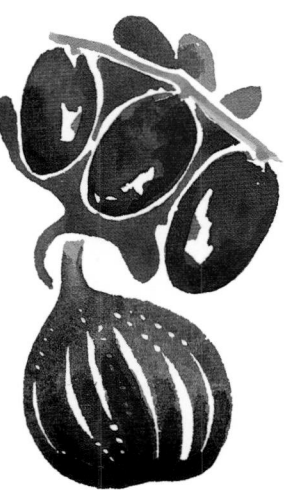

early Arab spice trade. Its common name is derived from the Arabic word for juice or sap, *araq*. Other easily fermentable products, such as dates and figs, gradually infiltrated the making of arak, and are still used in parts of North Africa and the Middle East. Finally, grape wine came to play its part in the old wine-making cultures of Greece and Cyprus, including that made from raisins.

In the West today, arak is most commonly encountered in the form of raki, the anise-tinged spirit of Greece and Turkey. Some colored raki is very fine, and is based on old cask-aged brandies, but most is a colorless and pretty raw-tasting spirit that can be anything up to 50% alcohol by volume (ABV). Raki is made throughout the Balkan countries of southeast Europe, sometimes from figs or plums rather than grapes.

TASTES GOOD WITH
Around the Mediterranean region, raki is nearly always drunk as an aperitif, but if you are lucky enough to find a particularly mellow example, it may be better drunk at the end of the meal, after coffee.

MIXING
If drunk as an appetizer, the more basic grade of raki may well be taken with ice in Greece and Cyprus.

BITTERS

FLAVORINGS

Numerous herbs and roots impart greater or lesser degrees of bitterness to all of these drinks.

Gentian is quite common. It is a flowering alpine plant, the root of which is rendered down to a bright yellow essence that has been used as a tonic and anti-fever remedy in folk medicine for centuries.

Quinine was the New World alternative to gentian. It is an extract of the bark of the cinchona tree, a native of South America.

Seville oranges The dried peel of this bitter variety is essential in Campari.

THE TERM "BITTERS" refers to any one of a number of spirits flavored with bitter herbs or roots, which are generally held to have medicinal properties. They range from products such as Campari, which can be drunk in whole measures like any other spirit, to those that are so bitter that they are only added in drops to flavor another drink.

Bitterness is the last of the four main taste sensations (the others being sweetness, saltiness and sourness) that developing taste buds learn to appreciate. A fondness for bitter flavors is often thought to be a sign of the palate having reached its true maturity.

The link between bitterness and health is evident in the fact that tonic water was originally conceived as an all-purpose pick-me-up containing the stimulant quinine, rather than as a mixer for gin, although these days its flavor tends to be drowned with artificial sweetening. The other unquestionably effective medicinal role of bitters is as an aid to digestion.

The origins of bitters lie in the flavoring elements that were commonly added to the very earliest spirits. These elixirs were taken as restoratives and remedies for any number of conditions, ranging from poor digestion to painful joints. The apothecaries who concocted them drew on the collected wisdom of herbal medicine, and added extracts of bark, roots, fruit peels, herbs and spices to enhance the healing powers of the drink.

Bitters are made all over the world. Perhaps the most famous of all is Angostura. An infusion of gentian root with herbs on a strong rum base, Angostura was invented in the nineteenth century by a German medic who was personal doctor to the South American revolutionary hero Simón Bolívar. He named it after a town in Venezuela, although today it is made exclusively in Trinidad, albeit still by the company founded by its inventor. Angostura is one of the few such medicinal drinks that can lay claim to actually having been formulated by a doctor.

In Europe the two major centers of production

UNDERBERG
An intensely pungent digestive bitter from Germany

CAMPARI
Italy's most famous bitter aperitif also comes in a ready-mixed bottle with a crown cap

MIXING

Negroni: Thoroughly mix equal measures of gin, Campari and sweet red vermouth with ice in a tumbler and add a squirt of soda.
Americano: As for Negroni, but leave out the gin and add a few drops of Angostura.
Pink gin (below): Sprinkle about half a dozen drops of Angostura into a goblet-shaped glass, roll it around to coat the inner surfaces, then toss it out. Add ice-cold gin, which will then take on the faintest pink tint.

of bitters are Italy and France. Italy has Campari—a bright red aperitif of uncompromising bitterness, which is made in Milan—and also Fernet-Branca. Like Germany's Underberg, it is sold in little bottles and is often recommended as a hangover cure. France's famous bitters include Amer Picon (which was invented as an antimalarial remedy by an army officer serving in Algeria), Toni-Kola and Secrestat.

English fruit bitters, such as orange and peach, were widely used in the cocktail era of the 1920s. Hungary's runner is Unicum, which balances its bitterness with a slight sweetness, while the Latvians add their own molasses-dark dry tonic, Melnais Balzams (Black Balsam), to their coffee.

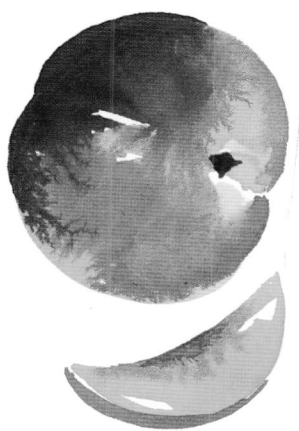

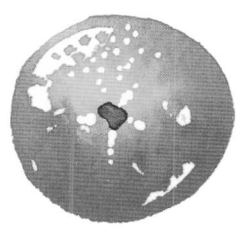

FERNET-BRANCA
The Italian bitter much prized as a hangover cure

UNICUM
A deeply colored bitter specialty of Hungary

ANGOSTURA
The most widely used bitter in the cocktail repertoire

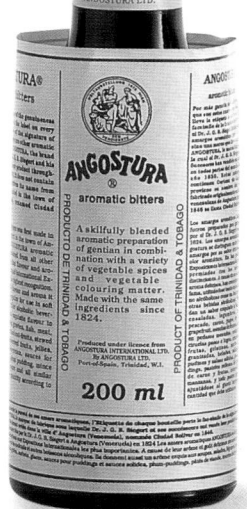

HOW TO SERVE
Campari is classically served with soda and a twist of lemon, but don't drown it. Amer Picon may be served the same way, or perhaps as a bitter element with gin for those whose need to be picked up requires more than a straight dry martini. Underberg and Fernet-Branca can be quaffed straight as stomach-settlers or just to aid digestion, while Angostura is essential in a pink gin—the drink of British officers and gentlemen.

BRANDY

STRICTLY SPEAKING, the term *brandy* applies to any grape-based spirit distilled from wine. There are "brandies" made from other fruits—such as Normandy's calvados, made from apples—but we shall deal with these under their own headings. The English name is a corruption of the Dutch *brandewijn*, in turn derived from the German *Gebranntwein*, meaning burned wine, which is an apt term for the product of distillation.

The most famous of all true brandies is cognac, named after a town in the Charente region of western France. It was to here that traders from northern Europe, particularly the Netherlands, came in the seventeenth century, putting in at the port of La Rochelle to take delivery of consignments of salt. They inevitably took some of the region's thin, acidic wine with them as well. Because of tax regulations, and to save space in the ships' holds—always a major consideration—the wines were boiled to reduce their volume by evaporation. On arrival at their destination, they would be reconstituted with water. However, it came to be noticed that the Charente wines positively benefited from the reduction process. It was but a short step from there to actual distillation.

HOW TO SERVE
The finest and oldest brandies should not be mixed. Younger products mix reasonably well with soda; the vogue for brandy and tonic being assiduously promoted in Cognac, of all places, is not one that finds favor with the author. In the Far East, brandy is mixed with plenty of ice water as a very long drink, and consumed with food.

MARTELL
The oldest
house in
Cognac is
still a brand
leader

HOW TO SERVE
Fine cognac should be drunk just as it comes, without mixers and certainly without ice. It is traditionally served in balloon glasses that allow room for swirling. Tradition is not often a reliable guide, and the aromas are much better appreciated in something resembling a large liqueur glass, which mutes the prickle of the spirit. The bouquet is also encouraged by a gentle warming of the glass in the hand (for which the balloon was indisputably better designed), but recourse to those lovely, old, silver brandy-warmers, which allowed you to barbecue the tilted glass over a little petrol flame, is not recommended.

Such was the fame and the premium paid for the distilled wines of the Charente that they came to have many imitators. None, however, could match the precise local conditions in which cognac is made. The region's chalky soils, the maritime climate and the aging in barrels fashioned from Limousin oak were the indispensable features that gave cognac the preeminent reputation that it enjoys to this day.

France's other brandy of note, Armagnac, is made in the southwest of the country. Armagnac is based on a wider range of grape varieties and made using a slightly different method than cognac. Although not as widely known as cognac, it has its own special cachet in the spirits market and is preferred by many as the better digestif.

There are grape brandies produced all over Europe and the Americas, as we shall see in the succeeding pages. The best are generally made by the potstill method of distillation. Some inferior spirit, artificially colored and flavored, also used to be known as brandy, but has been banned from using the term within the European Union following the introduction of a new law in 1989.

COGNAC

The Cognac region covers two *départements* on the western side of France near the Bay of Biscay: inland Charente, and Charente-Maritime on the coast. Cognac is a small town close to the border between the two. The vineyards are subdivided into six growing areas, the most notable of which are Grande Champagne and Petite Champagne, just south of Cognac itself.

As we have seen, the fame of cognac had been well and truly established in the Dutch and British markets by the end of

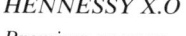

HENNESSY X.O
Premium cognac
in a singularly
shaped decorative
bottle

the seventeenth century. The industry's first great entrepreneur was Jean Martell, a Jersey-born opportunist who, in 1715, turned away from a life of crime (smuggling) in order to found the house that still bears his name. Cognac's other leading brands are Hennessy, Courvoisier and Rémy Martin. Smaller but no less distinguished companies include Hine and Otard.

The relative qualities of different cognacs depend almost entirely on the length of time they have been aged, and the cognacs are classified accordingly. No brandy that has earned the right to the cognac *appellation contrôlée* (AC) status may be blended from spirits that are less than two years old. At the bottom rung of the quality classification for the British and Irish markets is VS (historically known as three-star, and still designated by a row of three stars on the label). VS may contain brandies as young as three years old, but the basic products of most of the leading companies will contain some significantly older reserves.

The next stage up is VSOP, Very Special (or Superior) Old Pale, an old British term that arose in London in the nineteenth century to denote a particularly fine — but paradoxically light-colored — batch of cognac. (Although cognac derives most of its color from wood-aging, caramel can also be added to influence the color, provided it does not affect the taste. Any slight sweetness in the spirit derives from correction with sugar solution just before bottling.) VSOP is the five-star stuff because the youngest spirit it contains must have spent at least five years in wood.

Those blended from minimum six-year-old cognacs may be entitled XO, or given any one of a number of names the houses invent for themselves, such as Reserve, Extra, Cordon Bleu, Paradis or classically Napoléon — so named because the bottles supposedly contain brandies aged since the time of the *Empereur*.

The prices that the oldest cognacs command are breathtaking, yet the enjoyment can never be proportionately greater than that to be had from good VSOP. In many cases, you may be paying for something that looks like a giant perfume

COURVOISIER
Along with Martell, this is one of the most widely drunk cognacs in the world.

REMY MARTIN
The basic Rémy is a VSOP grade of cognac.

METAXA

Among the brandies produced on the mainland of Greece (and to some extent on the island of Samos), the abidingly popular Metaxa deserves a special mention. Despite the brouhaha with which it is treated in Greece itself, and a distinctly specious system of age-labeling, it is a fairly basic industrial product.

Greek brandy isn't ever going to fare well against aged cognac for the simple reason that the grape varieties that go into it are not generally of sufficiently high acidity to produce a suitable base wine. The mainstays are Savatiano (widely used in retsina) and the Muscat grape that produces the golden dessert wines of Samos and other islands, and the distillers are not above using base wines that contain some red grapes.

There are three grades of Metaxa, ascending in quality from three stars to five and seven. The last is sometimes said to have been cask-aged for around half a century, a claim we can take confidently with a cask of salt. It is relatively pale in color (which fact alone makes the age claim suspicious) and much sweeter on the palate than cognac, with an extravagant toffee or caramel quality.

AMERICAN BRANDIES

USA Brandy has been made in the United States since the days of the pioneers, most of it in what is now the premier wine-growing state, California. At one time, brandy production was simply a convenient means of using up substandard grapes that were considered unfit for quality wine production, as it still is in many of Europe's viticultural regions. In the last 30 years or so, however, a turn toward producing finer aged spirits has been made, and a number of these American products are capable of giving some of the famous VSOP cognacs a run for their money.

Not all are made in the image of cognac; some are discernibly more reminiscent of the Spanish style. The brandies are habitually matured in barrels of homegrown American oak,

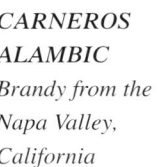

METAXA
The summer vacation favorite

CARNEROS ALAMBIC
Brandy from the Napa Valley, California

MIXING

Brandy Blazer: Put two measures of cognac in a saucepan with one sugar cube and the thinly pared rind from half an orange and one lemon. Heat gently, then remove from the heat and light the surface of the liquid. The alcohol will burn with a low, blue flame for about one minute. Blow out the flame. Add half a measure of Kahlúa and strain into a heat-resistant liqueur glass. Decorate with a toothpick threaded with a twist of orange rind.

which gives a more pronounced aroma to the spirit, accentuated by the heavily charred inner surfaces of the barrels. These conditions result in brandies of great richness and complexity. Names to look out for include Germain-Robin and RMS (the latter brand owned by Cognac star Rémy Martin). Some of the top California wineries have also turned out some impressive efforts, while bulk producer Gallo in Modesto make a passable version intended for mixing.

Latin America There is a long tradition of drinking fiery spirits all over Central and South America, in which grape brandy plays its part—particularly in the areas where the early Spanish colonists first planted vines. Mexico is the most important producer. Its flagship is a big-selling global brand called Presidente, made in the light, simple style of a rough-and-ready Spanish brandy.

The peculiarly South American offering, however, is pisco. There is still much dispute over whether it originated in Peru or Chile, the two centers of production (with a modest

contribution from Bolivia). I shall forbear to come down on either side of the fence, except to point out that the Pisco Valley and the seaport of the same name are in Peru, but the Chileans simply insist that that was one of the principal export destinations for their indigenous spirit, and the name just stuck.

Despite receiving some cask-aging, pisco is always colorless because the barrels it matures in are so ancient that they have no color left to give to the spirit. In Chile, the longer the maturation, the lower the dilution before bottling, so the finer grades (Gran Pisco is the best) are the strongest. Owing to widespread use of members of the Muscat grape family in the base wine, nearly all types and nationalities of pisco are marked by an unabashed fruitiness on the nose and palate.

The myth that pisco is a throat-searing firewater strictly for the peasants is probably based on the exposure of delicate European sensibilities to the lower grades. Top pisco has every right to be considered a world-class spirit.

PISCO
A top-quality
pisco from Peru

MIXING

Pisco Sour: Half-fill a small tumbler with smashed ice. Put in two measures of freshly squeezed lime juice and sweeten to taste with confectioners' sugar. Stir well to dissolve the sugar. Add a measure of pisco, and give the drink a final stir.

CALVADOS

IN AREAS WHERE wine grapes could not be grown with success, other fruits came to supplement grains in making fermented and distilled drinks. The most important fruit, after grapes, to act as a source of alcohol is the apple. Apple trees are capable of fruiting in much more wintry conditions than the vine, and since many varieties of apple are too tart or bitter to give much pleasure as eating apples, cider became the obvious alternative to beer in the cooler northern climates.

The distillation of cider is probably quite as old as the practice of distilling wine for grape brandy. In its heartland—the Normandy region of northern France—the earliest reference to an apple distillate dates from 1553, but we have no means of knowing how long, prior to the mid-1500s, it had already been going on.

If the name of the Normans' apple brandy, *calvados*, sounds more Spanish than French, that is because it derives from a story that tells of a ship, the *El Salvador*, from the mighty Spanish armada, which was dashed to smithereens off

OTHER NAMES
USA: applejack
UK: apple brandy/cider brandy

the Norman coast. The *département* came to be known as Calvados, and its traditional spirit was named after it. There is no historical corroboration of the story, and no one in Normandy seemingly expects you to believe it.

Like cognac and Armagnac, calvados received its *appellation contrôlée* status quite soon after the introduction of the AC system: 1942. At the heart of the region is one particularly fine area called the Pays d'Auge, prized for its soils and the lay of its land, which has its own designation. (The rest is straight appellation Calvados.) Both the potstill double distillation and the continuous method are used, although the calvados of the Pays d'Auge area may only use the former.

There are hundreds of different varieties of cider apple, classified into four broad taste groups: sweet, bittersweet, bitter and acid. The bittersweet ones make up the lion's share of the blend in a typical calvados. After distillation, the spirit goes into variously sized barrels of French oak for maturation. Supposedly, the younger a calvados is, the more likely it is to smell and

HOW TO SERVE
Younger calvados works surprisingly well with tonic, as long as you don't drown it. (I prefer half-and-half to one third-two thirds.) Hors d'Age, etc., must be drunk unmixed.

CALVADOS
The best calvados comes from the Pays d'Auge

CIDER BRANDY
A fine, powerful apple spirit from Somerset, England

MIXING

Depth Charge: Shake equal measures of calvados and cognac with half a measure of fresh lemon juice, a dash of grenadine and ice. Strain into a cocktail glass.

taste of apples; the older ones take on the vanilla and spice tones of the wood.

Age indications are not dissimilar to those of cognac and Armagnac. Three-star (or three-apple) calvados spends a minimum of two years in cask, Vieux or Réserve three years, and Vieille Réserve or VSOP four years. Those aged for six or more years may be labeled Hors d'Age or Age Inconnu ("age unknown!"). If a calvados is labeled with a period of aging, such as eight-year-old, then the age specified refers to the youngest spirit in it, not the average. Should you come across any of the small amount of vintage-dated calvados, note that the date refers to the year of distillation—the year *after* harvest.

In the United States, an apple spirit has been made ever since the first British settlers found that the apple trees they planted in New England proved hardier than grain crops. Applejack, as it is most commonly known, is made in much the same way as calvados, starting with good cider and distilling it twice in a pot still. The spirit is then aged in oak for anything up to about five years. The younger stuff is pretty abrasive, but on the eastern seaboard—as in Normandy—they like it that way. Laird's is one of the best-selling brands.

The alternative way of making applejack, now officially frowned on, was to freeze the cider. Water freezes before alcohol, so if the first slush to form was skimmed away, what was left would be virtually pure alcohol. (A derivative of this technique is used today in the making of both ice beers and ice ciders in order to strengthen them.)

Apple brandy, or cider brandy, is now being revived in the west of England. Somerset is, after all, considered by many to be capable of producing the world's best ciders. When properly aged, it can be quite impressive, although devotees of calvados are unlikely to be fooled by it in a blind tasting.

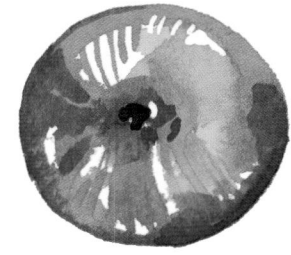

HOW IT IS MADE

Apples are harvested from September through December, depending on the variety. A precise blend of juices from the four types is fermented into cider at about 5–6% alcohol. This is subjected to a double distillation (or continuous distillation, except in the Pays d'Auge region of Calvados). The spirit is then aged in cask for anything up to 40 years, and bottled at 40–45% ABV.

APPLEJACK
America's answer
to calvados

HOW TO SERVE

In Normandy, there is a gastronomic tradition called the *trou normand* (literally "Norman hole"). A shot of neat calvados is drunk in place of a sorbet before the main course of a meal. The idea is that the spirit punches a hole through the food already consumed and allows you to go on eating in comfort.

EAU-DE-VIE

EAU-DE-VIE IS the French phrase for the
Latin *aqua vitae*, "water of life." Strictly
speaking, the term refers to all spirits distilled
from fermented fruits, starting with wine-based
cognac and Armagnac. By the same token,
calvados could therefore be considered an
eau-de-vie of cider. Since the names of these
individual spirits are legally protected by
France's geographical
appellation contrôlée regulations, they have come to
be known by those names
instead of being referred to
as eaux-de-vie.

Spirits can be produced
from many other fruits as
well as grapes or apples,
though, and these are

much less precisely defined. The term eau-de-
vie, therefore, tends now to be reserved for
these other fruit brandies. Apart from their basic
ingredients, the main attribute that distinguishes
eaux-de-vie from cognac and Armagnac is that
they are colorless because they haven't been
aged in wood like their more famous cousins.
The theory is

*LA VIEILLE
PRUNE*
*Pascall makes this
celebrated plum
eau-de-vie*

POIRE WILLIAMS
*Eau-de-vie flavored
with William pears*

that they develop in glass, which flies in the face of what is scientifically known about spirits—namely, that development stops once they are in the bottle.

Of the variety of fruits used, the most often encountered—and those producing the most delicious eaux-de-vie—are the various soft summer berries. Alsace, a wine region of north-east France that has lurched from French to German domination and back again since the late nineteenth century, is a particularly rich source of these spirits. Some of them are made by wine-makers, others by specialty distillers. What

they have in common is high alcohol (some-times around 45% ABV), absence of color and a clear, pure scent and flavor of their founding fruit. They are not sweetened, and should not be confused with the syrupy liqueurs of the same flavors, which tend to be colored, anyway.

Eau-de-vie of this kind is also made in Switzerland and Germany.

TASTES GOOD WITH
Served very cold in small measures, they can work well with certain desserts, particularly custard-based tarts topped with the same fruit as that used to make the eau-de-vie.

FRAMBOISE SAUVAGE
Eau-de-vie flavored with wild raspberries

FRAISE
A popular eau-de-vie from strawberries

EAUX-DE-VIE
Three less-common types—mirabelle, fleur de bière and kirsch—are available in miniature bottles

GIN

OF THE FIVE essential spirits (brandy, whiskey, rum, vodka and gin), gin is the only one that really has a reputation to live down. Over the years it has been the calamitous curse of the urban poor, the Mother's Ruin by which young girls in trouble tried to inflict miscarriages upon themselves, the bathtub brew that rotted guts during Prohibition, and the first resort of the miserable as the storm clouds of depression gathered. It was all so different in the beginning.

Although the English often claim to be the true progenitors of gin (as well as, more convincingly, of port and champagne), its origins in fact go back to sixteenth-century Holland. Like many other distilled drinks, the first inspiration behind the creation of gin was medicinal. The blend of herbs and aromatics used in it were believed to guard against all the ills that flesh was heir to. Principal among the elements of these concoctions was juniper, the

OTHER NAMES
Holland: genever or jenever
France: genièvre (although almost everybody in France now calls it "gin")

Dutch word for which—*genever*—is the linguistic root of the English word "gin."

The dark little berries of the juniper tree contribute to the characteristic strong perfume of gin. They are prized medicinally as a diuretic, to counteract water retention. Despite the predominance of juniper in the aroma and flavor of gin, however, it is not the only added ingredient. Precise recipes vary according to the individual distiller—they each have their own secret formula—but other common components include angelica, licorice, orris root, dried citrus peel, and caraway and coriander seeds.

HOW TO SERVE
The age-old mixer for gin is of course Schweppes tonic, the production of which is almost exclusively sustained by gin-drinkers. A gin and tonic is usually offered as a long drink with a slice of lemon and plenty of ice, but equal measures is a more sensitive way of treating the gin. Gin rubs along with any old mixer, though: orange juice, bitter lemon, ginger beer, whatever. (It isn't very good with cola perhaps, but then few things are.)

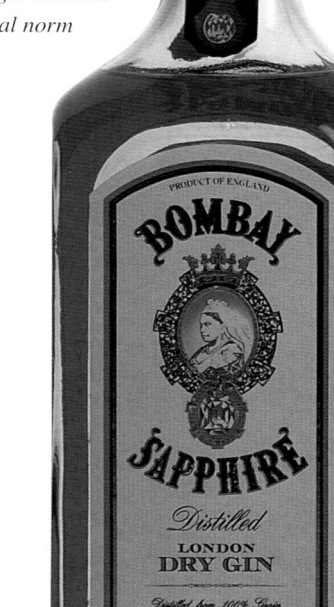

BOMBAY SAPPHIRE
More delicately aromatic gin than the commercial norm

GORDON'S
This is the brand leader among London gins

MIXING

The number of gin-based cocktails is legion, but here are a few of the more durable ones:

Gin Fizz: Shake a good measure of gin with a teaspoon of superfine sugar and the juice of half a lemon. Pour into a tall glass and top with fresh soda water. (This is not noticeably different from a **Tom Collins**, except that the latter may have a little less soda added. Then again, leave out the soda altogether, stir it in a tumbler rather than shaking it and call it a **Gin Sour**.)

Gimlet (below): Stir equal measures of Plymouth gin and Rose's lime cordial in a tumbler with a couple of ice cubes.

It may well have been British soldiers returning home from the Thirty Years' War who first brought the taste for Dutch genever across the North Sea. Then again, it may simply have been travelers to the continent starting or ending their journeys in Amsterdam. However that may be, a form of gin was being distilled in London in the seventeenth century, using the basic beer ingredients—hops and barley—and the essential juniper berries.

The meteoric rise in gin's popularity in Britain had two main causes. Firstly, periodic hostilities with the French led to the application of punitive tariffs to their exports and, just as port came to be the wine of patriotic choice among the elite, so gin replaced cognac. To compound that, reform of the excise system then produced an anomaly whereby beer was suddenly subjected to a much stricter levy than before, so that gin was actually cheaper. Not surprisingly, it became the staple drink of the poorest classes, who consumed it in much the same quantities as they had beer. The gin shops were born, and public drunkenness and alcohol-related illnesses soared.

For the great mass of the London poor, getting "blotto" was the only way of escaping grim reality. So began gin's long association with gloom and despondency (which still persists today in the enduring myth that gin is more of a depressant than the other spirits). The purveyors of gin sold their wares in terms that no

BELGRAVIA DRY LONDON GIN
One of the lesser-known London brands

MIXING

Gin Rickey: Half-fill a tall glass with ice. Add two measures of gin, the juice of half a lime or a quarter of a lemon and a generous dash of grenadine. Stir vigorously, then top with fresh soda.

White Lady: Shake a measure of gin with half a measure of Cointreau and half a measure of fresh lemon juice, with ice, and strain into a cocktail glass. (Some recipes also add a teaspoon of egg white. My bible, the *Savoy Cocktail Book*, clearly indicates the White Lady to be innocent of such a substance. It simply gives the drink a frothier texture, if that's what you like.)

FLAVORINGS

Juniper berries
(essential)
Coriander seeds
Caraway seeds
Orris root
Dried orange and
lemon peel
Angelica
Licorice, fennel or anise
Almonds
Cardamom pods

MIXING

Gin Smash: Dissolve a tablespoon of superfine sugar in a little water in a cocktail shaker. Add four large fresh mint sprigs and bruise, using a muddler to press the juices out of the mint. Half-fill the shaker with cracked ice and add two measures of dry gin. Shake the cocktail vigorously for 20 seconds, then strain into a small glass filled with crushed ice and a little finely chopped mint.

advertiser today could get away with; the wording on one signboard famously ran: "*Drunk for a penny. Dead drunk for tuppence. Clean straw for nothing.*" Such was the addiction of the masses to gin that it was actually made illegal by an Act of Parliament in 1736, but the law was hastily reversed six years later after it was predictably discovered that the contraband stuff that was now being drunk was considerably more toxic than the official spirit had been.

In 1750, the great social satirist William Hogarth produced his famous engraving *Gin Lane*. It depicted in minute detail the degradation and squalor that was being wrought by widespread consumption of gin. A century later, gin was still being blamed by critical commentators such as the author Charles Dickens as the corrosive solace of the destitute, although Dickens was more concerned with blaming social inequity for the condition of the poor, rather than seeing drink in itself as an evil. It was in this period, however, that the

great Temperance movements took root, and the poor were encouraged to fear drink as the devil's potion.

It was only in the late Victorian period that gin began to reassume a more dignified reputation. Because of its colorlessness and its absence of wood-derived richness, it was seen as a usefully ladylike alternative to Scotch whiskey and cognac. The all-too-recent association with the sordid doings of the idle poor meant that some euphemism had to be found for it—a facility Victorian society was supremely practiced in. For a while, it was improbably referred to as "white wine." Finally, the gin and tonic, the world's favorite aperitif, was born, and a new era in gin's fortunes was ushered in.

During the period of Prohibition in the United States (1919–33), gin became one of the more readily available sources of illicit hooch, largely because it was so

BEEFEATER
One of the most famous London gins

MIXING

Dry Martini: No cocktail recipe is more energetically argued over than the classic dry martini. It is basically a generous measure of virtually neat stone-cold gin with a dash of dry white vermouth in it. But how much is a dash? Purists insist on no more than a single drop, or the residue left after briefly flushing the glass out with a splash of vermouth and then pouring it away. (They puzzlingly refer to such a martini as "very dry," as if adding more vermouth would sweeten it. In fact, the terminology goes back as far as the original recipe, when the vermouth used was the sweet red variety.) Some go for as much as half a measure of vermouth, and I have a book that suggests a two-to-one ratio of gin to vermouth—guaranteed to send the purist into paroxysms of horror. I have to admit I incline more to the purist philosophy, though: The vermouth should be added as if it were the last bottle in existence. The drink should properly be mixed gently in a separate pitcher, with ice, and then strained into the traditional cocktail glass (the real name of which is a martini glass). A twist of lemon peel should be squeezed delicately over the surface, so that the essential oil floats in globules on top of the drink, but *don't* put the lemon twist in the glass. And hold the olive. (Add a cocktail onion, however, and the drink becomes a **Gibson**.)

easy for amateur distillers to throw together. All that was needed was to add whatever flavorings you could lay your hands on to a basic grain spirit, and then bottle it as soon as you wanted to. It is sometimes said that a lot of the more outlandish cocktails of the Jazz Era owed their inspiration to the need to disguise the disgusting taste of homemade gin.

The reason that gin continues to provide the base for so many cocktails is that it is such a good mixer. Its lack of color means that it doesn't turn an off-putting muddy hue when blended with fruit juices, as the brown spirits do, while its aromatic quality gives it something for the mixers to mingle with, as distinct from the absolute neutrality of vodka. Gin has inevitably lost a lot of ground to vodka in the more recent youth market, as its peculiar

PLYMOUTH GIN
Coates is the only producer of Plymouth gin.

BOOTH'S FINEST
Note that the company was established during the ban on gin in England

perfume is something of an acquired taste to untutored palates. In the 1990s, however, it suddenly found itself gaining new cachet among certain American rap artists, becoming the preferred tipple enthusiastically celebrated in their lyrics as "juice and gin" (in other words gin and orange, known to the F. Scott Fitzgerald set in the 1920s as an Orange Blossom).

TYPES OF GIN

English Gin There are two types. London dry gin is by far the more commonly known, although it doesn't necessarily have to be distilled in the capital. It is an intensely perfumed spirit, and varies greatly in quality between producers. Gordon's, Booth's and Beefeater are the most famous names, but some specialty products have established a conspicuous presence on the market in recent years, notably Bombay Sapphire in the pale-blue tinted bottle.

DUTCH GENEVER

The prototype for London gin

MIXING

Gin Swizzle: Beat together (as if you were preparing eggs for an omelet) a double measure of gin, a teaspoon of sugar syrup, the juice of a lime and a couple of firm dashes of Angostura in a large pitcher, with ice. When the drink is good and foaming, strain it into a tall glass. Alternatively, make the drink in the tall glass and stir it up with an old-fashioned swizzle stick.

The other type is Plymouth gin, of which there is only one distiller, Coates, at the Blackfriars distillery in the center of the city, not far from the waterfront. Plymouth is a distinctly drier gin than the big London brands; its spirit is impressively rounded and the range of aromatics used in it somehow give it a subtler bouquet than most gin drinkers may be used to. It makes an incomparable Pink Gin.

A very small amount of gin is cask-aged and referred to as golden gin, after the color it leaches out of the wood.

Dutch Genever This is quite a different drink than English gin, owing to the more pungently flavored grain mash on which it is based. The mixture of barley, rye and corn is often quite heavily malted, giving the older spirits a lightly beery tinge in color. There are basically two grades, labeled either Oude (old) or Jonge (young), the latter looking more like the English article. Genever frequently comes in an opaque "stone" bottle.

KIRSCH

KIRSCH IS THE ORIGINAL cherry spirit. It is a colorless pure distillate—a true brandy or eau-de-vie, in other words—made from cherries. It is included separately because it has traditionally been seen as a distinctive product from the other fruit brandies. A fair amount is made in the Alsace and Franche-Comté regions of eastern France, where they know a thing or two about such matters. It is also a particular speciality of the Schwarzwald, the Black Forest region of Bavaria in western Germany—hence its German name, which simply means "cherry." (Confusingly, kirsch is not related to cherry brandy.)

When the cherry juice is pressed for the initial fermentation, the pits are ground up too and left to infuse in it. The pits impart a characteristic slightly bitter note to the spirit, and bequeath a minute and harmless amount of cyanide to it in the process. It is generally given a short period of aging, but in large earthenware vats rather than barrels, so that it remains colorless. The true kirsch cherry is the black morello (the type that crops up in Black Forest cake, Bavaria's gift to the world's dessert

KIRSCH
A cherry eau-de-vie with an identity all its own

MIXING
Rose: Shake equal measures of kirsch and dry vermouth with a dash of grenadine and plenty of ice. Strain into a cocktail glass.

carts), but these days, red varieties are often used instead.

Kirsch is also made in Switzerland and Austria.

TASTES GOOD WITH
Use kirsch to add a touch of alcoholic richness to desserts, whether for soaking the sponge base for a mousse or moistening fresh fruit, such as pineapple. Indeed, its flavor blends unexpectedly well with all sorts of fruits. Beware any bottle labeled "Kirsch de Cuisine." It is an inferior product, smelling more like candle wax than cherries, whose roughness is supposedly disguised when used in cooking. And if you believe that...

HOW TO SERVE
Lightly chilled in small glasses, kirsch makes a refreshing after-dinner drink.

MARC

IN THE VINEYARDS of Europe, winemakers have long had to accustom themselves to the precarious existence that reliance on nature forces on them. A bumper harvest of ripe, healthy grapes means plenty of good wine and a healthy income. But what if frost decimates your crop in the spring and the sun doesn't shine when you most need it? In the lean years, you may well be grateful for a byproduct you can fall back on to ease the financial squeeze.

For many thrifty wine producers, marc has traditionally been the answer. After the grape juice has been pressed for fermentation, a mass of smashed skins and seeds, or pomace, is left, itself capable of fermentation. Marc is the distillate of this residue. In France, the most celebrated marc is made in Burgundy and Champagne, frequently by producers enthusiastic enough to buy other growers' leftovers, but there is also some made in Alsace, Provence and the isolated eastern region of the Jura.

In Italy, marc is known as grappa, and such is the connoisseurship surrounding it that varietal grappa, made from the skins of single grape varieties, has become

HOW TO SERVE
Their strong tannins make marcs unsuitable for mixing. They are intended for drinking neat, though their profoundly earthy flavor may come as a shock to the uninitiated. On the calvados principle that a strong spirit aids digestion, the Burgundians in particular value them as after-dinner drinks.

OTHER NAMES
Italy: grappa (also used in California)
Portugal: bagaceira
Spain: aguardiente (but that term may also be applied to any fiery grape spirit, including brandy)

something of a fad. An indication of its potential trendiness is that several producers in California (where the climate is sufficiently benign not to need such a standby) are making versions of grappa too. In all regions, the finer spirits may be treated to maturation in oak, resulting in a burnished golden color, but most of it is clear.

TASTES GOOD WITH
I once ate a sorbet in Reims that had been made with Marc de Champagne, and anointed with yet more of it. It was acutely horrible, but in a somehow intriguing way. More beguiling is the use of Marc de Bourgogne for marinating the rind of the powerful local soft cheese of Chambertin.

MARC DE CHAMPAGNE
Made by the champagne giants Moët & Chandon

GRAPPA
A varietal grappa made from moscatel grapes

MESCAL

MESCAL, OR MEZCAL, is one of Mexico's indigenous drinks. It is a pale yellowish spirit made from the juice of a species of cactus called the agave. The pressed juice is fermented to make *pulque*, a kind of beer of around 5–6% alcohol, which is known to have been consumed in Aztec times. It is then distilled once by the continuous method to produce mescal. (A second distillation removes more of the off-putting impurities in the spirit and results in the more highly prized tequila.)

It would be fair to say that mescal doesn't have a particularly illustrious image. It is the rapacious firewater that contributes to the downfall of the dissolute British

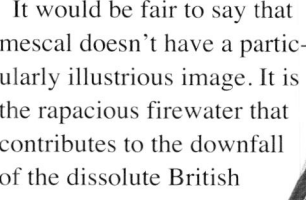

MESCAL
A little white worm lurks at the bottom of every bottle

HOW TO SERVE

If the idea of chewing the worm as it is doesn't appeal, try liquidizing it in a cocktail. I have swallowed it in sections like aspirins, but the promised heroism—not surprisingly—failed to appear.

consul in Malcolm Lowry's celebrated novel of alcoholism, *Under the Volcano*. In the past, it was considered to be capable of inducing gruesome hallucinations, a feature Lowry's novel reports, but it is hard to account for this since the agave cactus—or American aloe, as it is sometimes known—is not one of the hallucinogenic species.

Mescal is often sold with a pickled white agave worm in the bottle. It is genuine, and is intended to be eaten as the last of the drink is poured out. Supposedly, ingestion of the worm encourages great heroism in those already brave enough to swallow it. Again, the myth persists that the worm, which feeds on the agave plant, contains hallucinogenic properties. If that is likely to be your only motivation for trying it, don't bother. (The psychedelic drug mescaline was derived from the peyote cactus, not the agave.)

HOW IT IS MADE

The unlovely agave plant has an enormous core the shape of a pinecone, which is surrounded by great, spiny fat leaves. This core, or heart, is hacked away and the expressed juice—which is milky white and extremely bitter—is fermented into pulque. Mescal is the first rough distillation of the pulque. It may be given a short period of ageing in wood, but it is not intended to be a sophisticated product.

TASTES GOOD WITH

Agave worm.

HOW TO SERVE

If you want to tame its fire, try mixing mescal with a little freshly squeezed lime juice and topping it up with soda or tonic water. In Mexico, inevitably, they just knock it back as it is, like schnapps. It is hard to find a mescal, even commercially bottled, that doesn't smell dirty, an aroma that does tend to pierce through whatever it's mixed with.

RUM

RUM IS PROBABLY the least understood of the five main spirits, despite the fact that, in its white version, it is one of the biggest-selling of them all. Indeed, it is debatable whether many of those knocking back Bacardi-and-Cokes in bars around the world realize they are drinking some form of rum at all. In the popular mind, the drink is inextricably associated with a rather antiquated theatrical idea of "Jolly Jack Tars" and a life on the ocean wave.

There is some uncertainty over the origin of the spirit's name, but the favorite theory is that it is a shortening of an old West Country English word, "rumbullion," itself of unknown origin, but generally denoting any hard liquor.

The invention of rum probably dates from not long after the foundation of the sugar plantations in the West Indies, in the early six-teenth century. Until the voyages of Christopher Columbus, sugar was a luxury product, and much sought after in southern Europe, having originally been brought from

OTHER NAMES
France: rhum
Spain: ron

India into Venice by Persians and then by Arabs. When the Spanish explorers landed in Hispaniola (modern-day Haiti and the Dominican Republic) and the neighboring Caribbean islands, they saw in them promising environments for cultivating sugar cane and thereby breaking the stranglehold on the market that the Arabs had.

If yeast needs sugar to feed on in order to produce alcohol, then the sugar plant was always going to be an obvious source for some kind of distillate.

HOW TO SERVE
The best dark rums, and aged rums in particular, should be served straight, unchilled, as digestifs. They make stimulating alternatives to malt whiskey or cognac. Premium white rums from the independent producers are also best enjoyed neat, but they should be served cold.

NOTABLE PRODUCERS
Appleton, Myers
(Jamaica);
CSR (St Kitts);
Green Island
(Mauritius);
Clément, Rhum St
James, La Mauny
(Martinique);
Havana Club (Cuba);
El Dorado (Guyana);
Cockspur, Mount Gay
(Barbados);
Barbancourt (Haiti);
Pusser's (British Virgin
Islands)

CAPTAIN MORGAN
The leading brand dark rum

MIXING

Rum is the base for many of the more exotic cocktail concoctions available today, its heady richness contributing to the explosive power required. Here are two classics:

Bacardi Cocktail: The original, after which the brand is named. Shake a double measure of white rum with the juice of half a lime, a teaspoon of grenadine, and ice. Strain it into a cocktail glass.

Cuba Libre (below): Mix a generous measure of light or golden rum with a tablespoon or so of freshly squeezed lime juice, pour over ice, and top up with cola.

When first pressed, cane juice is a murky, greenish color and full of impurities. Boiled down, it eventually crystallizes into sucrose and a sticky brown byproduct, molasses, that would have readily fermented in the tropical conditions. Rum is the spirit derived from distilling the fermented molasses.

Sugar soon became a widespread, everyday product in Europe. The astronomical demand for it was serviced by one of the most notorious manifestations of European colonial history—the slave trade—and rum played a crucial part in the circular trade that came to be established. Settlers in New England financed their trips to West Africa by selling rum. A consignment of African slaves would be delivered to the West Indies and sold for molasses, which would then be shipped back to New England to be turned into more rum.

The association of rum with the British navy in particular derives from the fact that rum was provided to the ratings as a standard daily ration in the eighteenth century. The tradition continued throughout the most glorious period of Britain's maritime history, basically because rum could withstand hot weather more sturdily than beer could. The initial allowance was a fairly rollicking half-pint a day, which eventually was watered down into the despised "grog"

WOOD'S 100
A particularly rich
naval-strength
dark rum

MIXING

Petite Fleur: (from Michael Walker's *Cinzano Cocktail Book*): Shake equal measures of white rum, Cointreau and freshly squeezed grapefruit juice with ice and strain into a cocktail glass.

Mai Tai (below): Blend a measure each of dark rum and light rum with half-measures of tequila, Cointreau and apricot brandy, a measure of freshly squeezed orange juice, a splash of grenadine and a few drops of Angostura and ice cubes in a blender. Decant into a very large wine glass. Approach with trepidation.

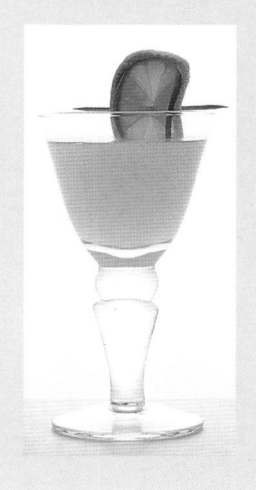

MIXING

Planter's Punch: Shake a double measure each of light rum and fresh orange juice with a couple of teaspoons of fresh lemon juice and ice, and strain into a large glass. (Some authorities insist on a dash of grenadine just for good measure.)

Ti Punch (below): Stir a generous measure of good white rum with a splash of cane syrup and the pounded rind and juice of a lime in a large tumbler with plenty of crushed ice. (Not to be confused with tea punch, which is actually based on tea.)

growing sugar cane specifically for distillation.

Some rum is made from the pressed cane juice itself, but most is made from the fermented molasses. In the former French colonies in particular, there is a distinguished tradition of *rhum agricole*, specialty products made on small sugar farms, in which rums are produced with different strains of yeast. They are individually appreciated in the same way that a wine drinker appreciates wines made from single grape varieties.

Both methods of distillation are practiced for rum

BACARDI
The world's favorite white spirit brand

HOW TO SERVE

Of the commercial products, white rum mixes famously well with cola, but also with orange juice or more tropical flavors such as pineapple or mango.

Dark rum has traditionally been seen as compatible with black currant or peppermint cordials, as well as the ubiquitous cola (below).

and then mixed with lemon juice as an antiscorbutic (but it was still not much less than a third of a pint of spirit). It was only as recently as 1970 that it was decided that perhaps encouraging the lads to drink around eight measures of spirit every day might not be the best guarantee of military efficiency.

Rum is today produced all over the West Indies and eastern South America, to a lesser extent in the Indian Ocean area—the Philippines and Mauritius—and in smaller quantities still in the United States and even in Australia. A lot of it is inevitably a byproduct of the sugar-refining industry, but the best grades are made by smaller, independent companies

MIXING

Hot Buttered Rum: In a tall glass, mix a teaspoon of demerara or brown sugar in a good double measure of strong dark rum. Add half a teaspoon of ground cinnamon and a knob of unsalted butter and fill with hot water. (Remember to stand a spoon in the glass to conduct the heat if the water has just boiled.) Stir well to dissolve the butter and sugar.

Piña Colada (below): Blend two measures each of white rum and pineapple juice, with a couple of teaspoons of shredded fresh coconut and ice, in a blender. (For that tropical touch, the drink should ideally be poured into a pineapple shell with a good lining of fruit left in it and drunk through straws.)

and, as with other spirits, the premium versions are double-distilled in a copper pot still. Continuous distillation and thorough rectification are used mainly by the bulk producers, particularly for the relatively neutral-tasting white rums that lead the market. Freshly distilled spirit from the pot still method is very high in impurities and must be allowed to mellow through a period of cask-aging, which in turn gives color to the darker rums. Some companies adjust the final color with caramel, but not to a degree that would affect the flavor.

After white rums, dark rum is the next most important category commercially, and it is certainly where the superior products are found. Leading brands are Captain Morgan and Lamb's, but there are many others. Some of them are bottled at the original naval strength of more than 50% ABV (Wood's Navy Rum, for example, is 57%), the traditional name for which was "overproof." The everyday dark rums are a more standard 40%, while Bacardi is adjusted down to 37.5% to put it on a level with the other commercial white spirits.

In between the two styles is the increasingly

MOUNT GAY BARBADOS
A major Caribbean brand of golden rum

MIXING

Daiquiri: Shake a double measure of white rum with the juice of half a lime or a quarter of a lemon, a teaspoon of superfine sugar and ice. Strain into a cocktail glass. (Adding half a measure of some fruit liqueur, together with 2 ounces of the equivalent fresh fruit, puréed, is a popular spin on the original Daiquiri. A strawberry version made with fraise liqueur is especially enticing.)

TEQUILA

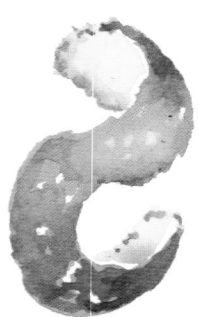

TEQUILA IS THE NATIONAL spirit of Mexico. It is one stage further down the road to refinement than its fellow cactus-based spirit, mescal, but several leagues ahead in terms of drinking pleasure. It starts life as pulque, the fermented beer-like juice of the agave plant, and is distilled twice before being aged in cask. It comes in two versions: clear, like vodka, and golden (or Oro), which spends a longer period in contact with the barrels. Virtually unknown in Europe until comparatively recently, Tequila made its first inroads into the world's liquor cabinets by traveling north from Mexico to the United States. It is now something of a cult drink in Europe's youth market.

The name *tequila* is echoed in the full botanical name of

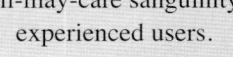

HOW TO SERVE
The correct way of drinking tequila: your drink is served to you cold and straight in a small shot glass. You then season your tongue with citrus and salt, by first squeezing a wedge of lime (lemon for the wimps) and then pouring salt onto the back of the hand and licking at each in turn. To be anatomically precise, the hand should be held at a 45° angle away from the body, with the thumb extended downward, and the juice and salt deposited along the groove between the bases of the thumb and forefinger. (Some make things easier by just sucking on the piece of lime.) The tequila is then thrown back in one gulp like schnapps, carrying the seasonings with it. The process is repeated ad infinitum.

Believe it or not, this really is how tequila is widely drunk in its native territory. If it sounds like a tricky and indescribably messy procedure, the answer is that it is, but long practice induces a sort of head-tossing, devil-may-care sanguinity in experienced users.

MIXING
Tequila and Orange: Avoid any fuss, and drink it on the rocks with fresh orange juice. It makes an enlivening change for those grown weary of vodka and orange.

CUERVO TEQUILA
The white version of Mexico's national spirit

MIXING

Margarita: Shake equal measures of tequila and Cointreau with the juice of half a lime and plenty of ice. Dip a finger in and run it around the rim of a cocktail glass. Up-end the glass briefly in a saucerful of coarse-ground salt, then strain the drink into it. (This is the classic tequila cocktail, but it is just a customized way of getting around the traditional salt-licking routine—with a slug of Cointreau for sweetly counteracting the salt. Some recipes add egg white too. No accounting for taste.)

the plant which is its source: *Agave tequilana*. Perhaps what prevented everybody else from trying it for so long was the thought of a spirit made from cacti, and indeed even the finest grades don't actually smell particularly inviting. It has a sweaty, slightly musty quality that must have come as something of a jolt at first to taste buds honed on squeaky-clean vodka.

In recognition of its cultural importance, the production of tequila has been strictly delimited within Mexico. It may be distilled in only a handful of towns, including Tequila itself, and in the area immediately surrounding Guadalajara. Two of the brands most commonly encountered on the export markets are Cuervo and Montezuma, the latter usually in an engraved bottle.

HOW IT IS MADE

Like mescal, tequila is distilled from the chopped, pressed and fermented hearts of agave plants. The juice is quite high in acidity, which lends even the refined spirit a certain piquancy. It is distilled a second time in a pot still, and then matured in wooden casks, briefly for the white version, and up to five years for the Oro.

GOLDEN MONTEZUMA
Gold tequila has aged in cask for longer than white

MIXING

Tequila Sunrise: Half-fill a tall glass with crushed ice. Put in a goodly measure of tequila and top up with fresh orange juice. Quickly drop a teaspoon of grenadine into the center of the drink. (The bright red grenadine sinks to the bottom and then blends upward into the orange in a very becoming way, hence the drink's name.)

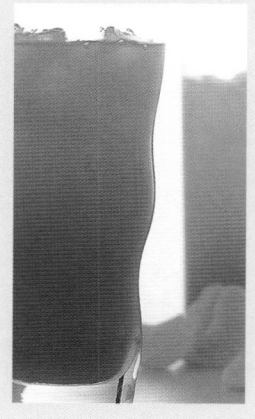

VODKA

IN ONE SENSE, vodka is the closest thing to perfection ever conceived in the long history of spirits. Had it been invented in the 1990s, in the era of wine coolers and ice beers, it would be hailed as a supremely adept piece of marketing wizardry. Nobody, other than a confirmed teetotaler, could possibly dislike it, for the simple reason that it tastes of nothing whatsoever. It is pure, unadulterated, uncomplicated alcohol. At least, most of it is.

The word *vodka* is a Russian endearment meaning "little water," from their word for water, *voda*. It doesn't denote the flavorlessness of the spirit, however, but derives from the widespread linguistic practice in Europe of referring to all distillates originally as a form of water (as in the Latin *aqua vitae* and French *eau-de-vie*).

Precisely because it is such a simple drink, it is almost impossible to pinpoint the origins of vodka historically. A potent spirit distilled from various grains, and

OTHER NAMES
Poland: wodka

indeed potatoes—still wrongly believed in the popular imagination to be its main ingredient—has been made in Poland, Russia and the Baltic states of Latvia, Lithuania and Estonia since the very early days of distillation in Europe.

But as to where a drink specifically recognizable as vodka first arose is a matter for the Poles and the Russians to sort out between themselves. (Most outsiders, it should be said, tend to come down on the Polish side of the fence these days.) What is certain is that, by the time home distillation had become a favored way of passing the long, grim northern winters in Poland, peasant families were producing their own vodkas on an extensive scale.

The discovery of rectification

HOW TO SERVE
Everything should be almost painfully cold. The bottle should be kept in the freezer and the glasses should also be iced. If there isn't a heavy mist of condensation on the outside of the glass, it isn't cold enough. Some shots are thrown back like schnapps, owing to an old folk belief that if you inhale the fumes for more than a split second, you will get too drunk too quickly. The aged vodkas, and specialties such as Zubrowka, are more often sipped appreciatively. A little shot glass is traditional, but in some homes, a rather larger, narrow tumbler, or even something like a goblet wineglass is used.

SMIRNOFF
The basic red label brand is the market leader

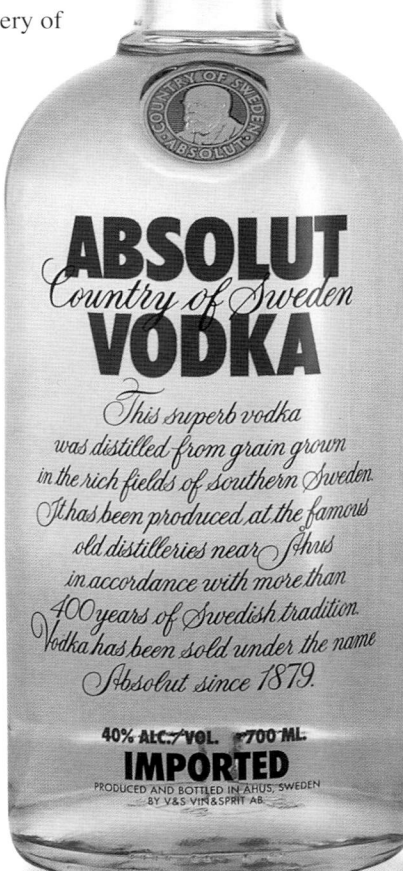

ABSOLUT
Blue label Absolut is the unflavored version

techniques did not take place until the beginning of the nineteenth century, and so these early distillates would have tasted pretty unclean, to say the least. Any herbs, seeds or berries that were on hand would be steeped in the spirit to mask its rankness. So the first vodkas were not the anonymous products preferred today, but the true ancestors of the flavored vodkas that are sometimes greeted as nothing more than novelty items by modern drinkers.

Nonetheless, it was the neutral, ultrapurified grain vodka—made from wheat or rye—that came to commercial prominence in the West. So prevalent is it now, particularly among younger drinkers who have yet to discover and appreciate the taste of unrectified, cask-matured spirits such as good whiskey and cognac, that it is hard to believe that hardly anyone in western Europe or America had heard of it until the late 1940s.

BLACK LABEL SMIRNOFF
A softer, mellower product.

BLUE LABEL SMIRNOFF
The strongest at 45%.

MIXING

Basic vodka has no scent or flavor, meaning it is not the most inspiring ingredient in the cocktail repertoire. All it can really do is confer an extra slug of alcohol for those hell-bent on the shortcut to oblivion. As a result, the sky's the limit.

Black Russian: The true Black Russian is simply equal measures of vodka and Tia Maria, or Kahlúa, mixed with ice cubes in a tumbler. However, the fashion in recent years has been to serve it as a long drink in a big glass, topped up with cola. Alternatively, leave out the cola, add a measure of single cream, shake it up and it becomes a **White Russian**. Then again, substitute dark brown crème de cacao for the Tia Maria and create a **Piranha**.

Black Cossack (below): Add a good slug of vodka to a half-pint of Guinness.

It all changed with the first stirrings of interest in California during the period of the Beat Generation.

Not only did vodka possess the aforementioned neutrality that made it such an obvious beginner's spirit, but it was also seen as a provocatively dissident thing to drink in the era of the onset of the Cold War. Vodka was the favored "hooch" of the Soviet bloc, and in the witch-hunting atmosphere of 1950s America, nothing was more guaranteed to inflame bourbon-drinking patriots than to see young folks imbibing the spirit of Communism with such evident glee. The late Alexis Lichine,

FLAVORINGS

Vodka will happily take up whatever flavoring a producer decides to give it, including:
Lemon peel
Bison grass
Red chili peppers
Cherries
Rowanberries
Black currants
Apples
Sloes
Saffron
Tarragon
Walnuts
Honey
Licorice
Rose petals (Seriously. Pound for pound, they are actually more expensive than gold.)

LIMONNAYA
A leading lemon-
flavored vodka.

Screwdriver: That nightclub favorite, vodka and orange juice. The name, according to one theory, originated among workers on American oil-rigs who—finding themselves short of swizzle-sticks—resourcefully used their screwdrivers to stir the drink. In the Baltic states, the freshly squeezed orange juice is served to you in a little jug and you mix to taste. Even here the cocktail name is in use, although, as I discovered in Riga, to make yourself clear, you must ask the barman for a "skrew." When first marketed on the west coast of the United States, it was suggested that it be drunk with ginger beer. Thus did the first **Moscow Mule** come to light.

drink historian, attributes the start of vodka's meteoric rise in the West to the purchase of a recipe for rectified vodka from a Russian refugee called Smirnoff by an American company, on the eve of the Second World War. The rest is history.

Vodka is still very much the drink of gastronomic choice in its native lands, drunk as aperitif, digestif and even as an accompaniment to food. It is nearly always taken ice-cold, preceded in Polish homes by the ritual wishing of good health—*na zdrowie*—to one's family and friends. The quantities consumed may raise eyebrows in our Western unit-counting culture, but a vodka hangover is very rare, owing to the relentless cleanup job the drink is given during distillation. This removes nearly all of its congeners, the substances that impart character to the dark spirits.

Fruit flavorings are very common, and make a drier, more bracing alternative to the equivalent liqueurs. Perhaps the most celebrated flavored product is Zubrowka, bison-grass vodka, which is generally sold with a

ABSOLUT
Kurant is
solidly fruity
and flavored
with black
currants

Bloody Mary: Everyone has his or her own proprietary recipe for the next-best hangover cure after aspirin. Some strange people even put ketchup into it. Others round out the alcohol with a splash of dry sherry. Here is my own formula.

Put a slice of lemon and two or three ice cubes in a tall glass, add a teaspoon of Lea & Perrin's Worcestershire sauce, a teaspoon of freshly squeezed lemon juice, a pinch of celery salt, a generous dash of Tabasco and black pepper—about half a dozen twists of the mill—and stir to coat the ice. Fill the glass to about an inch and a half from the top with tomato juice and pour on a generous measure of vodka. Stir well to combine the alcohol.

blade of grass in the bottle. Bison grass is the gourmet preference of the wild bison that roam the forests of eastern Poland, and the beast is usually depicted on the label.

Wisniowka (cherries), Limonnaya (lemon) and the Swedish Absolut company's Kurant (black currant) are all appetizing drinks. Pieprzówka, which is infused with chili peppers, is a variety for real aficionados: The spirit is emphasized by the hot spice burn of its flavoring component. Russia's Okhotnichya—"Hunter's Vodka"—is impregnated with orange peel, ginger root, coffee beans, juniper berries and even a drop of white port.

Neutral vodkas are produced all over the

world now, although most grades are only intended to be served in mixed drinks. Russian Stolichnaya, particularly the Cristall bottling, is an honorable, silky-smooth exception. Smirnoff makes three types, in red, blue and black labels to denote varying strength, and there are brands with such names as Black Death and Jazz Jamboree. Scandinavian vodkas such as Finlandia and Absolut have their deserved followings, while most British vodka tends to be little more than patent alcohol. At one time, vodka production had even traveled south from Russia into Iran, but the coming of Islamic rule brought that to a halt.

Also seen on the export markets is Polish Pure Spirit, bottled at around 70% ABV, and much beloved by reckless students as a dare.

HOW IT IS MADE

Although potatoes and other vegetables, and even molasses, have been used to make vodka at various times in its history, commercial vodka is nowadays virtually exclusively made from grains, the principal one of which is rye. A basic mash is made in the usual way by malting the grains and encouraging them to ferment with cultured yeast. The resulting brew is then continuously

PIEPRZÓWKA
This vodka has been colored and flavored with chilies

distilled in a column still apparatus to higher and higher degrees of alcoholic strength, thus driving off nearly all of the higher alcohols, or fusel oil. As a final insurance policy against flavor, the finished spirit is then filtered through a layer of charcoal, which strips it of any remaining character. It is then bottled at around 37.5% for commercial strength and released without further ado.

In the case of flavored vodkas, the aromatizing elements are added to the new spirit after rectification, and left to infuse in it over long periods—sometimes three years or more. Occasionally, a specialty vodka will be aged in cask and take on a tinge of color; others derive their exotic hues from the addition of spices, flowers or nuts.

TASTES GOOD WITH

Ice-cold vodka is the classic accompaniment to finest Russian caviar, itself served on heaps of ice. In the Scandinavian countries, it is also drunk, like aquavit, with marinated and smoked fish such as herring, mackerel and even salmon. Superchef Martin Blunos at Restaurant Lettonie, near Bristol in England, has created a sumptuously theatrical dish of scrambled duck egg served in the shell amid a slick of flaming Latvian vodka, topped with Sevruga caviar and with blinis and a shot of freezing vodka on the side.

STOLICHNAYA
This smooth vodka should be sipped appreciatively

MIXING
Balalaika: Shake a measure each of vodka and Cointreau with half a measure of lemon juice and plenty of ice, and strain into a cocktail glass.

Barbara: Shake a measure of vodka with half-measures of crème de cacao and light cream, with ice, and strain into a cocktail glass. (This is essentially a vodka-based **Alexander**.)
Katinka (from Michael Walker's *Cinzano Cocktail Book*): Shake a measure and a half of vodka with a measure of apricot brandy and half a measure of fresh lime juice with ice, and pour over a heap of slivered ice in a cocktail glass.
Vodkatini: Basically a classic martini, but with vodka replacing the gin.
Czarina: Stir a measure of vodka with half-measures of apricot brandy and dry vermouth and a dash of Angostura with ice in a mixing cup. Strain into a cocktail glass.

WHISKEY

WHISKEY (OR WHISKY, depending on where it hails from) is one of the world's leading spirits. Its history is every bit as distinguished as that of cognac and, like the classic brandies of France, its spread around the world from its first home—the Scottish Highlands, in whiskey's case—has been a true testament to the genius of its conception. Tennessee sour mash may bear about as much relation in taste to single malt scotch as Spanish brandy does to cognac, but the fact that they are all great products demonstrates the versatility of each basic formula.

Whiskeys are produced all over the world now. As the name is not a geographically specific one, they may all legitimately call themselves whiskey. In Australia and India, the Czech Republic and Germany, they make grain spirits from barley or rye that proudly bear the name. The five major whiskey-producing countries are Scotland, the United States, Ireland, Canada and Japan, which are covered in this chapter.

The name "whiskey" itself is yet another variant on the phrase "water of life" that we have become familiar with in the world of spirits. In translation, the Latin *aqua vitae* became *uisge beatha* in the Scots branch of Gaelic and *usquebaugh* in the Irish; it eventually was mangled into the half-Anglicized "whiskey" and was in

official use by the mid-eighteenth century.

In countries that lacked the warm climate for producing fermented drinks from grapes, beer was always the staple brew and, just as brandy was the obvious first distillate in southern Europe, so malted grains provided the starting point for domestic production further north. Unlike brandy, however, which starts life as wine, whiskey doesn't have to be made from something that would be recognizable, like beer. The grains are malted by allowing them to germinate in water and then lightly cooking them to encourage the formation of sugars. It is these sugars on which the yeast then feeds to produce the first ferment. A double distillation by the pot still method results in a congener-rich

HOW TO SERVE
The finest whiskeys are not necessarily drunk neat. It is widely believed that taming some of the spirit's fire helps to bring up the array of complicated scents and flavors in good whiskey. To that end, it is normally drunk with a dose of water, ideally the same springwater that goes into the whiskey itself, otherwise any pure, nonchlorinated water. Half-and-half are the preferred proportions in Scotland and Ireland, while in Tennessee and Kentucky they add a little less than half.

LAPHROAIG
One of the richest of the peaty styles of Scotch produced in Islay

MACALLAN
This 18-year-old whiskey is one of the best-loved Highland malts

spirit that can then be matured—often for decades for the finer whiskeys—in oak barrels.

Just as with other spirits that haven't had the life rectified out of them, whiskey is nearly always truly expressive of its regional origins and the raw materials that went into it. For that reason, a passionate connoisseurship of this spirit has arisen over the generations, similar to that which surrounds wine. Even more than brandy, whiskey handsomely rewards those who set out with a conscientious approach to the tasting and appreciation of the spirit.

SCOTLAND

Home distillation in Scotland can be traced back to the fifteenth century, when the practice of distilling surplus grain to make a potent drink for clan chieftains was established. Initially, the drink was—like all spirits—primarily valued

for its medicinal powers, and early examples were no doubt infusions of herbs and berries rather than the pure grain product we know today. Although other grains would have been used at first, the preeminence of malted barley was acknowledged relatively early on in the development of scotch.

Before the Act of Union that brought England and Scotland together politically in 1707, scotch was hardly known in England. Gin was the national drink south of the border. Once the English laid their administrative hands on Scotland, they did their level best to bring whiskey distillation under statutory control, but with only very partial success. Those whiskey makers within striking distance of the border fled north with their stills into the Highlands, and the production of scotch continued unabated as an almost wholly illicit activity.

Eventually, by a combination of threats and bribes, the authorities managed to place the whole enterprise under license so that, by the 1870s, there

GLENLIVET
A ten-year-old Spey-side malt from the Scottish Highlands

TASTES GOOD WITH

Scotch is naturally the only accompaniment to the ceremonial haggis on Burns Night (January 25). Whether it is a precise gastronomic match may be open to question, but to order a bottle of Rioja would be missing the point somewhat. Un-iced Scotch is also great with hearty soups: thick, barley-based Scotch broth or cock-a-leekie should ideally have a fair amount of whiskey in them anyway.

TALISKER
Talisker whiskey is the only malt whiskey produced on the island of Skye.

were just half a dozen arraignments in Scotland for illegal distilling (as against nearly 700 only 40 years earlier).

The advent of continuous distillation came to Scotland courtesy of Robert Stein, who invented a rudimentary version of the column still in 1826. Although scotch had traditionally been characterized by the richness and depth of flavor that marks all potstill products, the development of the new method allowed a lighter spirit of more obvious commercial appeal to be produced. By the late nineteenth century, the habit of blending true malt whiskey with straight grain spirit made by continuous distillation from unmalted barley (and corn) was widespread. These were the types of scotch that were introduced to cautious English palates.

In the early years of this century, a Royal Commission was set up to determine the parameters for Scotch whiskey production, i.e. the methods of distillation, rules on blending, minimum maturation times and, of course, the salient geographical point—that scotch could only be distilled and aged in Scotland. The commission reported in 1909, its conclusions were refined slightly in 1915, and it remains in force today as the legal textbook for an industry of worldwide importance that is also a central support of the Scottish economy.

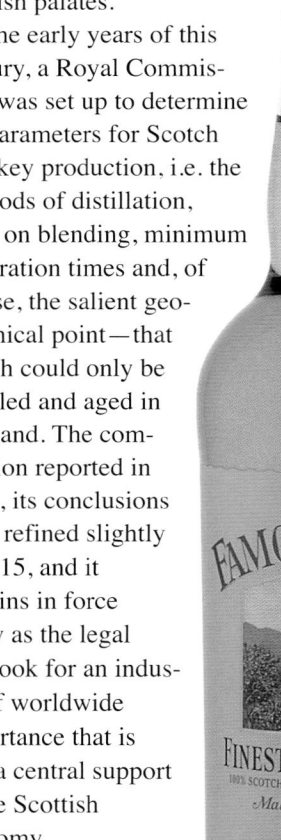

THE FAMOUS GROUSE
One of the leading brands of blended Scotch

TYPES OF SCOTCH
The most highly prized of Scotch whiskeys are the single malts. These are whiskeys that are produced entirely from malted barley, double-distilled, and made exclusively at a single one (hence the terminology) of Scotland's one hundred or so working distilleries. Some of these products are aged for many years. Twenty-five-year-old Scotch will be shot through with all sorts of profoundly complex flavors and perfumes picked up from the wood in which it has matured and perhaps, according to some, from the sea air that wafts around the coastal distilleries. Remember that—as with other spirits—aged malt can't continue to develop once bottled.

Some malts are the blended produce of several single malts, in which case they are known as vatted malts. They are often assembled from several distilleries within a particular region in order to illustrate the local style, comparable to specific regional subdivisions in a *vin de pays* wine area.

Whiskeys made from corn or unmalted barley are known as grain whiskeys and are always

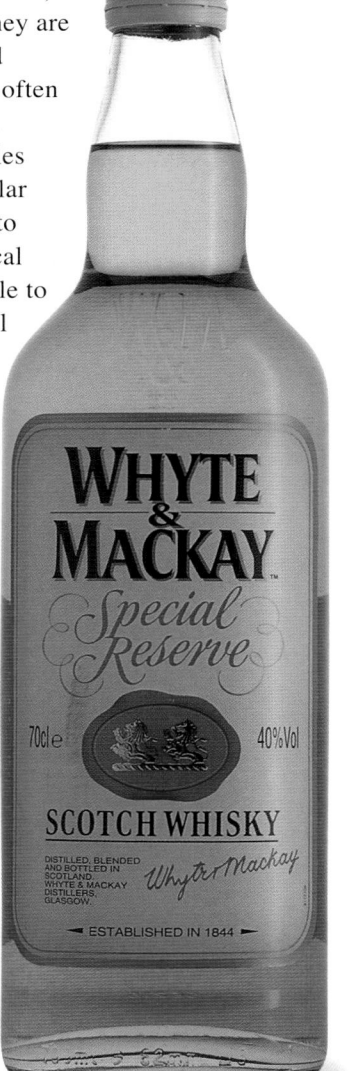

WHYTE & MACKAY
This whiskey is reblended for a second period of maturation

considerably lighter in style than the malts. They could be described as beginner's scotch, since they have far fewer of the aromatic components that account for the pedigree of great malt, but they should by no means be seen as worthless imitations. They have their role to play.

The greater part of that role is in the production of blended scotch, whiskey made from a mixture of malt and grain spirits. This is the market-leading category, occupied by virtually all of the big brand names, such as Bell's, J&B, Johnnie Walker, Ballantine's, Whyte & Mackay, The Famous Grouse, White Horse and Teacher's. Most of these have fairly low concentrations of malt in the blend, although Teacher's and Johnnie Walker's Black Label

J&B
This blended whiskey is popular in the American market; J&B stands for Justerini & Brooks

bottling are notable exceptions.

Scotch whiskey is mostly retailed at the standard dark spirit strength of 40% ABV, or perhaps slightly above (avoid any that are below). A small proportion of the best grades are bottled from the barrel undiluted. These are known as "cask strength" whiskeys. You are not intended to drink them as they come; the distiller is inviting you to dilute them with water yourself and find the precise level of potency that suits you.

AREAS OF PRODUCTION
For the purposes of whiskey production, Scotland is divided into four broad regions: the Lowlands, south of Stirling; the tiny Campbeltown, on a narrow peninsula west of Ayr; Islay and the Western

GLENMORANGIE
One of the most celebrated Northern Highland malts

TEACHERS
One of the maltier blended whiskeys.

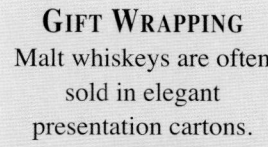

GIFT WRAPPING
Malt whiskeys are often sold in elegant presentation cartons.

FLAVORINGS

Discounting the whiskey-based liqueurs, the only case of a straight whiskey being flavored is that of certain Canadian products that have minute amounts of other drinks added to them: grape wine, wines from other fruits (prunes are a favorite), unfermented fruit juices, even sherry.

MIXING

Old-Fashioned: Grind up a sugar lump with a good shake from the Angostura bottle in the squat tumbler that is named after this drink. Add plenty of ice and a hearty quantity of Canadian or straight rye whiskey. Throw in a twist of lemon peel, a slice of orange and a cocktail cherry, and serve with a stirring implement in it.

which allows the spirit freer access to the vanillin and tannins in the wood. Nobody quite knows where the charring tradition came from, but it seems quite likely that it was the result of a happy accident.

There are two distinct styles of bourbon, sweet mash and sour mash, the differences arising at the fermentation stage of the grains. For sweet mash, the yeast is allowed to perform its work quite quickly over a couple of days, while for sour mash, some yeast from the preceding batch augments the brew. This doubles the length of the fermentation and ensures that more of the sugars in the grain are consumed.

Most bourbon is labeled "Kentucky Straight Bourbon," which means it is made from at least 51% corn, is aged for a minimum of two years in charred new barrels and has been made and matured within the prescribed areas. It is the equivalent category to single malt scotch. Some, sold as "Blended Straight," is made from more than one lot of straight bourbon, and corresponds to vatted malt. Most bourbon is bottled at a slightly higher strength than standard Scotch—about 43–45% ABV.

The leading brand by a long shot is Jim Beam, made at Bardstown and virtually synonymous with

bourbon on the export markets. Other brands include Wild Turkey, Evan Williams, Early Times, Old Grand-Dad and the pacesetting Maker's Mark (the one with the top dipped in red sealing wax).

TENNESSEE

South of the bourbon state of Kentucky, in neighboring Tennessee, an entirely different but equally distinctive style of whiskey is made. Tennessee sour mash is represented by just two distilleries—Jack Daniel's in Lynchburg, and George Dickel in Tullahoma. Their various bottlings represent some of the richest and smoothest whiskeys made.

Whereas bourbon is matured in charred barrels, Tennessee takes the principle a stage further by actually filtering the newly made spirit through a mass of charcoal. In the yards behind the distilleries, they burn great stacks of sugar maple down to ash and then grind it all into a rough black powder. This is

JACK DANIEL'S
By far the bigger
brand of the two
Tennessee whiskeys

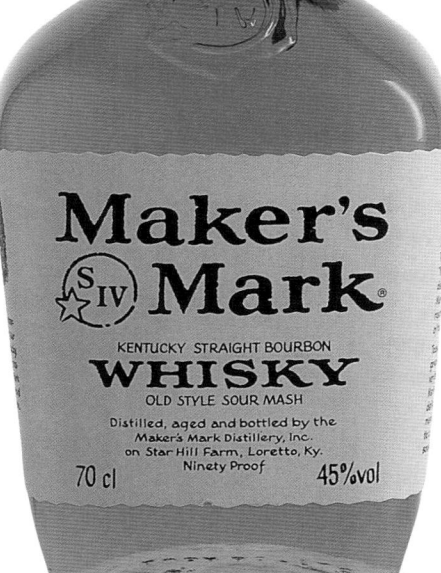

MAKER'S MARK
Small-volume
production allied
to top quality

piled to a depth of around ten feet into so-called mellowing vats, all sitting on a fleecy wool blanket. The whiskey drips at a painfully slow rate from holes in a gridwork of copper pipes above the vats, and filters gradually through the charcoal bed, before being cask-matured in the usual way.

Jack Daniel's is one of the world's best-loved whiskey brands. Its market-leading Old No. 7, in the famous square bottle, first established the kudos of JD by winning a Gold Medal at the 1904 World's Fair in St Louis. Its great rival, Dickel (which spells its product "whisky" in the Scottish way), matures its No. 12 brand for several years longer, and the results are evident in a more discreet and mellower nose and deeper color. Both are bottled at 40–45% ABV.

One of the great ironies of Tennessee whiskey is that both producers have their distilleries in "dry" counties where it is forbidden to sell alcohol, which means that they may not avail themselves of

the doorstep custom they could enjoy from public visits. A glass of soul-saving springwater is offered instead.

IRELAND

The origins of distillation in the Emerald Isle are lost in swathes of Irish mist, but are certainly of great antiquity, at least as old as those of scotch. There are those who have claimed that it was Irish missionaries who first brought the knowledge of distilling to France, and thus made brandy possible. Whether that is true or not, Irish whiskey once enjoyed an unrivaled reputation as a more approach-able style of spirit than Scotch malt. It was only when blended scotch began to be made on any significant scale toward the end of the nineteenth century that Irish whiskey was nudged out of the frame.

The reasons for the greater accessibility of Irish whiskey lie in its production process. No peat is used in the kilns, so there is none of the smoky pungency that is present in some degree in most scotch. Secondly, punitive taxes on malted barley in the mid-nineteenth century meant that the Irish distillers began to use a mixture of malted and unmalted grain in their mash, making it tradi-tionally a blended product long before the recipes for today's

JAMESON
The brand leader in the export market.

JIM BEAM
A particularly
popular bourbon

PADDY
This whiskey is
distilled at
Midleton, just
outside the city
of Cork

MIXING

Whiskey Sour: Mix the juice of half a lemon with a level teaspoon of superfine sugar in a tumbler with two or three cubes of ice. When the sugar is dissolved, add a generous measure of whiskey and stir again— American whiskeys are best for this preparation. (Some add a brief squirt of soda. If you find this formula a little *too* sour, add a little more sugar, but this is the way I like it.)

CANADIAN CLUB
The leading brand of Canadian whiskey.

standard scotch brands had even been dreamed about.

Most famously of all, Irish whiskey is subjected to a triple distillation by the copper pot still method. The third passage of the spirit through the stills results in a product with a softer, ultrarefined palate profile while still retaining all of its complexity. By law, the whiskey must then be cask-aged for a minimum of three years, although in practice most are aged for two to three times that period. It is usually bottled at 40% ABV.

The brand leader on the export markets is Jameson. Other notable names include Bushmills, John Power, Murphy's, Paddy, Dunphy's and Tullamore Dew. All but one are made in the Republic, mostly in the environs of Dublin or Cork. The exception is Bushmills, which is located in County Antrim in Northern Ireland.

(There is another Irish "whiskey," of course, made on illegal traveling stills that the authorities have always found notoriously difficult to track down. Perhaps they have more constructive things to do. For all its reputation as toxic brain-scrambler, poteen—pronounced *pocheen*—is an unassailable part of Ireland's folk history, and will continue to be so for as long as taxation rates on the official stuff are as rapacious as they are.)

CANADA

Canada's whiskeys are made from blends of different grains, the greater proportion of each brand based on an original mash that combines rye, corn and malted barley. They nearly always contain some spirit, however, that is produced entirely from the heavier-tasting rye, but it usually accounts for less than a tenth of the final blend. As a result, they have the reputation of being among the lightest classic whiskeys of all, even more so than the triple-distilled Irish.

The whiskey industry in Canada dates back only to the last century, when it arose as an offshoot of the agricultural production of grain. It was quite common at one time to pay the millers in kind with some of the grain, and distillation has long been a traditional way of using up surpluses all over the world. The

earliest producers—and, despite the country's size, there are still only a handful—were Hiram Walker, Seagram's and Corby's, all in the province of Ontario.

Distillation is by the continuous process, in gigantic column stills. Different spirits produced from different mashes, or fermented from different yeast strains, are painstakingly blended by the distiller—before the maturation in some cases, afterward in others. All whiskeys must spend at least three years in the barrels, which are of new wood, but there is a noble tradition of aged products in Canada for whiskeys that are 10, 12, even 18 years old on release. As elsewhere, the standard blends are sold at 40% ABV, but specialty aged bottlings may be somewhat stronger.

A curiosity of Canadian whiskey is that the regulations permit the addition of a tiny quantity of other drink products, such as sherry or wine made from grapes or other fruits. While this may account for no more than a hundredth part of the finished product, it makes its presence felt in the fleeting suggestion of fruitiness in the flavors of some whiskeys.

CROWN ROYAL
A Canadian brand owned by Seagram's

Most of the distilleries are situated in the eastern provinces of Ontario and Quebec. The leading label is Hiram Walker's Canadian Club, first blended in the 1880s, supported by the Burke's and Wiser's ranges from Corby's, McGuinness's Silk Tassel, Alberta Springs and Seagram's Crown Royal.

JAPAN

Of the countries under consideration here, Japan has by far the youngest whiskey industry—of even more recent provenance than its efforts at wine making. The first distillery was established in 1923, and it is only in the last 30 years or so that its products have come to the attention of whiskey drinkers other than the Japanese themselves.

The model for Japan's whiskey is single malt scotch, but there are equally successful spirits made in the idiom of blended scotch. The base is a mash of malted barley, dried in kilns fired with a little peat (though considerably less than is the case in Scotland, and so yielding a less aromatically defined product). Distillation is by the pot still method. Some of the brands are aged in used sherry or bourbon casks, as for scotch, others in heavily charred new American oak barrels, as for bourbon itself. Some distilleries buy a proportion of unused Scottish spirit for blending in with the home-grown whiskey. The premium brands are

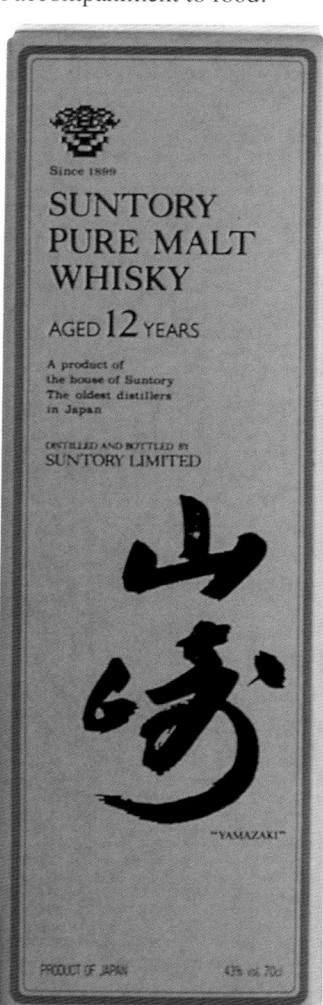

SUNTORY
The 12-year-old Yamazaki is a kind of Japanese single malt.

generally bottled at around 43% ABV.

The giant drinks company Suntory, which has a finger in all sorts of pies, from classed-growth Bordeaux to the green melon liqueur Midori, is also the biggest producer of Japanese whiskey, accounting for virtually three-quarters of the industry's annual output. Behind Suntory comes the Nikka company, and then the smaller producers Sanraku Ocean and Seagram's, which is anything but small everywhere else.

In Japan, whiskey is nearly always drunk heavily watered. Whereas in Scotland the mix is usually half-and-half, the Japanese prefer it as a long pale-yellowish drink in tall glasses filled to the top with springwater and with plenty of ice—about the most denatured form in which fine whiskey is commonly drunk anywhere in the world. It is drunk both as an aperitif and as an accompaniment to food.

Among the more illustrious products are Suntory's 12-year-old Pure Malt from its Yamazaki distillery on Honshu, the principal island; Nikka Memorial 50, Sanraku Ocean's single malt Karuizawa (also from Honshu); and Seagram's top labels Crescent and Emblem.

HOW TO SERVE
Whiskeys go well with soda for those who prefer a friskier drink, and to some extent with ginger ale (especially those fruity Canadian spirits). They should then be iced.

LIQUEURS

SINCE WE ARE CLEARLY distinguishing between spirits and liqueurs, it would be useful to arrive at a working definition of what constitutes a liqueur. Why is kirsch a spirit, for example, but cherry brandy a liqueur?

The distinction lies in the way that the various flavors of these drinks are obtained. Essentially, a liqueur is any spirit-based drink to which flavoring elements have been added, usually by infusion, and—in the vast majority of cases—enhanced by sweetening. Sometimes the flavorings are themselves subjected to distillation; sometimes they are merely soaked or macerated in an alcohol base. Although there are flavored spirits, such as lemon vodka (or, for that matter, gin) there are no *un*flavored liqueurs. To answer the question in the first paragraph, kirsch is a spirit because it is a straight, unsweetened distillate of cherries, whereas cherry brandy is a neutral spirit from other sources to which cherry flavor is added by infusion of the fruit.

Liqueurs have their origins in the practice of adding aromatic ingredients—herbs, fruit extracts, seeds, spices, nuts, roots, flowers, and so forth—to the earliest distilled spirits, in order both to mask the unappealing flavor of the impurities that had not been rectified out of them, and to endow the resulting potions with medicinal value. Given a source of basic spirit, they could and often would be concocted in domestic kitchens for use in cooking as well as for drinking—a tradition carried on in this book. As various proprietary liqueurs came on the market during the course of the nineteenth century, so home liqueur-making declined.

When the science of distillation was still in its infancy in Europe, the Catalan physician Arnaldo de Villanova advanced the theory that steeping certain medicinal herbs in alcohol extracted their beneficial qualities. This was a logical progression of the nonalcoholic distilling of essential oils that had been practiced in ancient Egypt and classical Greece. As an offshoot of the alchemical arts, distilling was intimately bound up with the doomed enterprise of attempting to turn base metals to gold, and so gold itself came to play a part in the formulation of alcohol-based remedies. (Arnaldo was saved from the Inquisition, it is said, because he had cured the pope of life-threatening illness by means of a tonic containing flakes of gold.) The tradition

Left: Le Palais de Bénédictine: Until recently Bénédictine was still made by the monastic order. Chartreuse is one of the few liqueurs still produced in the traditional way in the distillery (below) at Voiron, near Grenoble.

Above: Even today, small producers, such as this French artisan distiller, produce a wonderful variety of flavored liqueurs.

lives on today in the form of a drink called Goldwasser.

It was in the religious orders that many of the traditional liqueurs were first formulated, since the medicinal ingredients used were often grown in the monastery gardens. By the late Middle Ages, the Italians had become the most celebrated practitioners of the art of liqueur making. The marriage of Catherine de Medici to the future French king Henri II in 1533 brought a wave of Italians and their expertise into France. Some of the more notable products, such as Bénédictine, were made by French monastic orders until relatively recently. (Chartreuse still is.)

In the last century, liqueurs had an aura of being soothingly palatable afterdinner digestifs for those—women essentially—who were not fond of the stronger alternatives such as cognac.

Indeed, they were seen as more ladylike drinks altogether, an image enhanced by the introduction of the tiny glasses that are still depressingly enough seen as the appropriate receptacles. By now, they had shed most of their health-giving claims and become honest-to-goodness drinks, although it was still popularly believed by imbibers that they had prophylactic properties.

The cocktail era of the 1920s and 1930s that had to contend doggedly with universal prohibition in the United States, but suffered no such constraints in London, Paris, Berlin and Venice, freed liqueurs from the straitjacket of cultured politeness in which the Victorian period had imprisoned them. At a stroke, they transformed the old slings and fizzes, fixes, sours, punches, cups and smashes into drinks that were worthy of their names. A mixture of gin with lemon

Above: The museum of La Grande Chartreuse Monastery, Isère, France.

juice, sugar and soda may have been a pleasant way of drinking gin, but add a slug of cherry brandy to it and it became an altogether more exciting and hazardous proposition. That sense of playing with fire is inscribed in the names of the great cocktail recipes of the 1920s, in their evocations of gambling (Casino), sex (Maiden's Blush), spiritual danger (Hell, Little Devil) and even First World War munitions (Whizzbang, Depth Bomb, Artillery).

No drinking culture was ever happier or more heedless than that of the original and greatest cocktail era, and it couldn't have happened without the liqueurs. The following pages are a taster's tour of the famous and the not so famous.

ADVOCAAT

FLAVORINGS
Oranges
Lemons
Cherries
Vanilla

ADVOCAAT IS A Dutch specialty. It is essentially a customized version of the humble eggnog, without the milk: a mixture of simple grape brandy with egg yolks and sugar, as thick and as yellow as tinned custard. Most of it is sold in this natural form, although it is possible in the Netherlands to buy vanilla- and fruit-flavored versions. As a result of its velvety texture and bland wholesomeness, advocaat is often thought of as a drink for the elderly, and is commonly added to mugs of hot chocolate or strong coffee.

There are a few widely available brands of advocaat on the market: The red-labeled Warninks is probably the most familiar, but Fockinks, and the liqueur specialists, Bols and De Kuypers, also make it. The standard bottled strength is quite low for a liqueur—around 17% ABV, which is about the same strength as the average fortified wine.

HOW TO SERVE
In the Netherlands, advocaat is drunk both as an aperitif and a digestif. Unmixed, its texture is such that it is often consumed with a teaspoon. Taken in a hot beverage, it makes a comforting bedtime drink.

WARNINKS
Probably the most famous advocaat brand

MIXING
Snowball: Put a generous measure (a couple of fluid ounces) of advocaat in a tall glass and top up with ice-cold sparkling lemonade. If you require a bit more of a kick, add a teaspoon of sweet brown sherry to it as well. (This is the kind of "cocktail" generally considered safe to give to occasional drinkers, since it resembles nothing so much as a particularly rich milkshake.)

HOW IT IS MADE
Commercial grape spirit is sweetened with sugar syrup. Only the yolks of the eggs are added, along with an emulsifying agent to prevent the mixture from separating.

TASTES GOOD WITH
As the ready-made base of eggnog, it can be made into a long drink by topping it up with whole milk and a sprinkling of nutmeg.

ADVOCAAT
The only manufactured drink in this book to contain egg yolk.

AMARETTO

OF ALL THE LIQUEURS that rely on almonds for their principal flavoring, amaretto is the most famous. It has become widely associated in people's minds with one particular Italian brand, Disaronno Amaretto, made by a company called Illva, although there are other liqueurs that may properly be called amarettos. The famous amaretto comes in a rectangular bottle, with a label in the form of an old scroll and a disproportionately large, square screw-top. The flavor is not entirely derived from almonds but from the pits of apricots too. Resembling a kind of liquid marzipan, the taste is strong and sweet and is quite assertive even when mixed in a cocktail.

Legend has it that the recipe was given to an Italian painter, Bernardino Luini, in the sixteenth century by an innkeeper who was the model for the Virgin Mary in his fresco of the Nativity at Saronno. Whether or not there is much truth in the tale, the original domestic concoction was probably grape brandy in which apricot pits—with their strong almondy flavor—had been steeped.

HOW IT IS MADE

Almond extracts, along with apricot pits, are steeped in brandy, and the resulting drink is sweetened with sugar syrup and colored to a deep tawny brown.

DISARONNO AMARETTO
The most famous brand of Italian amaretto

MIXING

Godmother: Mix Disaronno Amaretto with an equal measure of vodka in a tumbler full of ice.
Godfather (below): As above, but substitute scotch for the vodka.

TASTES GOOD WITH

Just as a custard mixture, full of ground almonds, makes a good base for almost any fruit tart, so amaretto works well in the syrup for a fruit salad, or added to whipped cream or ice cream for most fruit-based desserts. It also marries deliciously with chocolate in super-rich *pot au chocolat*, and is excellent in a liqueur coffee, and perhaps with cognac too.

CASONI AMARETTO
Amaretto's flavor is like marzipan in a bottle

OTHER NAMES
France: crème d'amandes

FLAVORINGS
Almonds
Apricots

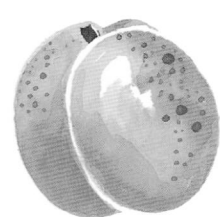

HOW TO SERVE

Although sweet, the flavor of Disaronno Amaretto is quite complex enough for it to be enjoyable on its own, but it works better chilled. Drinking it frappé (poured over crushed ice) is highly refreshing.

ANIS

CONFUSION REIGNS as to the precise differences between anis and pastis, and indeed whether there are any meaningful differences at all. They are both flavored with the berries of the anise plant, originally native to North Africa, and are popular all around the Mediterranean. They both turn cloudy when watered, and are both claimed as the respectable successor to the outlawed absinthe.

One august authority claims that pastis should be flavored with licorice rather than anise, although the two are very close in taste. Another claims that anis is simply one of the types of pastis. Still another claims that, whereas anis is a product of the maceration of anise or licorice in spirit, pastis should properly be seen as a distillation from either of the two ingredients themselves.

They can't all be right, of course, but for what it's worth, I incline to accept the last definition. For one thing, anis tends to be lower in alcohol than pastis— liqueur strength rather than spirit strength. The one thing we can be sure of

is that pastis is always French (the word is old southern French dialect), whereas anis can also be Spanish. In Spain, there are sweet and dry varieties, whereas French anise tends mainly to be dry.

Ever since the days of the medical school of Salerno, and probably earlier, extract of anis has been seen as a valuable weapon in the apothecary's armory. It is thought to be especially good for ailments of the stomach.

FLAVORINGS

Anise berries (anise). Sometimes the seeds of star anise—an Asian shrub that bears a fruit in the shape of an eight-pointed star— may be used. The flavor is fairly similar, though by no means identical.

HOW TO SERVE

The only true way to serve anis is to take it ice-cold in a little thick-bottomed tumbler. The addition of a small amount of water— usually about as much again—turns it milky but with a faint greenish tinge. It is considered a great appetite-whetter.

ANISETTE

Anisette is quite definitely a liqueur. It is French, sweetened, and usually somewhat stronger than anis. The most famous brand is Marie Brizard, from the firm named after the Bordelaise who, in the mid-eighteenth century, was given the recipe by a West Indian acquaintance.

ANIS
This liqueur is made in Spain as well as France

ANISETTE
The sweet liqueur form of anis, typified by this Marie Brizard anisette

AURUM

IF THE NAME of argentarium evokes silver, that of aurum hints at gold. One glance at its color will explain why. Made in the Abruzzi mountains, on the Adriatic coast of Italy, Aurum is a brandy-based proprietary liqueur in which a mixture of orange peel and whole oranges is infused, and the lustrous golden intensity of its appearance enhanced by saffron. It is claimed that the basic formula is of great antiquity. Aurum was given its Latin name by the celebrated Italian writer Gabriele d'Annunzio. The name hints that it may at one time have contained particles of genuine gold, harking back to the alchemical origins of distillation, and it has logically been argued that Aurum was the true forerunner of Goldwasser.

HOW IT IS MADE
No mere industrial spirit is used in aurum. The brandy in it is distilled by the makers from vintage Italian wines, and the distillate is cask-aged for around four years to take up wood color. The oranges (and other citrus fruits) are infused separately in more brandy, and then the infusion is triple-distilled. This, and the first brandy, are then blended and allowed another period of oak maturation.

GOLDEN AURUM comes from Abruzzo, eastern Italy

BÉNÉDICTINE

DEO OPTIMO MAXIMO ("Praise be to God, most good, most great"), exclaimed the Bénédictine monk, who formulated the liqueur that now bears his order's name, on first tasting the results. Or so the story goes. It was reputedly in 1510, so it isn't easy to verify. What is certain is that his monastery at Fécamp, in the Normandy region of northern France, produced this cognac-based herbal liqueur until the time of the French Revolution in 1789, when the monasteries were forcibly closed and production banned.

Bénédictine was officially extinct until the 1860s, when it was revived by a descendant of the monastery's lawyers, Alexandre Le Grand. On finding the secret recipe among a bundle of yellowing papers, he was inspired to build an extraordinary new distillery in the high Gothic style at Fécamp, and the now secularized liqueur—first christened Bénédictine by Le Grand— lived to fight another day.

Bénédictine is a bright golden potion of honeyed sweetness, containing an herbalist's pantheon of medicinal plants and spices. The exact formula is known only to three people at any given time, but it is thought to contain as many as 75 aromatizing ingredients.

BENEDICTINE One of the old monastic liqueurs

CHARTREUSE

UNLIKE BÉNÉDICTINE, CHARTREUSE really is still made by monks—of the Carthusian order—at Voiron, near Grenoble, not far from the site of their monastery, La Grande Chartreuse. Expelled from France at the time of the French Revolution, the order was allowed back into the mother country after the defeat of Napoleon, only to be kicked out again in 1903. It was then that a second branch of the operation was founded at Tarragona, in eastern Spain, and it continued as Chartreuse's second address until 1991, long after the production was finally reestablished in France in 1932.

The Carthusians are a silent order, which has no doubt helped to keep the recipe a secret; like its Norman counterpart, it is known only to a lucky trio. Proceeds from the worldwide sales of Chartreuse are plowed back into the order's funds, from which it goes to pay for all kinds of charitable works.

There is a premium version of Chartreuse (the original recipe is said to date from 1605) called Elixir, which is sold in miniature bottles at a fearsome 71% ABV, but it is principally sold in two incarnations today, green (55%) and yellow (40%). The latter is a deep greenish yellow hue, sweet, honeyed and slightly minty in flavor, while the green Chartreuse is a pale, leafy color, has a less pungent herbal scent and is distinctly less viscous.

Additionally, the order produces a rare higher grade of each color, labeled VEP, for *vieillissement exceptionnellement prolongé* (exceptionally long aging).

GREEN CHARTREUSE
Intensely powerful and aromatic.

YELLOW CHARTREUSE
Sweeter than green Chartreuse and of normal spirit strength.

HOW TO SERVE
If you find Chartreuse overwhelming on its own, do as the French do and serve it mixed as a long drink with tonic or soda and plenty of ice.

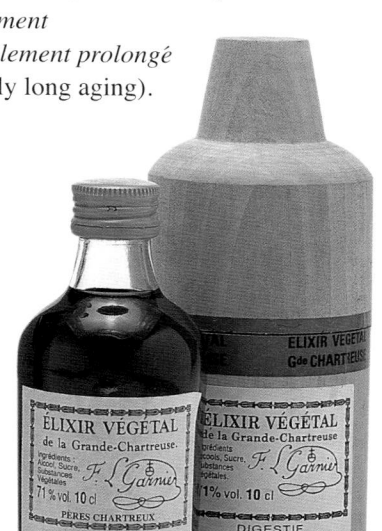

ELIXIR VEGETAL
This is the original Carthusian elixir, bottled at very high strength

MIXING
Alaska: Shake three-quarters gin to one-quarter yellow Chartreuse with ice and strain into a cocktail glass.

Bijou: Stir equal measures of Plymouth gin, green Chartreuse and sweet red vermouth with ice and a dash of orange bitters in a mixing cup. Strain into a cocktail glass. Add a cherry and a twist of lemon.

HOW IT IS MADE
By varying processes of distillation, infusion and maceration, over 130 herbs and plants are used to flavor a base of grape brandy. They were all once gathered from the mountains surrounding the monastery, but some are now imported from Italy and Switzerland. It is aged in casks for up to five years, except for the VEP, which receives twice that time.

TASTES GOOD WITH
The French sometimes fortify their hot chocolate with a reviving splash of the green Chartreuse. The yellow is thought more suitable for coffee.

COINTREAU

ONE OF THE MOST POPULAR branded liqueurs of all, Cointreau is, properly speaking, a variety of curaçao. This means it is a brandy-based spirit that has been flavored with the peel of bitter oranges. When it was launched in 1849 by the Cointreau brothers, Edouard and Adolphe, it was sold under the brand name Triple Sec White curaçao, but so many other proprietary curaçaos began to be sold as Triple Sec that the family decided to give it their own name instead.

The center of operations, as well as a distillery, is located in Angers, in the Loire Valley, but it is also made in the Americas. A variety of different bottlings is made at different strengths, including a cream version, but the best-loved Cointreau is the one that comes in a square dark-brown bottle at 40% ABV.

COINTREAU
One of the best-loved liqueurs of them all

MIXING

Cointreau is so versatile in cocktails that a list of recipes could easily fill a whole book. Suffice to say it can successfully be mixed in equal quantities with virtually any spirit (except perhaps whiskey) and the juice of half a lemon and shaken with ice. Start with gin and you have a **White Lady** (below), brandy for a **Sidecar**, vodka for a **Balalaika** and even tequila for a lemon (as opposed to lime) **Margarita**.

Despite its spirit strength, Cointreau tastes deliciously innocuous. It is sugar-sweet and colorless, but has a powerful fume of fresh oranges, with an underlying vaguely herbal note too. The oranges used in it are a clever blend of bitter green Seville-style varieties from the Caribbean (the island of Curaçao itself is close to Venezuela) and sweeter types from the south of France.

HOW IT IS MADE

Cointreau is a double distillation of grape brandy, infused with orange peel, sweetened and further aromatized with other secret plant ingredients.

TASTES GOOD WITH

If the balance of other seasonings is right, it works admirably in the orange sauce classically served with duck. It is excellent in a range of desserts, particularly so in rich chocolate mousse.

HOW TO SERVE

Absolutely everybody's favorite way of serving Cointreau is either on the rocks or frappé, depending on whether you like your ice in chunks or crystals. The cold then mitigates some of the sweetness of the liqueur, while the pure citrus flavor is exquisitely refreshing.

CREAM LIQUEURS

CREAM LIQUEURS ARE an ever-expanding category in the contemporary market. Whether the makers acknowledge it or not, cream liqueurs all owe something of their inspiration and appeal to the archetypal brand, Baileys Irish Cream. The manufacturers tend to push them particularly at Christmas, where they occupy a niche as the soft option for those who feel they need a spoonful of sugar and a dollop of cream to help the alcohol go down.

Baileys itself is a blend of Irish whiskey and cream flavored with coffee. It became suddenly chic in the 1970s, but was quickly saddled with the image of the kind of soft, svelte drink that unscrupulous boys plied unsuspecting girls with in nightclubs. Since then, cream liqueurs have gone on multiplying.

Coffee and chocolate flavorings are particularly common, and indeed some cream liqueurs are made by confectionery companies, such as Cadbury's and Terry's. Then again, some of the more reputable liqueur makers have produced cream versions of their own top products (for example, Crème de Grand Marnier) in order to grab a share of this evidently lucrative market.

I have to say I decline to take these products seriously. At best, they are substitutes for real cream cocktails, but they are always sweeter and less powerful than the genuine homemade article, and many of them contain an artificial stabilizer to prevent the cream from separating. In any case, why rely on somebody else's formula when you can follow your own specifications? Once you have made your own brandy Alexanders, you won't want chocolate cream liqueur.

The extreme was reached when another Irish drinks company of some repute launched a product called Sheridan's in the early 1990s. It came in a bifurcated bottle with two tops, one half filled with a black liquid that was coffee-flavored Irish whiskey, the other with thick white cream. The idea was that you poured first from one side of the bottle and then from the other—remembering to screw the top back onto the first half—in order to simulate the appearance of a liqueur coffee. (Little matter that Irish coffee is supposed to be served hot.) I am told the product has not so far proved conspicuously successful, perhaps because it involves such complicated moves when it comes to serving it in bars.

BAILEYS
The daddy of all cream liqueurs

CADBURY'S CREAM LIQUEUR
A ready-made brandy Alexander in a pinch

CRÈME LIQUEURS

A WHOLE RANGE OF liqueurs that use the prefix "*crème de*" may be bracketed together here. They have nothing at all to do with cream liqueurs, despite the terminology. They nearly always consist of one dominant flavor indicated in the name, often but not always a fruit, and are usually appropriately colored. In the main, they are bottled at 25–30% ABV, and may be considered among the more useful building blocks of the cocktail mixer's repertoire.

Originally, the term "crème" was used to indicate that these were sweetened liqueurs, as distinct from dry spirits such as cognac or calvados. They were mainly French in origin— the Marie Brizard

FRAISE DES BOIS
This version of crème de fraise uses wild strawberries

MIXING

The use of these liqueurs in cocktail-making is as limitless as the flavors themselves. Sometimes they work well with each other (try brown cacao and fraise, or banane and noyau, for example) but they will need a very dry base to counteract the cumulative impact of the sweetness. They all work well in cream cocktails, but one flavor is usually quite sufficient. Let your imagination off the leash.

Fruit Daiquiri: The original Daiquiri recipe of white rum shaken with the juice of half a lemon and a pinch of sugar can be adapted by adding a measure of any of the fruit liqueurs to it (and perhaps some puréed fruit as well), but you may then want to leave out the sugar.

Stinger: The adaptable Stinger is simply a half-and-half mixture of any spirit with white crème de menthe, shaken with ice and served over smashed ice in a cocktail glass. The prototype version is probably with Cognac.

Alexander: The recipe for this given in the brandy chapter can be adapted with other spirits too—gin is particularly successful— but it is always the brown crème de cacao that must be used.

FLAVORINGS

The flavors of such liqueurs are numerous, and the following list does not pretend to be exhaustive. The French names are given first, since that is how they are labeled.

Most commonly seen are: crème de banane (banana), cacao (cocoa or chocolate—comes in dark brown and white versions), cassis (black currant), fraise (strawberry), framboise (raspberry) and menthe (mint—comes in bright green and white versions).

company founded in the mid-eighteenth century in Bordeaux is still important in this field—but production soon spread to other specialty liqueur manufacturers, such as Bols and De Kuypers of Holland.

Before the widespread availability of such products, the sweetening element in a cocktail used to be sugar, pure and simple, or perhaps a sugar syrup. The crème liqueurs had the advantage of not only providing that sweetness, but also of introducing another flavor into the drinks they were added to. They have since become indispensable in extending the horizons of both the professional and amateur bartender, and are usually a recommended purchase in any guide giving advice on starting your own cocktail bar at home.

Most of these products will be based on a neutral-tasting, un-aged grape brandy, with the various flavoring ingredients either infused or

CRÈME DE FRAISE
A basic strawberry liqueur from Marie Brizard of Bordeaux.

HOW TO SERVE
If these drinks are to be taken as befitted their original purpose, as pleasant aids to digestion at the end of a grand dinner, they are best served frappé—i.e. poured over shaved ice—rather than neat. In that way, some of their sugary sweetness is mitigated.

MIXING
Oracabessa: Shake a measure of dark rum with a measure of crème de banane and the juice of half a lemon with ice and strain into a tall glass. Float some thin slices of banana on the surface of the drink and top it up with sparkling lemonade. Garnish lavishly with fruits.

Silver Jubilee: Shake equal measures of gin, crème de banane and cream with ice and strain into a cocktail glass.

Blackout (from Lucius Beebe's *Stork Club Bar Book*): Shake a measure and three-quarters of gin and three-quarters of a measure of crème de mûre (blackberry) with the juice of half a lime and plenty of ice and strain into a cocktail glass.

Stratosphere: A few dashes of crème de violette are added to a glass of champagne until a mauve color is obtained. The scentedness is then enhanced by adding a whole clove to the glass. (An American violet liqueur, Crème Yvette, was at one time the only correct product to use in this very ladylike aperitif.)

English Rose: Shake a measure and a half of London gin with three-quarters of a measure of crème de roses, the juice of half a lemon, half a teaspoon of superfine sugar and half an egg white, with ice, and strain into a wineglass. (Alternatively, you can make this in an electric blender for that extra frothiness.)

CRÈME DE CACAO
Cacao—cocoa or chocolate—is available in two versions, dark and white, to please chocoholics.

macerated in the spirit rather than being subject to distillation themselves. The difference, essentially, between infusion and maceration is that the former involves some gentle heating action, while the latter is just a cold soaking of the flavoring element in the spirit until it has been broken down and has imparted its aromatic compounds. Maceration is obviously a considerably slower process than infusion. In both cases, the ingredient has to be rendered water soluble, in the case of maceration particularly so.

Since these are intended to be rich but simple products, with one overriding flavor, the crème liqueurs are not generally treated to

CRÈME DE BANANE
Banana is one of the more versatile flavors

aging in wood. Oak maturation would interfere anyway with the often bold primary colors of the drinks, as well as obscuring the tastes.

They are more often than not sold in 11½-ounce bottles. You will find as you use them that a certain amount of powdery sugar deposit builds up underneath the screw tops; simply give them a good wipe down every now and then.

HOW THEY ARE MADE

After the infusion or maceration, during which absorption of flavor is obtained, the aromatized spirit may then have to be strained to remove any solid particles caused by making the flavoring agent water-soluble. It is then

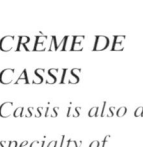

CRÈME DE CASSIS
Cassis is also a specialty of Burgundy

MIXING

Kir: The world-famous aperitif created in Burgundy, and originally named after a mayor of Dijon, consists of a glass of light, dry, acidic white wine with a teaspoon or two (depending on taste) of crème de cassis. The classic wine to use is a Bourgogne Aligoté of the most recent vintage, but any fairly neutral-tasting but *sharp* white wine will do. Add the cassis to a glass of non-vintage Brut champagne and the drink becomes a **Kir Royal** (below).

CRÈME DE FRAMBOISE

Red fruit liqueurs, such as framboise, are very good if added by the teaspoon to a glass of basic champagne or sparkling wine.

FLAVORINGS

More obscure flavors include: crème d'ananas (pineapple), café (coffee), mandarine (tangerine), mûre (blackberry), myrtille (blueberry), noyau (almond), roses (rose petal), thé (tea), vanille (vanilla), violette (violet)

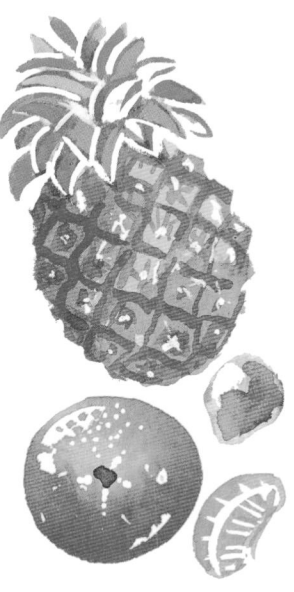

OTHER NAMES
Triple sec (only for the colorless version, strictly speaking)

HOW IT IS MADE
The blossom and dried peel of wild oranges are steeped in grape brandy or even neutral spirit; the resulting infusion is then sweetened, clarified and colored according to style.

CURAÇAO
Blue curaçao enjoyed something of a vogue in the cocktail renaissance of the early 1980s, though its color makes it hard to mix with.

TRIPLE SEC
The term tends to be used for the colorless curaçao

MIXING
Whip: Shake equal measures of cognac, dry vermouth and white curaçao with a dash of pastis (e.g. Pernod) and plenty of ice, and strain into a cocktail glass. (It should be noted that this lethal cocktail contains no non-alcoholic ingredient. Caution is advised.)
Rite of Spring (below): Mix a double measure of vodka and a measure of green curaçao with ice in a mixing cup. Decant into a tall glass and top up with clear lemonade. Dangle a long twist of lemon peel in the drink.

TASTES GOOD WITH
Indispensable in the classic crêpes Suzette. In the recipe given by the great French chef Auguste Escoffier, the pancake batter is flavored with tangerine juice and curaçao and the cooked crêpe sauced with butter, sugar and tangerine rinds. These days, it is generally Cointreau that is used in this ever-popular dessert.

CUARANTA Y TRES
Cuaranta is a sweet liqueur made in the Cartagena region of eastern Spain, based on a recipe that supposedly dates from classical times when the Phoenicians founded Carthage, in North Africa, and introduced viticulture. It is concocted from a brandy base with infusions of herbs, but has a noticeably predominant flavor of vanilla, which rather torpedoes the Carthaginian theory, since vanilla was only discovered in the sixteenth century by Spanish explorers in Mexico. Not much seen outside its region of production, it is nonetheless held in high regard locally.

DRAMBUIE

D RAMBUIE IS SCOTLAND'S (and, for that matter, Britain's) preeminent contribution to the world's classic liqueurs. Hugely popular in the United States, it is a unique and inimitable concoction of Scotch whiskey, heather honey and herbs. The story goes that the recipe was given as a reward to one Captain Mackinnon in 1745, after the defeat at Culloden, by Charles Edward Stuart—or Bonnie Prince Charlie, as the pretender to the English throne has ever since been known. The lad that was born to be king was of course ferried to Skye, and from there to France, away from the clutches of the nefarious English. Captain Mackinnon was his protector.

That story has inevitably since been debunked by meticulous historians. The truth is almost certainly the other way around. It was the Mackinnons who revived the spirits of the fugitive Prince with their own Scotch-based home concoction, which was very much a typical blend of the period, an unrefined spirit disguised with sweet and herbal additives.

Today, the spirit is anything but unrefined, being a mixture of fine malt and straight grain whiskey, to which the flavorings are added. The Mackinnon family still makes it, though near Edinburgh now rather than on Skye. They registered its name (from the Gaelic *an dram buidheach*, "the drink that satisfies") in 1892. It has been in private production since the time of the Bonnie Prince, but was only launched commercially in 1906—with spectacular success.

TASTES GOOD WITH
A hunk of rich Dundee cake doused in Drambuie is a sumptuous cold-weather treat.

DRAMBUIE Perhaps Britain's greatest contribution to the liqueur world

CYNAR
Cynar is a liqueur for the very brave. It is a soupy, dark-brown potion made in Italy, and flavored with artichoke hearts (its name derives from the Latin for artichoke, *cynarum*). All of the savory bitterness of the globe artichoke, boldly illustrated on its label, is in it, and if that sounds like fun, go ahead and try it. I once swallowed a modest measure of it in a little backstreet bar in Venice, and of all my shimmering memories of the watery city, Cynar is not, I have to say, the loveliest.

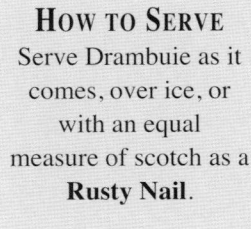

HOW TO SERVE
Serve Drambuie as it comes, over ice, or with an equal measure of scotch as a **Rusty Nail**.

GALLIANO

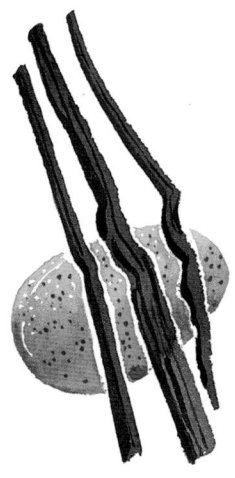

ANOTHER OF ITALY'S liqueur specialties, golden-yellow Galliano is chiefly known on the international cocktail scene for its matchless role of livening up a vodka and orange in the Harvey Wallbanger cocktail, and for its tall conical bottle. It was invented by Arturo Vaccari, a Tuscan distiller who named his new creation in honor of an Italian soldier, Major Giuseppe Galliano. In 1895 Galliano held out under siege at Enda Jesus in Ethiopia for 44 days against the vastly superior Abyssinian forces under the command of Haile Selassie's nephew.

The formula, as we are accustomed to hear in the world of liqueurs, is a jealously guarded secret, but it is said to be based on up to 80 herbs, roots, berries

MIXING
Harvey Wallbanger:
Pour a generous measure of vodka over ice in a highball glass, top up with fresh orange juice and float a measure of Galliano on top.

GALLIANO
This Italian classic comes in a distinctive conical bottle

MIXING
Milano: Shake equal measures of gin and Galliano with the juice of half a lemon and ice, and strain into a cocktail glass.

and flowers from the Alpine slopes to the north of Italy. Among its flavors is a strong presence of anise or licorice, and there is a pronounced scent of vanilla. It is also naturally very sweet. Despite the complexity of its tastes, it is a valuable addition to the bartender's battery.

HOW IT IS MADE
The various flavoring ingredients are steeped in a mixture of neutral spirit and water and then distilled; the resulting potion is then blended with refined spirits. It is bottled at 35% ABV.

FIOR D'ALPI
No liqueur makes more of a show of itself than Fior d'Alpi. Made in northern Italy, its name means "Alpine flowers," and those—along with a fistful of wild herbs—are its principal flavorings. It is a delicate primrose hue and comes in a tall narrow bottle. What catches the eye in the store window, though, is the gnarled little tree that sits inside every bottle. If you leave the bottle undisturbed for a while, the sugar in the drink will form a crystallized frosting on the twigs that can look touchingly Christmassy. That, coupled with the agreeable sweetness of the liqueur itself, is what keeps it popular—at least in Italy. Similar products are sold as Millefiori and—where else?—Edelweiss.

GLAYVA

IKE DRAMBUIE, Glayva is a Scotch whiskey-based liqueur made near Edinburgh, but it is of much more recent provenance. The drink was first formulated just after the Second World War. Its aromatizers are quite similar to those of Drambuie, although its flavor is intriguingly different. Heather honey and various herbs are used, and so is a quantity of orange peel, resulting in a noticeably fruitier attack on the palate.

The noble Scot commemorated in the case of Glayva is one Master Borthwick, the phlegmatic 16-year-old credited with carrying Robert the Bruce's heart back to Scotland after the king's defeat at the hands of the Saracens. Not content

GLAYVA

The original formula for Glayva is much older than the product itself

MIXING
Saracen: Shake a measure of Scotch whiskey, half a measure each of Glayva and dry sherry and a dash of orange bitters with ice. Pour into a tumbler and add a splash of soda. Decorate with a piece of orange rind.

with rescuing the regal heart, the indomitable lad cut off the head of a Saracen chieftain he had killed, impaled it on a spear, and brought that back, too, just to keep his spirits up. All of those pubs named the Saracen's Head recall the event, as did the Moorish head once depicted on the Glayva label.

TASTES GOOD WITH
Like the other Scotch-based liqueurs, Glayva is particularly good added to an ice cream, perhaps one flavored with honey and/or orange, like the drink itself.

FLAVORINGS
Heather honey
Orange peel
Various herbs

HOW TO SERVE
Glayva should be served just as it is, in a standard whiskey tumbler. Its fruitiness makes it slightly better for chilling than Drambuie, but don't overdo it.

GOLDWASSER

GOLDWASSER, OR Danziger Goldwasser to give it its archetypal name, recalls the great Catalan physician Arnaldo de Villanova who, in the thirteenth century, is reputed to have cured the pope of a dangerous illness by giving him an herbal elixir containing specks of gold. In so doing, he also saved his own skin from the Inquisition. Since the search for the elixir of life was intimately bound up with alchemy's project of turning base metals into gold, it was only natural that gold itself should be seen as being beneficial to health.

FLAVORINGS
Anise
Caraway seeds
Citrus fruits

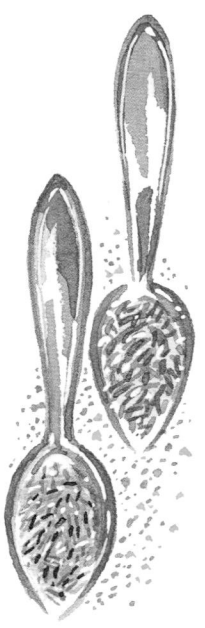

GOLDWASSER

All Goldwasser came originally from Gdansk, like this one

HOW TO SERVE
The prettiness can be enhanced by serving Goldwasser in a little cut-crystal liqueur glass.

OTHER NAMES
France: Liqueur d'Or or eau d'or

MIXING
Generally, there is no point in mixing Goldwasser, because you then bury the gold flakes. However, I am indebted to Lucius Beebe's 1946 *Stork Club Bar Book* for the following recipe for a layered cocktail (to be used only if you are sure your eggs are free of salmonella):

Golden Slipper: A measure of yellow Chartreuse is poured into a *copita*, or sherry glass. A separated egg yolk is then dropped whole onto the surface of it, and a measure of Goldwasser carefully poured on top of that. (I haven't tried this. I suspect it may look better than it tastes.)

The commercial prototype of the drink was first made in the Baltic port city of Danzig (now Gdansk in Poland). Based on the drink Kümmel, it is flavored with both anise and caraway seeds and is colorless, less sweet than many liqueurs, and it really does have a shower of real golden particles added to it, in memory of Arnaldo. When the bottle was poured, the gold specks flurried up to general approbation like the flakes in a snowstorm toy. (There was also for a time a silver version, Silber-wasser.) The Liqueur d'Or was a French version of the same thing. Some brands also had a citric fruit flavor—sometimes lemon, sometimes orange.

TASTES GOOD WITH
Soufflé Rothschild is a classic, hot dessert soufflé made from crème pâtissière and crystallized fruits that have been macerated in Danziger Goldwasser. It is served in individual soufflé dishes surrounded by strawberries.

GRAND MARNIER

GRAND MARNIER IS ONE of the best-loved of all the world's orange-flavored liqueurs. The original product is a little younger than Cointreau, its big French rival, but the style is quite different. In the sense that the oranges used in it are bitter varieties from the Caribbean, it may be classed as another type of curaçao, but it is a distinctly finer product than most ordinary curaçao.

The house that owns it was founded in 1827 by a family called Lapostolle. Louis-Alexandre Marnier later married into the family business and it was he who, in 1880, first conceived the liqueur that bears his name. Encountering the bitter oranges of Haiti on a grand tour, he hit upon the idea of blending their flavor with that of the finest cognac, and then giving it a period of barrel-aging that basic curaçao never receives.

Today, the production of the liqueur is split between two centers, one at Château de

GRAND MARNIER
Fully the equal of the higher grades of cognac

FLAVORING
Oranges

Bourg in the Cognac region, the other at Neauphle-le-Château, near Paris. The initial blending is carried out at the former site, the aging at the latter. What results is a highly refined, mellow full-strength spirit that has a warm amber color and an intense, festive scent of ripe oranges. It is sweet, but the distinction of the Fine Champagne Cognac on which it is based prevents it from being in any way cloying when served straight.

The Marnier-Lapostolle company also decided to try cashing in on the mania for cream liqueurs that has arisen in the last 20 years or so by launching a Crème de Grand Marnier at much lower strength, which I can't find it in my heart to recommend.

HOW IT IS MADE
The juice of Caribbean oranges is blended with top-quality cognac. After full amalgamation of the flavors, it is then redistilled, sweetened and given a period of cask-aging.

TASTES GOOD WITH
It is the classic ingredient in duck à l'orange, and may also be used in a whole range of desserts, particularly flamed crêpes and anything made with strong chocolate.

HOW TO SERVE
As reverently as the best cognac.

KAHLÚA

KAHLÚA IS THE only liqueur of any note to have been conceived in Mexico. It is a dark brown coffee-flavored essence packaged in a round-shouldered, opaque bottle with a colorful label. Although some of it is still made in Mexico using homegrown coffee beans, it is also made under license in Europe by the Danish company Peter Heering. It is inevitably often compared to the other, more famous coffee liqueur, Tia Maria, but it is slightly thicker in texture and somewhat less sweet than its Jamaican counterpart.

FLAVORING
Coffee

KAHLÚA
A liqueur with the stimulant properties of strong coffee

HOW TO SERVE
Kahlúa makes a very good chilled alternative to a liqueur coffee. Pour the Kahlúa over crushed ice in a tall glass and float some thick cream on top. Alternatively, add it to hot black coffee, and top it with cream and a dusting of cinnamon. Some think it mixes well with either Coca-Cola or milk as a long drink.

TASTES GOOD WITH
To enhance the flavor of a coffee dessert such as a soufflé or ice cream, Kahlúa somehow gives a smoother result than the more commonly used Tia Maria.

MIXING
Black Russian: Certain aficionados insist on Kahlúa rather than Tia Maria with the vodka. Either way, it is as well not to adulterate the drink with cola.
Alexander the Great: Shake a measure and a half of vodka with half a measure each of Kahlúa, crème de cacao and thick cream and plenty of ice. Strain into a cocktail glass. (This drink is reputed to have been invented by the great Nelson Eddy.)

IZARRA
Izarra is a sort of Basque version of Chartreuse, made in Bayonne in southwest France. It is flatteringly imitative to the extent that it comes in two colors—yellow and green—both full of aromatic herbs gathered wild in the Pyrenees. Green Izarra is higher in alcoholic strength. (It is, in fact, at 55%, exactly the same strength as green Chartreuse, but doesn't really have the same complexity of flavor.) The name means "star" in the local dialect. Izarra is based on Armagnac, which is given a redistillation with the aromatizing ingredients, followed by a period of cask-aging. Not surprisingly, it is not much seen outside its native region.

KÜMMEL

KÜMMEL IS ONE of the more ancient liqueurs. All we know is that it originated somewhere in northern Europe, although we do not know exactly where. The best guess is Holland, but the Germans have a respectable enough claim on the patent as well (its name is, of course, German). Certainly, it was being made in Holland in the 1500s, and it very much fits the image of such drinks of the time, in that it would have been an unrefined grain spirit masked by an aromatic ingredient.

The ingredient in this case is caraway seeds. A certain amount of needless confusion is created by the fact that the name looks as though it has something to do with the more pungent cumin. This is only because, in certain European languages, caraway is often referred to as a sort of cumin. They have nothing to do with each other, the misleading nomenclature only arising because the seeds are supposed to look vaguely similar.

KÜMMEL
Wolfschmidt
is the leading
brand of
kümmel

A key episode in Kümmel's history occurred at the end of the seventeenth century, during Peter the Great's sojourn in Holland. He took the formula for the drink, to which he had grown rather partial, back to Russia with him, and Kümmel came to be thought of as a Russian product, or at least as a Baltic one. The Baltic port of Riga, now capital of Latvia, was its chief center of production throughout the nineteenth century, and some was also made in Danzig (now Gdansk), where they eventually came to add flecks of gold to it and call it Goldwasser.

Versions of Kümmel are today made not just in Latvia but also in Poland, Germany, Holland, Denmark and even the United States. Not the least valued property of caraway, appreciated since Egyptian times, is its ability to counteract flatulence, which is why it was one of the traditional ingredients of colic water for babies.

HOW IT IS MADE
The base is a pure grain distillate, effectively a type of vodka, in which the seeds are infused. Most brands are fairly heavily sweetened but they are always left colorless.

TASTES GOOD WITH
Try adding it to the batter for old English seed cake, which is made with caraway seeds.

LIQUEUR BRANDIES

SOME FRUIT LIQUEURS have traditionally been referred to as "brandies," even though they are nothing of the sort in the sense that we now understand that term. There are essentially three fruit brandies—cherry, apricot and peach—and, although they are occasionally known by other names, it is as cherry (apricot or peach) brandy, that drinkers know them best.

Strictly speaking, these products belong to the same large category as those liqueurs prefixed with the phrase "crème de," in that they are sweetened, colored drinks, based on simple grape brandy that has been flavored with the relevant fruits, as opposed to being

FLAVORINGS
Apricots
Cherries
Peaches

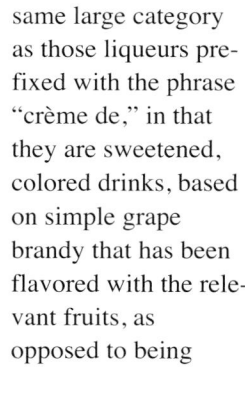

CHERRY BRANDY
Indispensable in the making of Singapore Sling

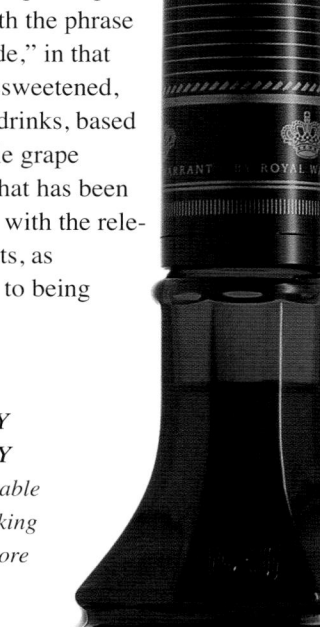

OTHER NAMES
France: Apricot brandy is sometimes known as Apry or Abricotine.
Liqueur brandies may eventually come to be known as apricot (cherry or peach) liqueur, if the term "brandy" is enforced for grape distillates only. (The alternatives could well be crème d'abricot, de cerise and de pêche.)

MIXING
Paradise: Shake a measure of gin with half a measure each of apricot brandy and fresh orange juice and ice, and strain into a flared wineglass.

primary distillates of those fruits themselves. The maceration of the fruit usually includes the pits or seeds as well, for the bitter flavor they impart and and—in the case of apricot pits especially—the distinctive flavor of almond.

Of the three, the apricot variant has probably traveled the furthest. There are true apricot distillates made in eastern Europe, of which the Hungarian Barak Pálinka is the most renowned, but they are dry like the fruit brandies of France. Good examples of sweet apricot liqueurs are Bols Apricot Brandy, Cusenier and Apry made by the Marie Brizard company.

Cherry brandy is one of the few liqueurs that may just have been invented by the English, the role of creator being claimed by one Thomas Grant of Kent. The original version was made with black morellos, although other cherry varieties may be used in modern products, depending on what is locally available. English

HOW TO SERVE
The best of these liqueur brandies make wonderful digestifs served in small quantities, provided they are not the very sweetest styles.

cherry brandy contributed to the downfall of the dissolute King George IV, who consumed it in ruinous quantities, perhaps to get over the memory of his doomed affair with Mrs. Fitzherbert in Brighton.

Among the more famous cherry liqueur brands are Cherry Heering, now properly known as Peter Heering Cherry Liqueur, which was first formulated in the mid-nineteenth century by a Danish distiller of that name. The Heering company grows its own cherries to make this product, which is cask-aged. Others include Cherry Rocher, de Kuyper, Garnier, and Bols, and there are brands produced in Germany and Switzerland.

Peach brandy is the one least frequently seen, its most famous manifestation probably being the one marketed by Bols.

HOW THEY ARE MADE

The pressed juice and pits of the respective fruits are generally mixed with a neutral grape spirit (more rarely a grain spirit), sweetened with sugar syrup and macerated until absorption of flavor is complete. If the fruit juice itself has fairly high natural sweetness, correspondingly less syrup will be added. In some cases, the liqueurs may be treated to a period of cask-aging, followed by adjustment of the color with vegetable dyes.

TASTE GOOD WITH

They all work well in fruit-based desserts that use the same fruits, for example hot soufflés, tarts and charlottes.

APRICOT BRANDY
Cusenier's liqueurs all come in these distinctive bottles

HEERING
Named after a Danish distiller in the last century.

MALIBU

WITH THE GROWTH of tourism in the Caribbean islands, it was only a matter of time before liqueurs flavored with coconut began to make their presence felt on the international market. Of these, the most famous is Malibu. Presented in an opaque white bottle, with a depiction of a tropical sunset on the front, it is a relatively low-strength blend of rectified Caribbean white rum with coconut extracts. The flavor is pleasingly not too sweet. Malibu was a better product than most of the range of liqueur concoctions with totally tropical names that bombarded the market during the cocktail renaissance of the early 1980s.

Another reasonably good product was Batida de Côco, a coconut-flavored neutral spirit made in Brazil that was also exported in quantity to the vacation islands of the Caribbean. Cocoribe was similar.

They are all colorless products, with an alcohol level slightly higher than that of light fortified wine. Since the success of these proprietary products, some of the famous Dutch and French liqueur manufacturers have got in on the act and also marketed variants of crème de coco.

HOW TO SERVE
These drinks are not great on their own, but make excellent mixers with ice and fruit juices, which is how they were intended to be served in the first place.

MALIBU
Perhaps the best of the coconut liqueurs

MALIBU
CARIBBEAN WHITE RUM WITH COCONUT
24% vol e70cl
PRODUCED UNDER LICENCE FROM THE
TWELVE ISLANDS SHIPPING CO LTD
BRIGHTON, BLACK ROCK, BARBADOS
CARIBBEAN SPIRIT

MIXING
Piña Colada: A simplified version can be made using Malibu instead of real coconut milk. Mix in equal measures with white rum and plenty of ice. Top up with pineapple juice.

Batida Banana: Mix equal measures of Batida de Côco with crème de banane and several ice cubes in a tall glass. Top up with whole milk. (This is a dangerously rich drink, effectively little more than a grown-up milkshake.)

HOW THEY ARE MADE
Most of the coconut liqueurs are based on ultra-refined white rum, although one or two are made with a neutral grain alcohol. The dried pulp and milk of the coconut are used to flavor the spirit, which is then sweetened and filtered.

TASTE GOOD WITH
A splash of coconut liqueur may productively be added to the sauces in Cajun or Far Eastern dishes, particularly those of Thai or Indonesian cuisine, where coconut itself figures strongly. Otherwise, it is splendid as a flavoring in a rich, creamy ice cream.

BATIDA DE CÔCO
Brazil's contribution to the coconut collection.

MANGAROC BATIDA DE CÔCO

MANDARINE NAPOLÉON

MANDARINE IS ANOTHER TYPE of curaçao, this time made with the skins of tangerines as opposed to bitter Caribbean oranges. By far the most famous brand is Mandarine Napoléon, the origins of which really do derive from the drinking preferences of the emperor Napoleon I. The key figure in its history is a French chemist, Antoine-François de Fourcroy, who rose to prominence in France as a key figure in public administration after the Revolution.

Following the demise of the Jacobin regime, de Fourcroy found favor with Napoleon Bonaparte to the extent that he was made a member of his Imperial State Council. When the tangerine first arrived in Europe from China (hence its synonym, mandarine) at the end of the eighteenth century, there was something of a craze for it. The fashion was to steep the peel in cognac after eating the fruit, and Antoine-François records in his diary that many was the night he was called on to share in the emperor's indulgence.

Mandarine Napoléon was launched in 1892 by a Belgian distiller, Louis Schmidt, who stumbled on the recipe in de Fourcroy's correspondence while pursuing

MANDARINE NAPOLÉON
A French invention now made in Belgium

HOW TO SERVE
Despite its sweetness, it does work well as an after-dinner drink taken straight or frappé in a traditional brandy balloon.

FLAVORING
Tangerines

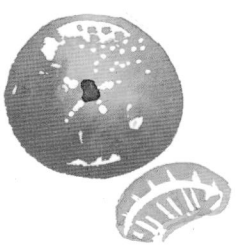

some chemical research. It was only after the Second World War, when the distillery was relocated from Belgium to France, that the Fourcroy family once again became involved, eventually taking on the worldwide distribution of Schmidt's liqueur. As it became ever more successful, they moved the production back to Brussels, where it remains.

The tangerines used in Mandarine come exclusively from Sicily. Other companies make versions of tangerine liqueurs—the Italians themselves of course make one from their Sicilian crop—but Mandarine Napoléon remains justifiably the preeminent example, a thoroughly individual product that has deservedly won international awards.

HOW IT IS MADE

For Mandarine Napoléon, tangerine skins are steeped in cognac and other French brandies. The spirit is then redistilled, sweetened, colored with carotene to a vivid yellowy orange and matured for several months. It is bottled at 38% ABV.

TASTES GOOD WITH

Add it to tangerine-flavored mousses or use it as the fuel to flame sweet pancakes.

MIXING
Titanic: Mix equal measures of vodka and Mandarine Napoléon over ice in a tumbler, and top up with soda water.

MARASCHINO

THE ORIGINAL MARASCHINO (which should be pronounced with a "sk" sound in the middle, not "sh") was a distilled liquor of some antiquity made from a sour red cherry. The Italian name for the cherry, which grew only on the Dalmatian coast, was *marasca*. When the Italian-speaking enclave of Dalmatia was incorporated into the then Yugoslavia, Italian production of maraschino was continued in the Veneto, where plantings of the marasca cherry were established from cuttings.

Maraschino is a clear liqueur derived from an infusion of pressed cherry

FLAVORING
Marasca cherries

MIXING
Tropical Cocktail: Shake equal measures of dry French vermouth, maraschino and white crème de cacao with a dash each of Angostura and orange bitters and plenty of ice. Strain into a wineglass.

skins in a cherry-pit distillate. (This secondary infusion is why maraschino should technically be considered a liqueur rather than a spirit, as distinct from kirsch.) After further distillation to obtain a pure, clear spirit, it is aged, ideally for several years. It always remains colorless, and should have a pronounced bitter cherry aroma, backed up by the nuttiness of the cherry pits.

A number of Italian firms are especially associated with the production of maraschino, notably Luxardo (which traditionally sells its product in straw-covered flasks at a knee-trembling 50% ABV), the venerable Drioli company and Stock.

HOW IT IS MADE
The pomace of pressed cherries is infused over gentle heat in a cherry distillate for several months. It is then rectified and transferred to neutral maturation vessels, made either from a light wood such as ash or from glass. It is sweetened with sugar syrup and left to age for several years.

TASTES GOOD WITH
It is incomparable for soaking the sponge in a layer cake, or poured over fresh cherries and many other fruits, such as peaches or apricots.

HOW TO SERVE
The best grades of maraschino should be smooth enough to drink on their own, but the sweeter it is, the more recourse to the ice bucket you may feel is necessary.

MARASCHINO
The traditional straw-covered bottle of Luxardo

MIDORI

N INSTANT HIT when it was launched in England in the early 1980s, Midori was another stroke of marketing genius from the giant Japanese drinks group, Suntory. Not content with its range of fine Scotch-style whiskey and classed-growth Bordeaux property, Château Lagrange, Suntory aimed for a slice of the cocktail action with this bright green liqueur in an idiosyncratic little bottle of textured glass.

The flavoring agent is melon,

MIDORI
Cornering the market in melon liqueurs

MIXING
Green Caribbean: Shake equal large measures of white rum and Midori with ice, strain into a tall glass and top up with soda water. Add a slice of lemon.

not a particularly common one in the liqueur world, but its vivid green color is achieved by means of a dye. Indeed, its greenness is its principal sales pitch, since *midori* is the Japanese word for green. The color is perhaps intended to evoke the skins of certain melon varieties, as opposed to the flesh that is actually used to flavor it. Having said that, Midori doesn't especially recall any melon variety; it is actually much closer to banana, in both aroma and taste. It is sweet and syrupy, and at the lower end of standard alcoholic strength for liqueurs.

TASTES GOOD WITH
It was seized on by chefs in some of the more adventurous restaurants for use in desserts that involve tropical fruit. Salads of mango, pineapple, melon, passion fruit and so forth are perfect choices, although again, there is that unapologetic color to contend with.

MERSIN
Mersin is a Turkish version of curaçao, a colorless liqueur based on grape spirit and flavored with oranges and herbs. It is commonly taken with a chaser of the fierce black coffee of Turkey.

FLAVORING
Melon

HOW TO SERVE
Midori is much better mixed than served straight, when its flavor quickly cloys. It blends beautifully with iced fruit juices, notably orange, except that the resulting color is horribly lurid. Lemonade may make a more visually appealing marriage, but a sweet mixer with a sweet liqueur is never a great idea.

NUT LIQUEURS

THE NUT-FLAVORED liqueurs deserve to be considered separately, as they form quite a large subgroup. Drinks relying on coconut for their principal taste are dealt with elsewhere (see Malibu); the flavorings here are those of hazelnut, walnut and almond.

In their French manifestations, the first two of those are straightforward enough. They are named noisette and crème de noix, after the French words for hazelnut and walnut respectively. In the case of almonds, it all becomes a little more complicated, basically because certain fruit pits, such as those of apricots and cherries, have an almondlike taste. A liqueur that contains

OTHER NAMES
Almond liqueurs: Amaretto (Italian), Crème d'amandes (French)
Hazelnut liqueurs: Noisette (French)
Walnut liqueurs: Crème de noix (French), Nocino (Italian)

almonds themselves is called crème d'amandes. However, a liqueur called crème de noyau—"noyau" being the French for the pit in which the almondlike kernel of a fruit is encased—will contain no actual almonds, only an approximation of the flavor.

These are all brandy-based drinks in which the chopped nuts are

HOW TO SERVE
These drinks are quite commonly taken with crushed ice as a digestif in France. Alternatively, they may be iced, slightly watered—about the same amount of water as liqueur—and drunk as aperitifs. The tradition in France is for a sweet appetizer (with the obvious exception of champagne), as distinct from the drier American and British taste.

FRANGELICO
A branded liqueur packaged to look like a monk

NOCINO
A strong walnut liqueur from Italy

steeped in a clear grape spirit and the resulting liqueur is clarified and bottled in a colorless state. The exception is crème de noyau, which more often than not has a faint pinkish hue if it has been made from cherry pits. They are all sweet, with fairly syrupy textures, and make invaluable additions to the cocktail repertoire.

Italy produces a range of nut-based liqueurs too. There is the distinctive almond-flavored Disaronno Amaretto, and also a walnut liqueur called Nocino. In the 1980s, a product called Frangelico was released. It was a delicate straw-colored liqueur flavored with hazelnuts and herbs, then dressed up in a faintly ridiculous dark brown bottle designed to look like a monk. The large brown plastic top represented his cowl, and around the gathered-in waist, a length of white cord was knotted. It looked like a particularly embarrassing tourist souvenir, but the liqueur itself turned out to be delicious, not too sweet, and with an intriguing range of flavors.

EAU DE NOIX
A rare French walnut liqueur

MIXING

Pink Almond: Shake a measure of scotch with half a measure each of crème de noyau, kirsch, fresh lemon juice and orgeat (a non-alcoholic almond syrup) with ice, and strain into a cocktail glass. (If you can't get orgeat, double the quantity of noyau.)
Walnut Whip: Shake equal measures of cognac, crème de noix and thick cream with ice and strain into a cocktail glass.
Mad Monk (below): Shake a measure each of gin and Frangelico with the juice of half a lemon and ice. Strain into a wineglass and add a squirt of soda.

HOW THEY ARE MADE

The nuts are crumbled up and left to infuse with the base spirit before sweetening and filtration. They are bottled at the average liqueur strength, around 25%. In the case of the crème de noix of Gascony, the walnuts are beaten off the trees while still green, then the spirit is sweetened with honey and subjected to a further distillation. For crème de noyau, fruit pits are the infusion agent. They are usually either cherry or apricot, but peach and even plum may also be used.

TASTE GOOD WITH

They work well with nutty desserts—anything using almond paste or praline—but also in a chocolate mousse, or drunk alongside a piece of rich, dark fruitcake. Frangelico served chilled makes an unlikely table-fellow for a piece of mature Stilton.

FLAVORINGS
Almonds
Walnuts
Hazelnuts
Fruit pits
Honey (in the case of some crème de noix)

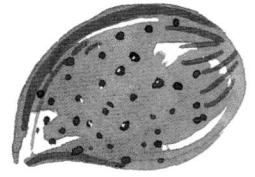

PARFAIT AMOUR

THE LONG ASSOCIATION of drinking with seduction is celebrated in the name of purple Parfait Amour, "perfect love." In the eighteenth century particularly, the use of alcohol in amorous pursuits had less to do with getting your intended too stupefied to know what he or she was doing than with stimulating the erotic impulses with artful concoctions of spices and flowers mixed with the alcohol.

Parfait Amour liqueur is really the only surviving link to that noble tradition. It is almost certainly Dutch in origin; its name, as with all such potions,

FLAVORINGS
Lemons or other citrus fruits (such as the larger, shapeless citron of Corsica)
Cloves
Cinnamon
Coriander seeds
Violets

HOW TO SERVE
It is best to serve Parfait Amour unmixed, or else blended with something colorless such as lemonade, in order not to interfere with your beloved's enjoyment of the color. It tastes better chilled, although you may feel that an excessively cold drink may numb the erogenous zones, which wouldn't do at all.

PARFAIT AMOUR
Indelibly associated with romance

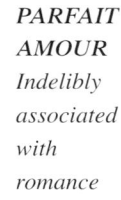

MIXING
Eagle's Dream: Blend a measure and a half of gin, a measure of Parfait Amour, the juice of half a lemon, half a teaspoon of superfine sugar and the white of an egg with smashed ice in a blender, and strain into a large wineglass.

is French because that was considered the romantic language par excellence. As its (added) color would lead you to expect, it is subtly scented with violets, but the flavor owes more to fruits and spices than flowers, which distinguishes it from the colorless crème de violette. The main components are citrus fruits—usually lemons—and a mixture of cloves and other spices.

The drink enjoyed great popularity during the cocktail boom in the 1920s. Apart from anything else, no other liqueur is quite the same color. There was once a red version of it too, but somehow purple has come to be more inextricably associated with passion. Today, Parfait Amour is made not only by the Dutch liqueur specialists Bols, but by certain French companies as well.

HOW IT IS MADE
The various aromatizing elements are macerated in grape spirit, which may then be redistilled, and the purple color is achieved by means of a vegetable dye.

TASTES GOOD WITH
What else but a box of chocolate truffles?

PASTIS

Pastis is one of the most important traditional drinks of Europe, despite having only minority status in Britain and the other northern countries. Around the Mediterranean fringe of Europe, from southeast France to the Greek islands, in its various derivatives, pastis functions in the same thirst-quenching way as beer does further north. It is important in terms of the quantity consumed locally, and is of great cultural significance too. It is an in-between-times drink rather than just an aperitif; it's a drink for lazy afternoons watching *boules* being played in the village square. There is also the tradition of illicit home distillation.

Drinkers all over the

RICARD
The famous
pastis
of southern
France

OTHER NAMES
France: pastis *Greece*: ouzo *Spain*: ojen

MIXING
Monkey Gland: Shake two measures of gin with a measure of fresh orange juice and three dashes each of pastis and grenadine and plenty of ice, and strain into a large wineglass.

world have, on first contact with pastis, usually been fascinated by its most famous property—that it clouds up when mixed with water. This attribute, indeed, is what gives the drink its name, *pastis* being an old southern French dialect word meaning "muddled," "hazy" or "unclear."

PERNOD AND ABSINTHE
The very close similarities of pastis to anisette have been noted elsewhere (see Anisette). Depending on which authority you consult, the principal flavoring element in pastis is either licorice or anise—perhaps more often the former—but there are other herbal ingredients in it as well. A neutral, highly rectified alcohol base, generally of vegetable origin, provides the background for the aromatizing agents, which are steeped in it before essence of licorice or anise is added and the whole mélange is sweetened and diluted.

Anise has been known as a digestive aid in medicine since the time of the Egyptians, which is why, to this day, many over-the-counter stomach-settling remedies contain a hint of its flavor. (Oxyboldene, a popular French brand, is a case in point.) The history of pastis is somewhat entangled, however, with a similar type of drink that came to be seen as anything but health-giving. By the beginning of the twentieth century, the name of absinthe was mud.

Apart from home distillates, and excepting individual brands, the only category of drink that has ever become extinct is absinthe. It was considerably stronger than much of today's commercial pastis, but what really doomed it was that it contained

wormwood in concentrations that were held responsible for poisoning the brains of those who habitually drank it. During the late nineteenth century, absinthe became known as the house drink of decadent Parisian artists, Symbolist poets and others, many of whom died the kinds of squalid deaths associated with laudanum use during the English Romantic period 60 and 70 years earlier.

When absinthe was given its marching orders in France by a governmental decree of 1915, other countries soon followed suit. One of its chief manufacturers—the firm of Henri Pernod, which had been making it for over a century—then turned to making a similar product without wormwood at lower alcoholic strength, and using anise as its main flavoring agent. In effect, Pernod was the sanitized version of absinthe. The reissued edition of that great reference work, *The Savoy Cocktail Book*,

MIXING
Yellow Parrot: Shake equal measures of pastis, yellow Chartreuse and apricot brandy with ice, and strain into a cocktail glass over crushed ice.

HOW TO SERVE
Pastis should ideally be served in a small, thick-bottomed glass with about the equivalent amount of water. The water should be very cold, so as to eliminate the need for ice. Those with slightly sweeter tastes may add sugar to it. The best way to do this is to balance a perforated spoon or metal tea strainer with a sugar cube on it across the top of the glass and then pour the water over it. (This was the traditional way to sweeten absinthe.)

PERNOD
Ricard's northern French counterpart

MIXING

Bunny Hug: Shake equal measures of gin, Scotch whiskey and pastis and strain into a cocktail glass. (Not for the novice cocktail drinker, this one.)

specifically recommends using Pernod as a substitute in those of its recipes that originally called for absinthe.

Pernod is perhaps the most familiar pastis on the market today. The other main French brand, Ricard, is now part of the same group, although they are made at opposite ends of France. Berger is the other company of note making this sort of product. In northern European countries, where there is often an ambivalence about the flavor of anise or licorice in a drink, Pernod and Ricard have been much favored as bases for a fruit-juice mixer, but the only unimpeachably authentic way to drink them in their native regions, particularly around the town of Marseille, is diluted with a small quantity of water.

Somewhat unexpectedly, absinthe has made a cautious comeback in certain European countries, notably Switzerland and Portugal. Presumably it contains considerably less wormwood and therefore is only vaguely comparable to the real thing. A theory has gained currency that it was really only banned because it was

highly alcoholic (in which case the hallowed Chartreuse might have been expected to find itself in more difficulties than it has). A scientific writer, Harold McGee, points out that wormwood contains a toxic oil called thujone, which was almost certainly linked to the formation of lesions on the cerebral cortex of the recklessly heavy user.

SPAIN

The Spanish equivalent is *ojen* (pronounced "oh-hen"). It is named after the town where it is made and is sold in two versions: sweet and dry.

MIXING

In northern Europe and the United States, pastis is often mixed with fruit juices. Its colorlessness makes it a useful base: Sharper flavors such as grapefruit are the most successful. A fashion for drinking it with black currant cordial was quite the thing in Britain in the 1970s. It perhaps reminded the drinker of a certain type of childhood candy with a chewy center that combined the flavors of licorice and black currant. **Pernod-and-black** topped up with sweet cider—known in the bars of the north of England as **Red Witch**—was a popular way of achieving oblivion in my own misspent youth.

FLAVORINGS
Licorice
Anise

MIXING
If you come across absinthe, and are feeling daring, this was the recipe for the original **Absinthe Cocktail**: Shake equal measures of absinthe and water with a dash of sugar syrup, a dash of Angostura and ice, and strain into a cocktail glass.

GREECE

After pastis, the most familiar relative of this family of drinks is Greek ouzo, much beloved drink of vacationers in the Peloponnese and the islands, perhaps even more so than retsina. The flavoring agent is anise and, like pastis, the drink turns milky-white when water is added. It is drunk in much the same way, except perhaps with somewhat more water than is common in France, and generally as an aperitif. The bottled strength is around 35–40% ABV, again similar to pastis.

FLAVORINGS
Herbs—possibly including cilantro, camomile, parsley, veronica (which was once used in France as a substitute for tea), even spinach!

HOW TO SERVE
Ouzo should be served cold in a small, thick-bottomed glass, either on its own, with about the equivalent amount of water, or with an ice cube or two.

OUZO
The drink of the sunny Greek islands

MIXING
Cocktails that include pastis tend to be among the most dramatic in the repertoire. Many of these contain no nonalcoholic ingredients. That is because a relatively small amount of pastis will have plenty to say for itself in even the most ferocious of mixes, concoctions that would drown the presence of many of the more delicate liqueurs.

Block and Fall: Stir together a measure each of cognac and Cointreau with half a measure each of pastis and calvados, over ice, in a tumbler.

Hurricane: Shake a measure and a half of cognac with half a measure each of pastis and vodka and ice, then strain into a cocktail glass.

Ojen Cocktail: Shake a double measure of dry ojen with a teaspoon of sugar, half a measure of water, a dash of orange bitters and ice, and strain into a small tumbler.

HOW THEY ARE MADE
The various herbs and plants are usually infused in a straight, highly purified vegetable spirit base and essence of anise or licorice is added. Further blending with rectified alcohol is followed by sweetening, and the drink is bottled at an average 35% ABV.

TASTE GOOD WITH
The combination of aromatizers in pastis is a particularly successful one with fish, either for marinating or adding to a sauce. Try marinating chunks of tuna in olive oil, pastis and dill and then grilling them on skewers.

PIMM'S

FOREVER ASSOCIATED with the English summer, Pimm's No. 1 Cup is a proprietary version of a fruit cup created by the eponymous Mr. Pimm in the 1820s. James Pimm originally devised his recipe in order to mark out his own establishment in the City of London from the run of common-or-garden oyster bars—oysters being not much more than ten a penny in those days—which traditionally served stout ale to wash the bivalves down.

He did such a roaring trade with his fruit cup that Pimm began to market it ready-mixed in 1859, the asking price for a bottle being a substantial three shillings. Since that time, Pimm's has gone through a number of owners, including—at the turn of the century—the then Lord Mayor of London, Sir Horatio Davies. Popular throughout the British Empire during colonial times, it came to enjoy a sudden vogue in France and Italy after the war.

In the early years of the twentieth century, Pimm's was elaborated into six different versions, each based on a different spirit. The market has since whittled these down to just two, Pimm's Vodka Cup and the original—still sold as No. 1 Cup, and based on London gin, with an unmixed strength of 25% ABV. Pimm's has suffered somewhat from being seen as too fussy to prepare. Its present owner, one of Britain's biggest drinks companies, has tried to combat that by launching little cans of premixed Pimm's.

TASTES GOOD WITH

Classic English picnic foods—cucumber sandwiches, hard-cooked quail's eggs, crackers with cream cheese and crudités—are all made the more splendid with plenty of Pimm's. Take a big pitcher and throw in half a bottle of Pimm's and a liter of lemonade.

FLAVORINGS

All highly secret of course, but it contains fruit extracts—notably orange—and at least one other alcoholic ingredient, perhaps curaçao. Who knows?

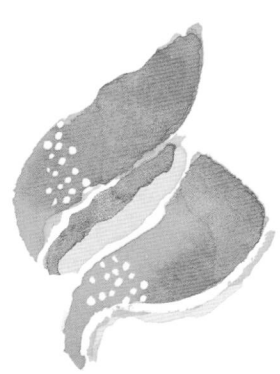

HOW TO SERVE

A generous measure of Pimm's No. 1 should be poured over ice in a tall glass. (In Mr Pimm's oyster bar, they knocked it back by the pint.) It is then topped up with lemonade or soda, and garnished with slices of orange, lemon and lime, a wedge of apple and a dangling twist of pared cucumber rind. If you can find fresh borage, use some of its smaller leaves instead of the cucumber. Float a little bundle of mint leaves on top. If that sounds like too much of a production, just throw in a slice of lemon and get on with it.

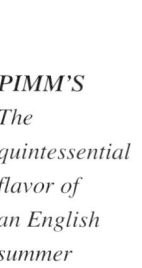

PIMM'S
The quintessential flavor of an English summer

POIRE WILLIAM

FLAVORING
Williams pears

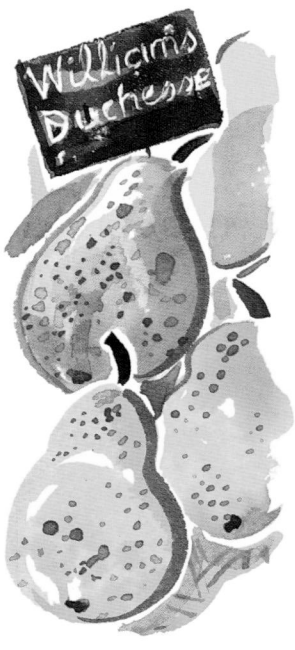

HOW TO SERVE
Served well chilled, or perhaps with a single piece of ice, it makes a good aperitif. Alternatively, add a splash of lemonade.

POIRE WILLIAM IS NOT to be confused with true pear brandy, which is a colorless spirit, eau-de-vie de poire, made in Alsace and Switzerland. The big liqueur companies nearly all make a sweet pear-flavored liqueur, traditionally lightly colored and made by the usual method of infusing crushed fruit in neutral grape spirit. Some may have a brief period of cask-aging, but most don't.

One of the curiosities of Poire William—which is so named after the particular variety of pear used—is that, while its aroma is very strong and evocative, the flavor is often disappointingly mild. This is true of pears generally. The Williams is a gorgeously aromatic fruit when fully ripe but, used in cooking, its flavor often all but vanishes, which isn't at all true of the best apple varieties. As such, I find the liqueur has to be used in fairly enthusiastic quantities in a cocktail in order to get the most out of it.

Pear-flavored liqueurs are made in France (about the best brand is Marie Brizard), Italy (which has Pera Segnana), Germany and Switzerland. A novelty product is Poire Prisonnière, which comes with a whole pear in the bottle. I remember as a student seeing one in a store window in Venice and debating with a friend how on earth they managed to get the pear in. We eventually concluded they must somehow hand-blow the bottle around the fruit. So much for

POIRE PRISONNIÈRE
The pear is painstakingly grown in the bottle

MIXING
Old William (from G. Marcialis and F. Zingales's *Cocktail Book*): Pour a double measure of Poire William over ice in a tumbler. Add a half-measure each of maraschino and fresh orange and lemon juices, and mix thoroughly. Decorate with orange and lemon slices.

youthful ingenuity. The pears are in fact *grown* in the bottles, which are attached to the tree, so that each fruit has its own private greenhouse. Before the bottles are filled with the liqueur, the pears are pricked in order to release their juices.

TASTES GOOD WITH
Poire William is excellent poured over certain fresh fruits, notably pink grapefruit segments, pineapple or, of course, pear.

POIRE WILLIAM
Delicately flavored French pear liqueur

PUNSCH

UNSCH IS MORE FAMILIARLY known in English-speaking countries as Swedish punch, although even then it isn't a drink many people have come across. Its lineage can be traced back to the eighteenth century, when Sweden's ocean going trading vessels began doing business in the East Indies. Among the commodities they brought back was some of the arak that is the traditional spirit of those regions. Some arak is rice-based, some a distillate of sugar cane, and therefore more like rum.

In its raw state, it wasn't much to northern European tastes, and so a few drink companies took to blending it with grape brandy and various wines and cordials, in effect creating a kind of powerful punch in the process. Like a traditional punch, the mixture is also highly spiced—just what the doctor ordered in the depths of the grim Scandinavian winter.

The punch was a British colonial invention, but by the eighteenth century, a vogue for it had spread not only to

PUNSCH
The real thing—
a cask-aged
punch from
Sweden

MIXING
Diki-Diki: Shake a double measure of calvados, half a measure each of punsch and grapefruit juice, with ice, and strain into a cocktail glass.
Grand Slam (below): Mix a double measure of punsch with a measure each of dry white and sweet red vermouth, with ice, in a pitcher, and then strain over crushed ice in a wine glass.

FLAVORINGS
Sweet spices, such as cinnamon and cloves

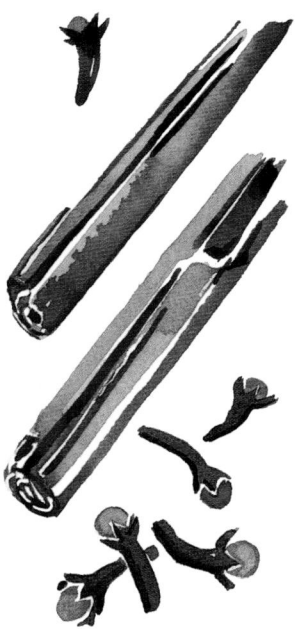

HOW TO SERVE
To relive the old days, warm the punsch gently (without letting it boil) in a small saucepan and serve it in big, heat-proof wineglasses.

Scandinavia but into France as well. Rum was a favored base ingredient, variously boosted with hot tea, lemon juice and sweet spices such as cinnamon. Punch was, in every way, the granddaddy of the cocktail.

In an echo of the British habit, Swedish punch was usually served hot, at least until the end of the last century. Since that time, the universal fashion for alcoholic drinks to be served cold has meant it is now drunk straight or even iced.

HOW IT IS MADE
These days, punsch is exclusively a rum-based drink, to which other forms of alcohol—including wine—are added, together with a quantity of fragrant spices, such as cinnamon and cloves. It is sweetened and then aged for several months in cask.

TASTES GOOD WITH
Punsch goes well with little salty appetizers made with strong cheese.

RATAFIA

RATAFIA WAS, CENTURIES AGO, a forerunner of the liqueur, in that it involved steeping fruits or nuts in a sweetened spirit base. That wouldn't in itself earn it a separate entry in this guide, were it not for the fact that the term ratafia has come to be applied mainly now to a type of aperitif made in the brandy-producing areas of France. The brandy is mixed with fresh fruit juice.

Ratafia is not a geographical name. It derives from the old French practice of concluding any formal agreement, such as a legal contract or business transaction, with a shared drink—a "ratifier," if you like. The original phrase is Latin: *rata fiat* ("let the deal be settled").

There are also ratafias made in wine areas—particularly Burgundy and Champagne—in which the naturally sweet grape juice is mixed in with some of the regional wine. The most celebrated ratafia, however, is Pineau des Charentes, made in the Cognac region from grape juice fortified with cognac. It can't be considered a fortified wine, though, for

the very good reason that the grape juice has not undergone fermentation. It comes in white and rosé versions, and always has the sweetness of ripe grape juice about it.

In Armagnac, not to be outdone, they make their own version of this drink by exactly the same method. Called Floc de Gascogne, its production—like that of Armagnac itself—is on a much more modest commercial footing than its Charentais counterpart.

There is also a variant of this type of ratafia made in the Calvados region of Normandy, in which fresh apple juice is fortified with apple brandy. It is called pommeau, and is a considerably more palatable proposition (to the author's taste at least) than either Pineau or Floc.

HOW IT IS MADE

By adding grape brandy to unfermented grape juice, or conversely apple brandy to apple juice, in each case to an average bottled strength of around 17% ABV.

TASTES GOOD WITH

Ratafia works quite well as an accompaniment to a slice of aromatic melon— better than most wine, at any rate.

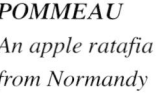

PINEAU DES CHARENTES
The ratafia of the Cognac region

POMMEAU
An apple ratafia from Normandy

SAMBUCA

AN ITALIAN LIQUEUR that became quite fashionable beyond its home region of Rome in the 1970s and 1980s, Sambuca Romana is a clear, moderately sweet, quite fiery drink, flavored with elderberries and anise. Its name is derived from the botanical name for elderberry, *Sambucus nigra*. There are other herbs and roots in it too, but these are the two predominant flavors.

In the days when every drink had to be dignified with its own particular serving ritual, it was decreed that Sambuca was to be garnished with coffee beans and set alight. Aficionados of the custom differed quite sharply as to whether the correct number of beans was two or three. Such detail scarcely mattered, since what mostly preoccupied the drinker was how to swallow it without burning the nose.

To earn your Sambuca stripes, you have to blow out the flame on a glassful and then swallow the drink in one gulp, like an oyster. In Rome, they will ask you whether you want it *con la mosca*, literally "with the fly" (i.e. with the coffee beans). There, they are not merely for garnish. If you say *si*, you will be expected to crunch the beans up as you drink.

MIXING
Matinée (from Michael Walker's *Cinzano Cocktail Book*): Shake a measure of gin, half a measure each of Sambuca and thick cream, half an egg white and a dash of fresh lime juice with plenty of ice, and strain into a cocktail glass. Sprinkle with finely grated nutmeg.

TASTES GOOD WITH
A chilled glass of Sambuca makes a good accompaniment to a genuine Italian *torta*, one of those heavenly sticky cakes made with dried fruits, almonds and lemon zest.

FLAVORINGS
Elderberries
Anise

SABRA
This is Israel's entry in the spirits and liqueurs stakes—a svelte concoction flavored with a clever mélange of Jaffa orange and chocolate. Despite the bitterness contributed by the orange peels, the resulting drink is exceptionally sweet. Try mixing it with cognac and ice to lighten the effect.

SAMBUCA
A fiery liqueur in more ways than one

HOW TO SERVE
If you are going to try the flaming Sambuca trick, it helps to serve the liqueur in a narrow glass like an old-fashioned sherry schooner, because the flame will take more easily on a smaller surface.

SLOE GIN

SLOE GIN, AND its French equivalent prunelle, rely for their flavor and color on a type of small bitter-tasting plum, the fruit of a shrub called the blackthorn. English sloe gin, as marketed by companies such as Hawker's, is nothing more than sweetened gin in which sloes have been steeped and then strained out once they have stained the spirit a deep red. The fruits contribute a strong, rather medicinal taste to the drink.

Prunelle, from the French word for the fruit, is not red but green, and is made by macerating the fruit kernels in a grape spirit base. Although the color may be added, it does reflect the green-ish flesh of the fruit. Liqueur companies such as Garnier and Cusenier (theirs is called Prunellia) make it, and it is especially popular in Anjou, in the

FLAVORING
The fruit of the wild blackthorn bush

SLOE GIN

A sloe gin from one of the big names in gin

OTHER NAMES
France: Prunelle/Prunellia

western part of the Loire Valley. They also make eau-de-vie from sloes in Burgundy and Alsace.

The plant itself is a wild shrub that grows quite plentifully throughout Europe, its little sour fruits only ripening properly in early winter. Sloe gin is still quite widely made at home in country areas of England, but only with commercial gin, of course.

HOW IT IS MADE
Sloe gin is easy to make at home if you have access to the fruits. The best ratio is about half a pound of sugar to a pound of the fruit, but if the fruit is very sour, you may want to increase the sweetening by a couple of ounces. The fruit should be partly squashed or pierced to encourage absorption of the flavor. Top up your bottle with gin (or vodka, if you prefer, but gin makes a more interesting marriage of flavors). Leave it sealed for at least three months, shaking it up occasionally, and then strain the spirit off the solids.

TASTES GOOD WITH
Like cranberries or rowanberries, sloes make a good, tart jelly for garnishing strong, gamy meats. A shot of sloe gin in the accompanying sauce or gravy enhances the flavor.

HOW TO SERVE
Sloe gin is best served as it comes and at room temperature. A marketing push for a brand of sloe gin a few years ago suggested adding a teaspoon or two of it to a glass of sparkling wine, which isn't a bad idea—especially if the sparkling wine is a bit rough.

SOUTHERN COMFORT

THE FOREMOST AMERICAN liqueur is Southern Comfort, a fruitier counterpart to the scotch-based liqueurs. Naturally, American whiskey is used as its starting point. As so often in the world of proprietary liqueurs, the exact composition of Southern Comfort is a closely guarded commercial secret, but what we do know is that the fruit flavoring it contains is peach.

Its origins probably lie in the mixing of bourbon with peach juice as a traditional cocktail in the southern states. In New Orleans, there was once a mixed drink called a Sazerac. A recipe for it is given in the *Savoy Cocktail Book*. It consists of a shot of rye whiskey, with a sprinkling of

SOUTHERN
COMFORT

A fruity whiskey
liqueur of the
Deep South

MIXING

Southern Peach: Shake a measure each of Southern Comfort, peach brandy and thick cream with a dash of Angostura and plenty of ice, and strain into a tumbler. Decorate with a wedge of peach.

peach bitters, a lump of sugar and a dash of absinthe. So traditional is it that a New Orleans company has been producing a premixed version of it since around the middle of the nineteenth century.

Peaches themselves are grown in great quantities in the southern states; the Georgia peach is one of America's proudest agricultural products. The practice of blending the peach juice with whiskey in the bars of New Orleans undoubtedly also played its part in influencing the creation of Southern Comfort.

Today, the company that owns the brand is the same one that has the leading Tennessee whiskey brand, Jack Daniel's. The Southern Comfort distillery is located in St Louis, Missouri. The bottled strength is high—40% ABV—which is perhaps one of the reasons it appealed so much to the late great rock legend Janis Joplin.

TASTES GOOD WITH

Southern Comfort makes a good substitute for bourbon poured over the traditional light fruitcake at Thanksgiving or Christmas. Quantities should be extremely generous, though: a whole bottleful is not unknown.

FLAVORING
Peaches

HOW TO SERVE
Southern Comfort is intended to be meditatively sipped, like other fine American whiskeys, but you could try taming its fire and emphasizing its fruitiness with a mixer of peach nectar. It's also fine with orange juice on the rocks.

STREGA

STREGA, the name of a popular proprietary liqueur produced in Italy, is Italian for "witch." It is so called because it is supposedly based on a witches' brew, an aphrodisiac love potion guaranteed to unite any pair of lovers who drink it in eternal togetherness. You have been warned.

It is a bright yellow concoction full of all sorts of complex flavors. The fruit base is a citrus blend and reputedly contains around six dozen different botanical herbs, making it not dissimilar in style to the yellow version of Chartreuse. It has

STREGA
This Italian liqueur is full of complex flavors

MIXING
Golden Tang (from Michael Walker's *Cinzano Cocktail Book*): Shake a double measure of vodka, a measure of Strega, and half a measure each of crème de banane and fresh orange juice with ice, and strain into a large wineglass. (Alternatively, double the quantities all around and strain into a tall glass.)

the same kind of syrupy texture, too, and is considered an especially good digestif.

Although the color resembles that other Italian liqueur specialty, Galliano, Strega's flavor is quite different, more obviously herbal and with a stronger citrus element.

TASTES GOOD WITH
Strega works particularly well as an accompaniment to freshly cracked nuts at the end of a meal.

HOW TO SERVE
Strega is more appealing served frappé, on crushed ice, which takes the edge off its sweetness, than on its own.

SUZE

I F I HAD TO NOMINATE one other product to make up a perfect trinity of aperitifs with champagne and pale dry sherry, it would unhesitatingly be Suze. Some may consider that Suze, and the various related Swiss and German products, should technically be considered under "bitters," but they are not always direct distillates; some are actually wine-based. What they do all have in common is that they rely for their impact on gentian.

Gentian is a wild mountain plant found in the Alps and the mountains of the Jura, in France. It has large yellow flowers, but it is principally valued for its roots, which can grow up to a yard long and have one of the most uncompromisingly bitter flavors found anywhere in the plant world. It was once the quinine of its day, before that plant was brought to Europe from the Americas in the seventeenth century. Like quinine, gentian has had a distinguished history in the pharmacist's repertoire; it was thought to be particularly good for ailments of the liver.

The Suze brand is owned by pastis manufacturers Pernod-Ricard, and it has a very

SUZE
*Well worth
a journey to
France to
taste*

MIXING
Drought: Shake equal measures of gin and Suze with a small splash of fresh orange juice, and strain into a cocktail glass. (This is an unimaginably dry mixture, and particularly good at whetting the appetite.)

FLAVORING
Gentian root

delicate primrose color. It is based on wine, and its flavor is so dry and bitter, even when mixed with a little water or served on ice, that it acts as an extraordinarily powerful appetite-rouser.

Other similar products may be labeled Gentiane in France and Switzerland, or Enzian in Germany. The German products tend to be direct distillates of the gentian root, though, rather than wine-based.

HOW IT IS MADE
In the case of Suze and similar products, an extract of gentian is steeped in a white wine base, which imparts a little faint color to the liquid. It is then clarified and bottled at fortified wine strength.

TASTES GOOD WITH
Suze is great served with any bitter nibbles, and is extremely appetizing with the more pungent varieties of green olive.

HOW TO SERVE
Pour a measure of Suze into a tumbler with either the merest splash of very cold water or a single cube of ice just to freshen it up.

GENTIANE
An alternative French brand of gentian aperitif.

TIA MARIA

JAMAICA'S CONTRIBUTION to the world of liqueurs, Tia Maria has turned into one of the best-loved of all such products in both America and Europe. It is a suave, deep brown coffee-flavored drink that proves itself highly versatile on the cocktail circuit and as an after-dinner drink.

It is based, not surprisingly, on good dark Jamaican rum of at least five-year-old standard and flavored with the beans of the highly prized coffee variety Blue Mountain. In addition to the coffee, the palate is further deepened by the addition of local spices. Although the liqueur is sweet, noticeably sweeter than its Mexican counterpart Kahlúa, for example, the aromatic components in it prevent it from being cloying. This makes it one of the few such drinks that is actually quite acceptable to savor on its own.

Not the least reason for its popularity in Europe was the craze for the cocktail Black Russian, usually mixed with Coca-Cola, in

FLAVORINGS
Coffee
Spices

TIA MARIA
The world's most famous coffee liqueur

HOW TO SERVE
On the rocks is a pleasant way to serve Tia Maria as a digestif. Otherwise, it is one of the few liqueurs to make a truly appetizing mix with cola. Some like it with orange juice, but the resulting muddy color is somewhat unattractive.

Tia Maria
LIQUEUR
World famous for the unique smoothness of its flavour derived from an original Jamaican coffee liqueur recipe which has been closely guarded for generations

700 ml e   26,5% vol

MIXING
Sunburn: Shake equal measures of cognac and Tia Maria, half a measure each of fresh orange and lemon juices and ice, and strain into a cocktail glass.
Proportions of the classic **Black Russian** (below) vary according to taste. Two parts vodka to one part Tia Maria on ice, with no mixer, makes a very adult drink.

which it provides a luxurious note of richness to what is otherwise a fairly prosaic mix.

HOW IT IS MADE
Coffee beans and spices are infused in a base of cask-aged rum, which is then lightly sweetened. It is bottled at just under 27% ABV.

TASTES GOOD WITH
Tia Maria is excellent for lacing chocolate desserts, and of course makes a good liqueur for coffee—particularly when the coffee used is Blue Mountain.

TRAPPISTINE
Another of the few remaining liqueurs made by religious orders, Trappistine is made at the convent of the Abbaye de Grâce de Dieu in the eastern French *département* of Doubs, not far from the Swiss border. A naturally pallid, yellowy green color, it is based on Armagnac and contains macerations of many wild herbs.

VAN DER HUM

Van der hum is South Africa's equivalent of curaçao, made by several producers in the Cape, including the giant national wine consortium KWV. The whimsical name translates as "What's-his-Name." Its base is Cape brandy, of which there is a large annual production, and the citrus fruit used is a tangerine-like orange variety locally known as *naartjies*. Much in the way of curaçao, the peels of the orange are infused in the brandy and supplemented with an herb or spice element. The precise formula may vary from one producer to the next, but nutmeg is a favored addition.

Rather like Mandarine Napoléon, the drink derives from the practice of steeping citrus peels in the local brandy. Such a concoction would have been widely produced domestically by early Cape settlers, and the formula came to be replicated on a commercial scale. It is a reliable and attractive liqueur, its pale gold color and pronounced bitter orange scent adding to its appeal. The bottled strength is generally 25%-plus.

VAN DER HUM
South Africa's
answer to orange
curaçao

MIXING

Sundowner: Shake a measure and a half of South African brandy or cognac and a measure of Van der Hum with half a measure each of fresh orange and lemon juices and ice. Strain into a cocktail glass.

LA VIEILLE CURE

The correct translation of this liqueur's name is "The Old Rectory," not—as it would seem—"The Old Cure." The mistranslation would be right on at least one score, though. It was once a golden potion made by the monastic order at the abbey of Cenons, near Bordeaux. It used over 50 different curative wild herbs macerated in blended brandies, and was very much a typical medieval alcohol remedy, first conceived in the days when distillation went hand in hand with the pharmacist's art. The flavor has been compared to that of Bénédictine. To enjoy it to the fullest, La Vieille Cure should be served neat and un-iced in small liqueur glasses. In the 1980s, the production passed into the hands of one of the large French drinks companies of the region, but the liqueur's manufacture should not be confused with the wine-producing château of the same name in Bordeaux.

VERVEINE

Verveine du Vélay, to give it its full title, is another of those liqueurs that models itself stylistically on Chartreuse, to the extent that it comes in green and yellow, with the green the stronger. It is a brandy-based herbal concoction made near Puy, in the Auvergne region of central France. Verveine is the French for verbena, a flowering herb whose leaves have been used in folk medicine for centuries as a restorative for the liver and also for neurological complaints. Its bitter flavor is apparent in the liqueur named after it (though there are other herbs in it too), the sharpness gentled with a little honey.

FLAVORINGS
Naartjie peels
Nutmeg and other spice and herb aromatizers

HOW TO SERVE

Traditionally, Van der Hum is quite heavily sweetened by the manufacturer. For those who prefer a drier drink, the customary thing is to mix it half-and-half with brandy. Some companies bottle it ready-mixed as Brandy-Hum—the Cape equivalent of B & B.

FORTIFIED WINES

THE DRINK PRODUCTS in this final section are, technically speaking, wines. If they were wines pure and simple, however, they would have no place in a book dealing with spirits and liqueurs. These wines have one important difference from ordinary table wines. They have all been fortified, and what they are fortified with is spirit, grape spirit more often than not. In that respect, none of these types of wine could have existed before the discovery of distillation.

In most cases, the creation of the classic fortified wines was a chance discovery occasioned in the course of trying to find ways of preserving ordinary wines. It wasn't that some clever person in Portugal once thought, "Let's add some brandy to our wines and see what they taste like." The addition of spirit was intended to keep wines from spoiling on the long and often arduous sea voyages they had to undergo en route to their customers abroad.

In the days when the chemistry of fermentation was much less thoroughly understood than it is now, wine was often shipped, in the barrel, in a micro-biologically unstable state. It may have been that its fermentation had only been interrupted by a sudden drop in the cellar temperature, as opposed to having run its natural course. When such wines arrived

at their destinations, it was often found that they begun refermenting or, worse, that they would referment *after* being bottled.

The yeast that ferments in grape juice and result in the production of alcohol can only continue to do its work as long as there is enough natural sugar in the liquid for it to feed on, and as long as the amount of alcohol generated doesn't exceed a certain level—usually estimated in the range of 16–17% by volume (ABV). After that, it dies off, and the wine becomes stable. If you add a healthy dose of brandy or other spirit to wine that has apparently finished fermenting (or to one that is still in the process of fermenting, for that matter), you raise the alcohol level to such a degree that the yeast is killed off.

In addition to then having a stable

Left: The essential flor (yeast cells) growing on the surface of a barrel of fino sherry.

Above: For tasting, sherry is still taken from the barrels in the traditional way using a long-handled venecia.

Left: Neat rows of vines and fermentation tanks bake in the hot sun in the Douro Valley at Pinhão, Portugal.

wine on your hands, you also of course have a product that is quite a bit higher in alcohol than most ordinary wines. The normal strength of unfortified table wines is in the region of 11–13% ABV. Some German and Italian wines make a virtue of being particularly low in alcohol (as little as 5%, perhaps), while certain Italian and Californian wines made from grapes that have grown in raging hot climates may climb up to around 15%. But 15% is the *starting* point for fortified wines, and they can be fortified up to 22%, bringing them close to the strength of the average liqueur.

Each of the world's classic fortified wines (they originated in southern Europe, but are now made in most wine-making countries) has its own particular method of production. The majority are made from white grapes, the most

notable exception being port, most of which is red. They tend to be sweet, but don't have to be—fino and manzanilla sherry are the driest of the dry. Most of them contain only wine and grape spirit, but in the case of vermouth and related products, a whole bunch of aromatizing ingredients (familiar to us from some of the herbal liqueurs) creates a style that is halfway between a fortified wine and a liqueur.

Fortified wines may once have seemed a good way of using up a substandard harvest, either through the distillation of grapes to make the fortifying agent, or in masking a poor wine's faults by adding spirit to it. By the time the nineteenth century dawned, however, most of these wines were seen as premium products— vintage port and Madeira particularly were as highly acclaimed as claret and

Above: At one time, on the Douro River, Porto, Portugal, small boats were used to bring barrels of port from high in the valley.

burgundy. Until about the time of the Second World War, they were held in special regard by the British, who have always had a taste for strong and fiery wines. Since that time a progressive decline has occured as international tastes in wine have tended to the dry and light end of the spectrum, and away from the sort of sinew-stiffening brew to be sipped by the fireside on winter nights.

Despite that, there will always be a place for the traditional fortified wines. In a world where table wine is often accused of being infected by a bland homogeneity of taste, the fortifieds are, in a variety of ways, unashamedly unique styles of wine.

MADEIRA

OF ALL THE CLASSIC fortified wines of southern Europe, Madeira is the one with the most singular history. It comes from the island of the same name in the Atlantic Ocean; a volcanic outcrop, Madeira is actually slightly nearer to the coast of North Africa than it is to Portugal, of which it is an autonomously governed region.

The evolution of this wine belongs to the days of the trading ships that plied the East India routes in the late 1600s. Madeira's geographical position made it a natural port of call for north European vessels on their way to Africa and the East Indies, and so they would load up with wine at the port of Funchal, the island capital. It gradually came to be noticed that, whereas many table wines would be badly spoiled by the combination of violent

shaking and the torrid heat in which they traveled the oceans, Madeiras were eerily improved by the experience.

The shippers were so sure of the benefits the sea voyage conferred on the wine that they began to send wines that were only destined for the European markets all the way to Indonesia and back. Some went the other way, and a great connoisseurship of Madeira grew up in the newly independent United States. Until virtually the end of the nineteenth century, this is how the most highly prized Madeiras were all made.

Eventually, it simply wasn't financially practical to keep treating Madeira to an around-the-world cruise, and so the conditions it endured at sea—the tortuous heat, especially—were recreated in the wineries, or "lodges," where the wines originated. Some Madeira is heated simply

HOW TO SERVE
Serve Madeira in a good-size sherry glass or small wineglass. The drier styles may benefit from a little light chilling, but the richer, darker styles, with their overtones of toffee and Christmas cake, should be served at room temperature.

RICH MALMSEY
This is the sweetest style of Madeira

VERDELHO
The second-driest style— this five-year-old Madeira is only very slightly sweet

MIXING

It was common in America once to substitute sweet Madeira for the brandy in a **Prairie Oyster**, that most challenging of hangover cures, involving a raw egg yolk, salt and cayenne pepper and a dash of Worcestershire sauce.
Boston (below): Shake equal measures of dry Madeira and bourbon with half a teaspoon of superfine sugar and an egg yolk. Strain into a small wineglass and sprinkle with grated nutmeg.

HOW IT IS MADE

A light, white base wine is made from any of the four main varieties, perhaps supplemented with some juice from the local red grape tinta negra mole (though it is theoretically of declining importance). For the sweeter styles, bual and malmsey, the fermentation may be interrupted early on by the addition of grape spirit, meaning that some natural sugar remains in them, while the drier wines (sercial and verdelho) are fermented until more of the sugar has been consumed before being fortified. The wines are then subjected to heat during the cask-aging, either by one of the heating systems known as an *estufa* (stove), or else by just being left in the hottest part of the lodge, in which case it may be known as a *vinho canteiro*.

by being left under the roof of the lodge to bake in the heat of the tropical sun. Some is stored in rooms where fat central heating pipes run around the walls throughout the summer swelter, and even the lowest grades are matured in vats that have hot-water pipes running through them.

There are four basic styles of Madeira, named after the grape varieties that go into them. The palest and driest style is sercial. Then comes verdelho, a little sweeter and darker, then bual, and finally malmsey (the last is an English corruption of the Portuguese name "malvasia"). The wines are also graded according to how long they have been aged. This may be given as a minimum age on the label (5-year-old, 10-year-old and so on), or one of the accepted descriptive terms may be used. "Reserve" equates roughly to 5-year-old, "Special Reserve" to 10, "Extra Reserve" to 15. Some Madeira is vintage-dated, meaning it is the unblended produce of the stated year's harvest.

SERCIAL
The palest and driest style of Madeira

TASTES GOOD WITH

The driest styles present the answer to that age-old problem of what to drink with soup. They are particularly good with clear, rich consommé. As you proceed to the sweeter end of the scale, drink them with mincemeat pies, Christmas cake and other dense fruitcakes or, of course, Madeira cake.

MARSALA

SICILY'S VERY OWN fortified wine is named after the town of Marsala, in the province of Trapani at the western end of the island. Like many of the fortified wines of southern Europe, it has an English connection. It was effectively invented by a wine merchant, John Woodhouse, in 1773, in direct imitation of the sherry and Madeira in which he was something of a specialist. In the rough-and-ready way of the time, he simply added a quantity of ordinary brandy to the traditional white wines of western Sicily, and found on shipping them that the result was a reasonably close approximation of the already established fortified wines.

Woodhouse founded a commercial operation on the island at the end of the eighteenth century, and won valuable orders

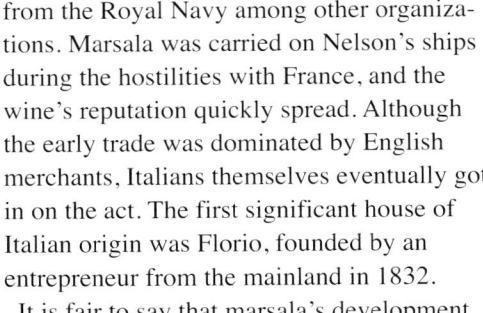

from the Royal Navy among other organizations. Marsala was carried on Nelson's ships during the hostilities with France, and the wine's reputation quickly spread. Although the early trade was dominated by English merchants, Italians themselves eventually got in on the act. The first significant house of Italian origin was Florio, founded by an entrepreneur from the mainland in 1832.

It is fair to say that marsala's development since that period has been one of slow decline as a result of conflicting theories about how it should be made, and the widespread use of irrigation in the vineyards where it is grown. Irrigation can result in grapes of lower sugar concentration, which means that alternative methods of sweetening the wine have had to be found.

The rules and regulations governing the production of marsala

TERRE ARSE
A vintage-dated marsala from Florio

SECCO
The driest style of marsala

HOW TO SERVE
Dry and medium-dry marsala, of which there is a regrettably small amount, should be served chilled in sherry glasses as an aperitif. The sweetest styles should be served at room temperature as digestifs or with certain types of aged, dry cheese.

MIXING

Casanova: Shake a measure of bourbon with half a measure each of sweet marsala and Kahlúa, a measure of thick cream and plenty of ice. Strain into a cocktail glass.

Inigo Jones (from Michael Walker's *Cinzano Cocktail Book*): In a mixing-cup, stir together a measure of cognac, a measure of sweet marsala, a measure of dry rosé wine and a dash each of fresh orange and lemon juices with plenty of ice. Strain into a tumbler half-filled with crushed ice.

were only finally codified in 1969, and are considerably more flexible than those controlling the manufacture of the other famous fortified wines. Perhaps the least satisfactory aspect of them is the nature of the sweetening agents that may be added. It can be either a fortified grape juice, or just grape juice whose sweetness has been concentrated by cooking. This latter ingredient, known in Italian as *mosto cotto*, is not in itself alcoholic. The best marsalas have natural sweetness from ripe grapes, which is retained through interrupted fermentation.

Marsala is classified by age—Fine is one year old, Superiore two, Superiore Riserva four, Vergine five, Stravecchio ten—and by sweetness. Dry is labelled "secco," medium-dry, "semisecco" and the sweetest, "dolce." It also comes in three colors. The better grades are both shades of tawny, either amber (*ambra*) or golden (*oro*), but there is a red version, too (*rubino*). Producers of note include de Bartoli, Pellegrino and Rallo.

HOW IT IS MADE

Light white wines from local grape varieties grillo, inzolia and catarratto are turned into marsala by one of three methods. They can be fortified with grape spirit in the traditional way, or sweetened and strengthened with either alcohol-boosted juice from ultrasweet, late-ripened grapes or with cooked grape juice concentrate. Concentrate is only permitted in the Ambra Marsala. The wines are then cask-aged for varying periods.

TASTES GOOD WITH

Marsala has come to be seen as even more of a kitchen ingredient than Madeira. It is indispensable as the alcohol element in both zabaglione and tiramisù, while scaloppine of veal, a popular dish in Italian trattorias all over the world, is often sauced with a syrupy brown reduction of marsala.

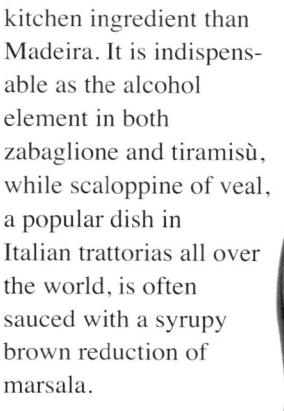

DOLCE
This is best suited for classic Italian desserts

FINE
Fine marsala is the youngest style.

RISERVA
Superiore Riserva marsala is four years old.

MUSCAT *and* MOSCATEL

SWEET FORTIFIED WINES are made from muscat all over the world. It is easy to think muscat is a single grape variety, but it is in fact a grape family. Some of its offshoots are of the highest pedigree, notably a type the French call muscat blanc à petits grains. Others, such as muscat of Alexandria and muscat Ottonel, are of humbler extraction, and produce correspondingly less exciting wines. Moscatel is the name the family assumes on the Iberian peninsula.

This is a quick global tour of the styles of sweet wine the muscat relatives make. All should be served chilled as dessert wines or on their own. They tend to be in the range of 15–18% ABV,

except for the first category, Australian muscats, which reach up to 20%.

AUSTRALIAN LIQUEUR MUSCATS

These are extremely rich, strong, fortified muscats made in and around the town of Rutherglen, in the northwestern corner of the Australian state of Victoria. They are produced by a method that seems to combine a little of all the ways of making fortified wine. The grapes are left to overripen and shrivel on the vine, so that they are halfway to becoming raisins. After pressing, they ferment partway, but the fermentation is arrested by fortification with grape spirit, keeping massive quantities of natural sugar in the wine. The cask-aging they then receive combines elements of the *solera* system used in Spanish brandy and sherry, and the action of searing sunshine, as in *canteiro* Madeiras. Among the more notable producers are Stanton & Killeen, Mick Morris and Chambers.

VIN DOUX NATUREL MUSCATS

A group of muscat wines made in southern France are made by virtually the same method as port. Their collective name, *vins doux naturels*, means "naturally sweet wines." The grapes are picked very ripe and the normal process of fermentation is stopped by adding a powerful grape spirit, so the natural grapey sweetness of muscat is retained. There are six appellations for this type of wine, the most famous of which comes from the southern Rhône Valley—muscat de Beaumes de Venise. Best producers are Domaine Durban and Domaine de Coyeux.

Four of the others are located down in the Languedoc. They are Muscat de Frontignan, de Lunel, de Mireval and de St Jean de Minervois. The sixth, Muscat de Rivesaltes, is grown even further south, in Roussillon, near the Spanish border. De Rivesaltes does not have to be made from the noblest muscat, though, and the quality varies hugely between producers.

SETÚBAL MOSCATEL

This is a highly traditional fortified wine based on the muscat of Alexandria grape, together with a couple of its more obscure cousins. It is made on the Setúbal peninsula in western Portugal, southeast of Lisbon, and was recognized

MUSCAT DE BEAUMES DE VENISE
Domaine de Coyeux is one of the best producers of muscat

as a regionally demarcated wine in the first decade of the twentieth century. The process is the same as for the French *vins doux naturels*, except that after fortification, the grape skins are allowed to macerate in the finished wine for several months. Some Setúbal moscatel is released after five years or so, when its color is already a vivid orange from the wood. Other wines are aged for a couple of decades, deepening to burnished mahogany until they are a molasses-thick essence of pure muscat flavor. The most significant producer is José Maria da Fonseca.

MOSCATEL DE VALENCIA

Around Valencia, on the eastern coast of Spain, they make what the French would call a *vin de liqueur*, that is, a wine that hasn't

SETÚBAL MOSCATEL

A 20-year-old moscatel from Portugal's Setúbal

really fermented as such but for which the grapes have merely been pressed and then fortified with grape spirit. (In that respect, they could be considered similar to the ratafias made in the brandy regions of France.) Moscatels of Valencia are not made from the most distinguished muscat variety and are more often than not seen in screw-top bottles. When very fresh and very well chilled, these can be pretty refreshing drinks, particularly in the intense heat of a Spanish summer.

JEREPIGO

Jerepigo is the South African version of Moscatel de Valencia, except that it most emphatically does use the aristocratic muscat Blanc à Petits Grains variety, here known— just to confuse everybody —as muscadel or muskadel. Otherwise, the production is the same, with grape spirit being added to the very sweet, freshly pressed grape juice. Vintages of Jerepigo (the name is Portuguese in origin) are occasionally released at around 15 years old, and are found to retain much of their initial freshness.

MOSCATEL DE VALENCIA

A highly ornate bottle for what is in fact a very simple drink

JEREPIGO

An old vintage of South Africa's answer to fortified moscatel.

PORT

ORT IS THE ONLY one of the major fortified wines to be based on a red wine. True, there is such a thing as white port, but it only accounts for a fraction of the production. Port hails from only one delimited area, the Douro Valley in northern Portugal. It has been so popular for so long as a style of wine that many non-European wine-making countries have been trying their hands at making port since the nineteenth century. The difference today is that, in the countries of the European Union at least, they are no longer allowed to be called port.

The drink originated during one of the frequent periods of hostilities between the English and the French in the 1600s, as a consequence of which the English authorities declared a punitive tax levy on goods imported from

France. This hit the wine trade hard. Wine shippers had to look to Portugal, England's oldest European ally, with whom there were preferential trade tariffs, to supply their customers. Journeying inland along the river Douro, the English merchants happened upon the fierce red wines of the region and found them pretty much to the domestic taste. As was common practice at the time, they fortified them with a little brandy for the sea voyage.

Thus was port born. Originally, it was of course a dry wine, since these were fully fermented wines that were being augmented with brandy. However, it only took the chance discovery of the effects of fortification

***COCKBURN'S
1991***
*A vintage port from
one of the English
shippers*

***GRAHAM'S
1989 LBV***
*Port from a single
year matured in the
shipper's cellars*

HOW TO SERVE
Good port should be served in wineglass quantities, not in silly little liqueur glasses, unchilled except in the case of white port. Older wines that have thrown a sediment may need to be decanted.

on an extremely ripe, sweet wine to remodel port in the image with which we are familiar today. To preserve that sweetness, the wines would have their normal fermentation interrupted (or "muted") with brandy, so that some of the grape sugars would remain unconsumed by the yeast.

Eventually, it was considered that using a simple local grape spirit was cheaper than buying fine cognac for the fortification. Also, port was coming to be seen as a fine wine in its own right, and so it was desirable that the fortifying agent should be as neutral as possible, in order to allow the characteristics of the underlying wine to be shown off.

Port styles have since multiplied almost *ad infinitum*. At the top of the quality tree are the vintage ports, wines of a single year that must be bottled within two years of the harvest and are intended for long aging. Late-bottled vintage (LBV) is also the product of a single year, but one that has been kept in cask in the shipper's premises for longer—around six years, usually—in order to be more mature on bottling, and readier to drink on purchase. Vintage Character port is an everyday blended product and nothing special, while the fine old tawny ports are often aged for many years in barrel so that their initial full-blooded red fades to an autumnal brown.

Other countries producing good port-style fortified wines are Australia (where the favored grape variety is the spicy shiraz), South Africa and the United States. There is a very good Greek fortified red called Mavrodaphne that makes an agreeable alternative to the more basic offerings of the Douro.

HOW IT IS MADE

The fermentation of Douro wines is stopped partway through by the addition of grape spirit, to produce a sweet, strong, wine. Various periods of cask-aging are given to the various grades. The bottled strength is in the region of 18–20%, but can be as high as 22%.

TASTES GOOD WITH

Port is excellent with nuts and with mature, strong hard cheeses, such as Cheddar, but less good with its traditional partner, Stilton.

QUINTA DO CRASTO
An LBV from a small Portuguese producer

TAYLOR'S 20 YEARS OLD
Twenty years is the average age of the blend

GRAHAM'S SIX GRAPES
A fairly basic ruby port

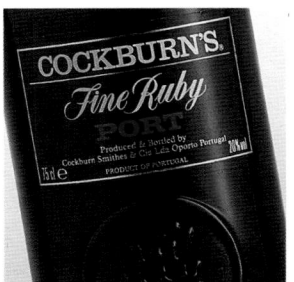

COCKBURN'S FINE RUBY
This is the lowest port designation

QUADY'S
A port-style fortified wine from the United States

SHERRY

ALTHOUGH FORTIFIED WINES bearing the name of sherry have been produced around the world for well over a century, true sherry comes only from a demarcated region in the southern Spanish province of Andalucía. There are three main centers of production—Jerez de la Frontera, Puerto de Santa María and Sanlúcar de Barrameda. The last is the traditional home of a type of pale, delicate dry sherry called manzanilla.

The production process for sherry is one of the most complicated of any fortified wine. When the new white wine is made, it

TIO PEPE
Muy Seco is the very driest style of sherry

OTHER NAMES
Spain: Jerez *France*: Xérès

is fermented until fully dry, and then transferred into large butts. Some sherries, the ones that are destined to end up as the pale dry style known as fino (or manzanilla), develop a film of yeast culture called *flor* on the surface of the wine. In some barrels, the layer of *flor* dies out because it has consumed all the remaining nutrients in the wine, whereupon it breaks up and sinks to the

HARVEYS
BRISTOL CREAM
A big-selling brown cream sherry

HOW TO SERVE

Fino and manzanilla, and the sweetened pale sherries, should be served very well chilled, preferably from a freshly opened bottle. In Spain, they think nothing of drinking a bottle of dry sherry as we would a table wine. The other styles should be served at room temperature.

Finos are brilliant aperitifs, old olorosos best at the other end of the meal.

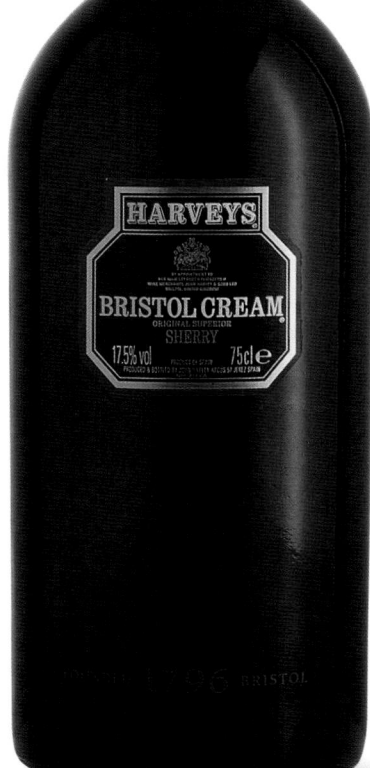

MIXING

Parkeroo (from Lucius Beebe's *Stork Club Bar Book*): Mix a double measure of pale dry sherry and a measure of tequila in a pitcher with ice. Decant into a champagne flute filled with shaved ice and add a twist of lemon peel.

bottom of the butt. With the subsequent greater exposure to the air, the color of the wine deepens through oxidation, and the style known as amontillado results.

Some wines develop no *flor* at all and go on to turn a deep, woody brown color. These are oloroso sherries. The fortification of the wine varies according to the style. Fino may be fortified to only 15% ABV, whereas oloroso is generally bottled at around 20%. At this stage, all of the wines are naturally dry, and some— the true connoisseur's sherries—will be bottled in that condition after aging in cask.

Many commercial sherries, however, are made sweet by the addition of a quantity of *mistela*, the juice of raisined grapes to which grape spirit has been added. The best sweet sherries are sweetened with PX, which stands for Pedro Ximénez, the name of a grape variety whose berries are left to dry in the sun until loss of moisture has concentrated their sugars to an almost unbelievable degree. Some houses bottle some of their PX separately as a specialty product.

Other countries that produce sherry-style wines are Australia (which makes about the best outside Jerez), the United States, South Africa and Cyprus. Within Spain itself, there are two other regions near Jerez that produce similar fortified wines in the same range of styles, but they are not as distinguished as sherry. One is Montilla-Morilés, the other the virtually forgotten Condado de Huelva.

Spain's other great, now sadly nearly extinct, fortified wine is Málaga, made around the Mediterranean port of that name. Its finest wines are deep brown, caramel-sweet creations of great power, once extremely popular in Britain, now forsaken by fashion.

TASTE GOOD WITH

Dry sherries are good with salted nuts such as almonds, with piquant snacks such as olives and salty fish like anchovies, and with Serrano ham or its Mediterranean equivalents. The sweet old olorosos are wonderful with rich, dark fruitcake and hard Spanish sheep's milk cheeses such as Manchego.

MIXING

Adonis: Mix a double measure of dry sherry, a measure of sweet red vermouth and a dash or two of Angostura in a cup with ice, and strain into a wineglass.

Sherry Flip: Shake a double measure of brown cream sherry, half a teaspoon of superfine sugar and a whole egg, with ice, and strain into a wineglass. Sprinkle grated nutmeg on top. (Alternatively, mix this up in a blender.)

Sherry Cocktail (below): A good double measure of pale dry sherry is mixed with three dashes each of dry vermouth and orange bitters, and plenty of ice, and strained into a large wineglass.

EMVA CREAM
A Cypriot wine, no longer labeled as "sherry"

VERMOUTH

ERMOUTH IS AS FAR removed from the natural produce of the vine as it is possible for a fortified wine to get. Not only is it strengthened with spirit, but it is also heavily aromatized with herbs and botanical ingredients in order to make a distinctive type of drink that is usually intended for drinking—either mixed or unmixed—as an aperitif. There is no particular connoisseurship of vermouth, as there is for aged sherries and vintage ports. This is an everyday product made to a consistent and unchanging recipe by each manufacturer.

The presence in vermouth of that cocktail of herbs

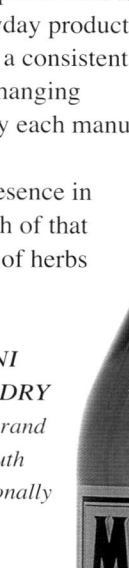

MARTINI EXTRA DRY
The top brand of vermouth internationally

HOW TO SERVE

A drop or two only of dry French vermouth is needed for the perfect dry martini or "Vodkatini."

All these drinks should be served as aperitifs or at the cocktail hour.
Vermouth is not as fragile once opened as pale dry sherry tends to be. It doesn't have to be drunk within a few days, and is able to withstand extremes of temperature far more hardily than the other light fortified wines.

MIXING

Merry Widow: Stir equal measures of gin and dry vermouth with two dashes each of Pernod, Bénédictine and Angostura with ice in a mixing cup. Strain into a large wineglass.

and roots alerts us to the fact that this was originally a medicinal drink. That said, the practice of adding herbs to wine goes back to ancient Greek times, when the extra ingredients may have been put in as much to disguise the taste of spoiled wine as for their curative powers. A popular early additive was wormwood, the villain of the now-outlawed absinthe, yet much prized as a tonic for the stomach from classical antiquity through to medieval times and the beginnings of distillation in Europe.

As far as a drink identifiable as the precursor of modern vermouth is concerned, we have to travel back to the 1500s in order to find a merchant called d'Alessio selling a wormwood wine in Piedmont (now in northwest Italy). The inspiration had come from similar German products, probably produced on a domestic scale, and it is from the German word for wormwood, *Wermuth*, that the modern English word is derived. It was already popular in England by the middle years of the following century.

Two centers of vermouth production came to be established. One was in d'Alessio's part of Italy, close to the alpine hills that were a handy wild source of the various botanical ingredients that went into the wine, and the other over the border in eastern and southeastern France. As the big commercial companies were founded, two distinct styles of vermouth emerged, one pale and dry with pronounced bitterness, the other red and sweet and not quite so bitter. The former was the style associated with France, the latter with Italy. So ingrained did these

NOILLY PRAT

A bone-dry vermouth produced in the south of France

MIXING

Lily: Shake equal measures of gin, Lillet and crème de noyau with a dash of fresh lemon juice and ice, and strain into a wineglass.
Perfect Cocktail (below): Shake equal measures of gin, dry vermouth and sweet vermouth with ice, and strain into a cocktail glass. (Substitute Pernod for the gin and you have a **Duchess**.)

FLAVORINGS

May include quinine, coriander seeds, cloves, juniper, ginger, dried orange and lemon peels, hyssop, camomile, raspberries, rose petals, and so on.

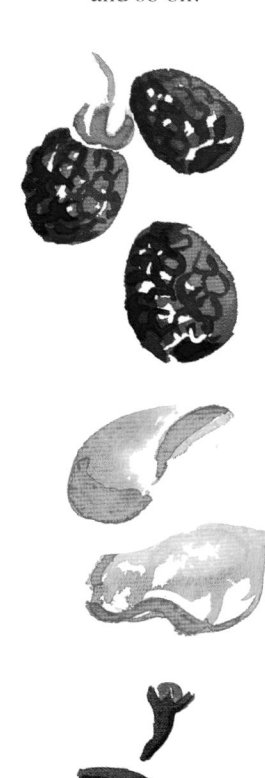

definitions become that even now drinkers refer to "French" and "Italian" to mean dry and sweet respectively, when these may not necessarily be the geographical origins.

In fact, sweet and dry vermouths are made in both countries, and indeed elsewhere, including the United States. Brands vary according to the number and type of the herbal ingredients added, but the basic style remains the same from one batch to the next. Cloves, cinnamon, quinine, citrus peels, ginger, perhaps a touch of wormwood still (although the banning of absinthe sharply decreased the amount of wormwood that was considered acceptable in other drinks) are typical elements in the potpourri of aromatizers that go into the modern vermouths.

As with many of the traditional liqueurs, the medicinal image of vermouth was—by the onset of the twentieth century—something of an albatross around its neck, rather than a marketing opportunity. It was once again the cocktail era that rode to its rescue, finding multifarious uses for both styles of vermouth. After all, if the traditional dry martini was destined to be the only use to which dry vermouth could be put behind the bar—one drop at a time—then not a great deal of it was ever going to be sold. Because it is quite as perfumed, in its own way, as gin, vermouth proved extremely versatile in mixed drinks, and the

demand for it today—thanks in part to the big proprietary brands—remains reasonably steady.

The bulk-producing Italian firm of Martini e Rossi, based in Turin, is still the vermouth name that springs most readily to mind for consumers today. Other Italian producers are Riccadonna, Cinzano and Gancia. In France, the Marseillan producer Noilly Prat makes one of the more highly regarded dry vermouths, but also has a sweeter style. The region of Chambéry in eastern France has been awarded the *appellation contrôlée* for its vermouths, which include a strawberry-flavored fruit version called Chambéryzette. As well

CINZANO BIANCO
Very popular brand of sweet white vermouth

CARPANO PUNT E MES
A deep red vermouth produced at Turin

MIXING
Bronx: Shake a measure of gin, half a measure each of dry and sweet red vermouth and the juice of no more than a quarter of an orange with ice, and strain into a cocktail glass.

as red and white styles of vermouth, there is a golden or amber variant, and a rosé.

Other similar branded products include Lillet of Bordeaux, owned by one of the classed-growth claret châteaux, which blends a proportion of fruit juice in with the wine base along with the customary herbs; the French Dubonnet, a red or white sweet vermouth also full of highly appetizing quinine bitterness; and Punt e Mes, a similar but dark-colored Italian product that combines sweetening and bittering elements in intriguing balance.

DUBONNET
The red version
mixes well with
lemonade

MIXING
Bamboo: Shake two measures of dry sherry and three-quarters of a measure of sweet red vermouth with a dash of orange bitters and ice, pour into a large cocktail glass. Add one or two ice cubes if desired.

HOW IT IS MADE
A low-alcohol, mostly white wine is produced and may be allowed a short period of aging. For the sweeter styles of vermouth, it then has a quantity of sugar syrup added to it before the fortification with spirit. This is usually grape spirit but may occasionally also be derived from vegetable sources such as sugar beet. The wine is then transferred into large barrels or tanks to which the dried aromatizing ingredients have already been added. Occasionally, the mixture is stirred manually with wooden paddles. After absorption of the flavorings, the vermouth will be bottled at around 17% ABV. Some producers insist their vermouths will continue to age in the bottle for a couple of years if kept. There are no vintage vermouths.

TASTES GOOD WITH
Dry vermouths are particularly useful in the kitchen for adding to sauces to accompany fish. The herbal ingredients in the vermouth add an attractive savory note to the dish. A seasoned reduction of Noilly Prat, lemon juice and light cream is a fine way to sauce good white fish such as sole or halibut.

MIXING
Bentley: Shake generous equal measures of calvados and red Dubonnet with plenty of ice, and strain into a cocktail glass.
Midsummer Night: Shake equal measures of gin and Punt e Mes with a half-measure of cassis and ice. Strain into a cocktail glass.

NONALCOHOLIC MIXERS

ALTHOUGH MANY of the drinks talked about in this book are commonly drunk unmixed, such as single malt whiskeys, aged brandies and rums, and the fortified wines, the great majority of them would not be consumed at all were it not for nonalcoholic mixers. Some of these are so familiar as to need no explanation; others may be more rarely used, but nonetheless constitute an important element in the mixed drink and cocktail repertoire.

FRUIT JUICES

Of all the fruit juices, orange is probably the most important for mixing with single spirit shots, most notably with the white spirits that don't muddy its color. To the cocktail maker, freshly squeezed lemon juice is undoubtedly the most versatile ingredient. The juice of lemons has the uncanny ability to accentuate the flavors of other fruits, almost in the manner of a seasoning (try tasting a fresh fruit purée with and without lemon juice to demonstrate this point), and so it complements the fruit-flavored liqueurs very well. Additionally, its sourness mitigates the syrupy sweetness of many of the classic liqueurs. Lime juice is even more sour and is used in drinks that should have a particularly biting tang. Pineapple makes a sweetly exotic element in some rum-based mixtures.

ORANGE JUICE

FRESHLY SQUEEZED LEMON JUICE

SPARKLING BEVERAGES

To achieve the diluting effects of water without changing flavor, and add a refreshing sparkle to a mixture, soda water is the required ingredient.

At one time, no bar (or home for that matter) was complete without a soda siphon. They were charged with tablets of sodium bicarbonate and dispensed a stream of bubbling water through a pressurized nozzle. Nowadays, there is effectively no difference between bottled or canned seltzer and carbonated mineral water.

TONIC WATER

Tonic water and gin go together like Fred Astaire and Ginger Rogers. A sweetened fizzy water flavored with the bittering component, quinine, tonic is medicinally named for the antimalarial properties it demonstrated in tropical climates. It blends well not just with gin, but with vodka and even

SODA SIPHON

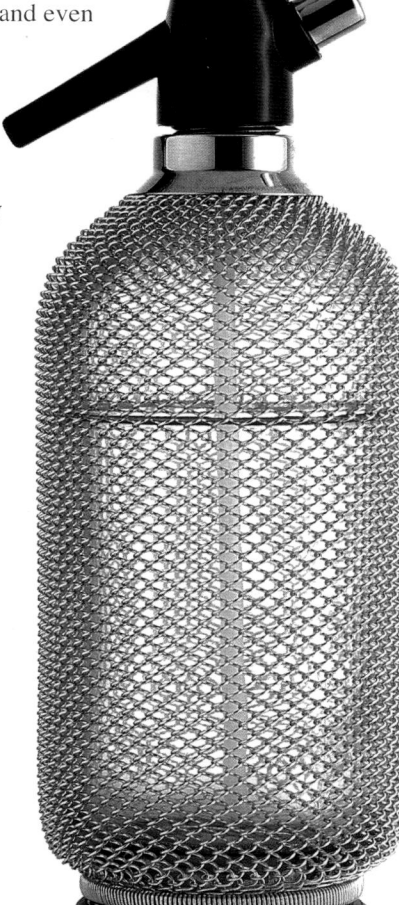

WATER
The simplest of all mixers is the one that dilutes the strength of ardent spirits without altering the character of their basic flavor. Water is indispensable to whiskey drinkers, who claim that it enhances rather than mutes the aromatic personalities of their favored spirit. Water softens the olfactory impact of the alcohol while allowing the complexities of grain, peat and wood to announce themselves.

Pastis drinkers use plain water, too, for the cloudiness that gives the drinks their collective name can only be obtained by mixing. In all cases, good springwater or mineral water is preferable to heavily chlorinated tap—especially so in the case of Highland and Lowland malts.

calvados—wherever the dryness of a drink can be made more appetizing with bitterness.

Lemonade should not be thought of solely as a children's drink, as it provides a useful way of administering citric sourness and tang to a long drink. The best lemonades for bar use are not as sweet as the kids may like them, and some are actually still, in which case you may just as well use lemon juice and a pinch of sugar.

LEMONADE

All cola is derived from the invention of Coca-Cola in the United States in the late nineteenth century by John Pemberton. It was originally intended as a stimulating tonic drink, and included the ground nuts of the cola tree, along with crushed coca leaves. The latter are also the source of the drug cocaine, which came to be frowned on in the early years of this century, and so Coca-Cola removed them from the recipe. Rum and neutral vodka seem to be the main spirits with which cola mixes most happily, coffee-flavored Kahlúa and Tia Maria its closest liqueur companions.

COCA-COLA

Ginger ale or ginger beer also have their uses, with scotch for example, but perhaps most famously with vodka as a Moscow Mule. Vodka maker Smirnoff now makes a premixed version of this drink.

SYRUPS

Cocktail making would not be quite what it is without the availability of a range of flavored nonalcoholic syrups to add complexity and interest to a drink. Of these, the most famous is grenadine, used to give a strong red coloring to otherwise clear mixtures, and to create the red-orange-yellow color spectrum in the

classic Tequila Sunrise. Grenadine is made principally from the juice of the pomegranate, the peculiar Asiatic fruit that looks like a thick-skinned onion but, when cut, reveals a mass of jewel-like seeds within. It is thick, ruby-colored and intensely sweet; some brands are made with a small alcohol quotient, but no more than about 3% ABV.

Orgeat is a somewhat uncommon syrup that was once used very widely in cocktails. Its flavoring element was almonds and it added that telltale taste of marzipan to a drink, even when used in very sparing quantities. Its name derives from the French word *orge*, meaning barley, which was once one of its ingredients.

Other syrups, flavored with a whole fruit stand of exotic ingredients, are now available. Pineapple, apricot, strawberry, banana, even kiwi fruit are produced, and can add an appetizing dash of fruit flavor to a mixed drink, without the extra alcohol that liqueurs bring.

In addition to the flavored syrups, it is also possible to buy a bottled neutral sugar syrup, but as it consists only of sugar and water, you may as well make your own.

GRENADINE
The principal flavor of this red syrup is pomegranate

GOMME
This is simply a straight sugar and water syrup

ORGEAT
An almond-flavored syrup once widely used

GINGER BEER
A traditional English summer concoction, ginger beer works well as a mixer for basic Scotch, and with vodka for a Moscow Mule.

RECIPES

Cooking with alcohol is a traditional and exciting feature of the cuisine of many countries. This collection of new and traditional recipes uses the best seasonal produce, the rich culinary traditions of Europe, Asia and America, and just a splash or two of liquid nectar to develop and intensify the dishes' flavors. The alcohol used for the traditional dishes is indigenous to the places or regions in which they arose. For many other recipes, unfamiliar combinations of food and alcohol have been brought together.

Over the years, cooks have been adding a little alcohol as an essential ingredient to many classic dishes, and here are time-honored recipes such as pepper steak with chive butter and brandy, crêpes Suzette with Cointreau and cognac, and zabaglione with marsala. Explore as well the hidden potential of the wide variety of foods that are now available, and mix and match foods and alcohol to discover exciting combinations, such as scallops sautéed with green Chartreuse, or the thrilling flavors of roasted fennel with Pernod in a warm walnut salad.

The alcoholic drinks used in these recipes range from aperitifs and vermouths to spirits and liqueurs: Those of universal appeal include gin, brandy and Madeira, and there are fine regional drinks, such as Pernod, calvados and Noilly Prat or other dry white vermouth.

Whether you are looking for recipes that are quick and easy, want to attempt a restaurant classic, or wish to try something more innovative and surprising, you will enjoy this bold and exciting approach to using spirits and liqueurs with food.

SOUPS AND APPETIZERS

A successful first course will invariably set the tone for the meal to follow by stimulating the appetite without overwhelming it and by setting up an anticipation of the succeeding flavors and textures. Choose from this wide selection, which includes: crisp, crunchy tempura vegetables served with a piquant sherry dipping sauce, refreshing melon and cucumber infused with the flavors of port and ginger, the surprising combination of gin with salmon seviche and brandied Roquefort tarts.

PUMPKIN SOUP *with* ANISETTE

Licorice-flavored liqueur adds a touch of excitement to this winter soup.

SERVES 4

1¹/₂ pounds pumpkin
2 tablespoons olive oil
2 large onions, sliced
1 garlic clove, crushed
2 fresh red chilies, seeded
  and chopped
1 teaspoon curry paste
3 cups vegetable or chicken stock
1 tablespoon anisette
²/₃ cup light cream or half-and-half
salt and pepper
hot bread, to serve

COOK'S TIP
*Use hollowed-out small
squashes or pumpkins as individual
soup bowls.*

---

1 Peel the pumpkin, remove the seeds and chop the flesh coarsely.

2 Heat the oil and fry the onions until golden. Stir in the garlic, chilies and curry paste. Cook for 1 minute, then add the chopped pumpkin and cook for 5 minutes more.

3 Pour in the stock and season with salt and pepper. Bring to a boil, lower the heat, cover and simmer for about 25 minutes.

4 Process until smooth in a blender or food processor, then return to the clean pan. Add the liqueur and reheat. Taste and season if necessary. Serve the soup in individual heated bowls, adding a spoonful of cream to each portion. Hot bread makes an ideal accompaniment.

FRENCH ONION SOUP *with* COGNAC

Cognac adds a delicious kick to this classic French soup.

SERVES 4

2 tablespoons olive oil
2 tablespoons butter
3 medium onions (about 1 pound),
 sliced
1 teaspoon light brown sugar
2 garlic cloves, crushed
5 cups vegetable or chicken stock
¼ cup cognac
4 slices French bread
1 tablespoon Dijon mustard
1 cup grated Gruyère cheese
salt and pepper

COOK'S TIP
Don't rush the browning of the onions. Their sweetness emerges through long, gentle cooking.

1 Heat the oil and butter in a heavy-bottomed saucepan and cook the onions very gently for 30 minutes, until they are very soft. Sprinkle the brown sugar and garlic on top and cook until the onions are golden brown.

2 Stir in the stock and cognac, with salt and pepper to taste. Bring to a boil, then lower the heat and simmer for 30 minutes.

3 Just before serving, toast the bread under a hot broiler on one side only. Turn the slices over, spread them with the mustard and cover with the grated cheese. Broil until all the cheese has melted and is golden.

4 Spoon the soup into bowls and float the toasted bread on top. Serve immediately.

CANTALOUPE *with* PORT

In this refreshing dish, the port forms a syrup when infused with the melon, ginger and cucumber.

SERVES 4

1 medium cantaloupe
¼ cup port
1 tablespoon chopped candied ginger
½ cucumber, peeled, halved lengthwise and seeded

COOK'S TIP
To test whether melons are ripe, use your nose—ripe melons have a strong perfume. The blossom end will yield slightly to pressure.

1 Cut the melon in half and remove the seeds. Using a small spoon or melon baller, scoop the flesh into a bowl. Stir in the port and chopped ginger.

2 Cut the cucumber into long thin ribbon strips with a vegetable peeler. Stir into the melon mixture and chill before serving. Garnish with mint leaves.

BRANDIED CHICKEN LIVER PÂTÉ

The rich flavor of chicken livers in this delicious appetizer is enhanced by the addition of a little brandy.

SERVES 4–6

12 ounces chicken livers
8 tablespoons (1 stick) butter
1 rindless lean bacon strip, chopped
1 shallot, chopped
2 garlic cloves, crushed
2 tablespoons brandy
2 tablespoons chopped fresh parsley
salt and ground black pepper
fresh bay leaves and peppercorns, to garnish
olive bread, to serve

1 Rinse, trim and coarsely chop the chicken livers. Melt half the butter in a large frying pan. Add the chopped bacon, shallot and garlic and fry for 5 minutes. Add the chicken livers and fry gently for 5 minutes more.

COOK'S TIP
If properly sealed, the pâté will keep in the fridge for 3–4 days.

2 Stir in the brandy and chopped parsley, with salt and pepper to taste. Bring to a boil and cook for about 2 minutes, then remove from the heat and process in a blender or food processor until smooth.

3 Spoon the pâté into individual dishes. Melt the remaining butter and pour carefully over the surface of each pâté to seal. Garnish with bay leaves and peppercorns.

4 When cool, chill the pâté until firm. Serve with olive bread.

SCALLOPS *with* PASTIS *on* VEGETABLE FRITTERS

The anise flavor of pastis combines wonderfully with shellfish.

SERVES 4

2 carrots
1 large zucchini
1 parsnip
1 small potato
1 egg, lightly beaten
oil, for frying
2 shallots, chopped
1 green bell pepper, seeded
  and chopped
8 large scallops, halved
3 dill sprigs, chopped
1 tablespoon pastis
$^2/_3$ cup chicken or fish stock, or
  bottled clam juice
$^1/_2$ teaspoon lemon juice
salt and ground black pepper
dill sprigs, to garnish

VARIATION

*Oysters can be cooked in the same
way as these scallops.*

---

1 Coarsely grate the carrots, zucchini, parsnip and potato into a bowl. Bind the mixture with the egg.

2 Heat a little oil in a large frying pan and drop 3–4 heaped spoonfuls of the vegetable mixture into the pan. Flatten a little, then cook for 8–10 minutes, until golden, turning once. Remove from the pan and keep hot while cooking successive batches.

3 In another frying pan, heat a little oil and sauté the shallots and green pepper for 6–8 minutes.

4 Add the scallops, chopped dill, pastis, stock or clam juice and lemon juice and poach for 2 minutes. Season to taste. Spoon the mixture onto the vegetable fritters, garnish with dill and serve immediately.

SALMON SEVICHE *with* GIN *and* LIME

Marinating in a mixture of gin and lime juice "cooks" fresh fish and gives it a marvelous flavor.

SERVES 4

$1^1/_2$ pounds skinless salmon fillet
1 small red onion, thinly sliced
6 chives
6 fennel sprigs
3 parsley sprigs
2 limes
2 tablespoons gin
3 tablespoons olive oil
sea salt and ground black pepper
mixed greens, to serve

VARIATION

*For a tasty alternative, marinate
strips of very fresh sea bass, bream,
halibut or cod.*

1 Cut the salmon fillet into thin slices, removing any large bones with tweezers. Lay the pieces in a wide, shallow glass or ceramic dish. Scatter the onion slices, chives, fennel and parsley sprigs on top.

2 Using a vegetable peeler, remove a few fine strips of rind from the limes and reserve for the garnish. Cut off the remaining rind, avoiding the pith, and slice it coarsely. Squeeze the lime juice into a cup and add the sliced rind, with the gin and olive oil. Add sea salt and black pepper to taste. Pour over the fish and mix gently.

3 Cover the dish and chill for 4 hours, stirring occasionally. Sprinkle with the reserved strips of lime rind just before serving with the mixed greens.

DUCK *and* CALVADOS TERRINE

A classic dish from Normandy, using the regional apple brandy.

SERVES 4

1¼ pounds boneless duck meat,
* coarsely chopped*
8 ounces pork stew meat, ground
2 shallots, chopped
grated rind and juice of 1 orange
2 tablespoons calvados
10 lean bacon strips
2 eggs, beaten
2 tablespoons chopped fresh
* parsley*
salt and pepper
mixed greens and hot toast,
* to serve*

1 Grease and line the bottom of a 2-pound loaf pan. Place the chopped duck meat in a bowl with the ground pork, shallots, orange rind and juice, calvados and seasoning. Mix well, cover and chill for 1–2 hours.

2 Stretch the bacon strips with the back of a large knife and use them to line the loaf pan or dish, leaving any excess hanging over the edge.

3 Stir the eggs and parsley into the meat mixture, then spoon it into the prepared pan or dish. Smooth the surface, fold the bacon over, then cover with foil. Preheat the oven to 350°F.

COOK'S TIP
Marinating the duck for a
few hours will develop the flavors.

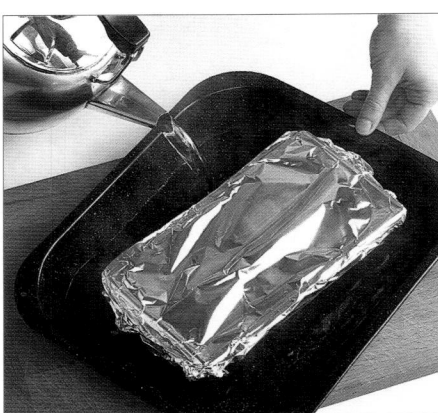

4 Stand the terrine in a roasting pan and pour in boiling water to come about two-thirds of the way up the sides of the pan or dish.

5 Bake for 1¼ hours, then remove the terrine from the water bath, lift off the foil and allow to cool. Cover with clean foil and a weight and chill for 3–4 hours, until firm. Slice and serve with mixed greens and hot toast.

BOURBON PANCAKES *with* ASPARAGUS

Double your delight by adding bourbon to the batter and the dressing for the asparagus and prosciutto.

SERVES 4

¹/₂ cup self-rising flour
¹/₂ teaspoon mustard powder
1 egg, beaten
¹/₄ cup milk
1 tablespoon bourbon
8 cooked asparagus spears,
* to serve*
8 slices of prosciutto, to serve
FOR THE DRESSING
3 tablespoons olive oil
1 tablespoon bourbon
salt and pepper

1 Sift the flour and mustard powder into a bowl. Make a well in the center and add the egg, milk and bourbon. Whisk the batter until smooth.

2 Heat a griddle or heavy-bottomed frying pan. Grease it thoroughly. Drop spoonfuls of the batter onto the hot griddle to make four pancakes. Cook for 2–3 minutes, until bubbles rise to the surface of each pancake and burst.

3 Turn the pancakes over with a spatula and cook for 2–3 minutes more, until golden brown. Remove and keep hot while making four more pancakes in the same way.

COOK'S TIP
For evenly shaped pancakes pour the batter into greased baking rings.

4 Mix the dressing ingredients together in a bowl. Taste and adjust the seasoning if necessary.

5 Place two pancakes on each plate. Put an asparagus spear on top of each pancake, drape decoratively with a slice of prosciutto and spoon over a little of the dressing on top.

QUAIL'S EGG *and* VERMOUTH TARTLETS

Eggs hard-cooked in this way have an attractive marbled surface like Chinese hundred-year-old eggs.

SERVES 4

10 quail's eggs or 5 hen's eggs
2 tablespoons soy sauce
2 tablespoons mustard seeds
1 tablespoon green tea leaves
6 filo pastry sheets
4 tablespoons (½ stick) butter
1 small avocado
3 tablespoons dry white vermouth
2 tablespoons mayonnaise
2 teaspoons fresh lime juice
salt and pepper
paprika, for dusting
mâche or baby lettuce, to serve

1 Put the quail's or hen's eggs in a saucepan. Add cold water to cover. Add the soy sauce, mustard seeds and tea leaves. Bring to a boil, then lower the heat and simmer for 3 minutes.

2 Remove the pan from the heat and lift out the eggs with a slotted spoon. Gently tap them on a firm surface so that the shells crack all over. Put the eggs back into the liquid and leave in a cool place for 8 hours or overnight.

COOK'S TIP
Pack cooked shelled eggs into wide-necked sterilized jars and cover with dry sherry or vermouth. Seal, label and store in a cool place. Use within six weeks.

3 Preheat the oven to 375°F. Grease four 4-inch tartlet pans. Brush each sheet of filo pastry with a little melted butter and stack the six sheets on top of each other. Stamp out four rounds with a 6-inch cutter.

4 Line the tartlet pans with the pastry and frill the edge of each. Put a crumpled piece of foil in each filo shell and bake for 12–15 minutes, until cooked and golden. Remove the foil and set aside to cool.

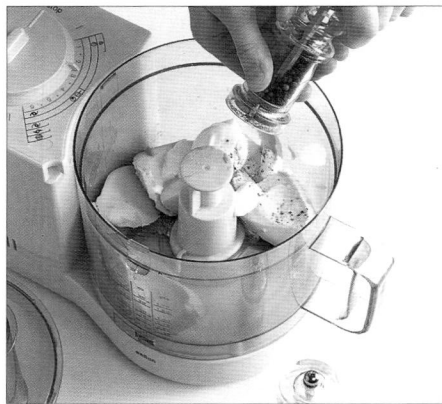

5 Cut the avocado in half, remove the pit and scoop the flesh into a blender or food processor. Add the vermouth, mayonnaise and lime juice, and season to taste with salt and pepper. Process until smooth.

6 Shell the quail's eggs and cut them in half (or quarters for hen's eggs). Pipe or spoon the avocado mixture into the pastry shells and arrange the halved eggs on top. Dust the eggs with a little paprika and serve at once, with the mâche.

BRANDIED ROQUEFORT TARTS

Light puff pastry rounds topped with the irresistible combination of brandy and Roquefort cheese.

MAKES 6

5 ounces Roquefort cheese
2 tablespoons brandy
2 tablespoons olive oil
2 red onions (about 8 ounces
 total), thinly sliced
8 ounces puff pastry, thawed
 if frozen
beaten egg or milk, for glazing
6 walnut halves, chopped
2 tablespoons chopped
 fresh chives
salt and pepper
chive knots, to garnish
mixed greens, diced cucumber
 and tomato wedges, to serve

1 Crumble the Roquefort into a small bowl, pour the brandy over and let marinate for 1 hour. Meanwhile, heat the oil in a frying pan and gently fry the onions for 20 minutes, stirring occasionally. Set the pan aside.

2 Preheat the oven to 425°F. Grease a baking sheet. Roll out the pastry on a floured surface and stamp out six rounds with a 4-inch fluted cutter. Put the rounds on the baking sheet and prick them with a fork.

3 Brush the edges of the pastry with a little beaten egg or milk. Add the walnuts and chives to the onion mixture, with salt and pepper to taste. Divide the mixture among the pastry shapes, leaving the edges clear.

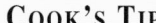

COOK'S TIP
To make the chive knots, simply tie chives together in threes, with a central knot. Blanch the chives briefly if they are not very pliable.

4 Spoon the brandied cheese mixture on top of the pastries and bake for 12–15 minutes, until golden. Serve warm, garnished with chive knots, on a bed of mixed greens, diced cucumber and thin tomato wedges.

FISH AND SEAFOOD

Fish is fashionable and healthy. Flat fish, round fish, shellfish in their many varieties lend themselves to speedy and stylish dishes. If your inclination is for shellfish, green Chartreuse adds the tastes and aromas of brandy and herbs to a creamy scallop dish, while mussels with dry sherry are given Thai flavors with a spiced coconut sauce. A stew can sound very mundane, that is, unless it is one made with carp and trout, laced with a little Marc de Bourgogne.

LOBSTER NEWBURG *with* MADEIRA

A traditional shellfish dish in which the lobster is sautéed in a rich cream sauce flavored with Madeira.

SERVES 4

2 cooked lobsters, about
  1¹/₂ pounds each
2 tablespoons butter
²/₃ cup Madeira
3 tablespoons fish stock or
  bottled clam juice
1 cup heavy cream
3 egg yolks
¹/₄ teaspoon grated nutmeg
salt and ground black pepper
fresh parsley and lemon wedges,
  to garnish

1 Preheat the oven to 400°F. Crack the lobster claws and legs, remove the cooked meat and chop it into neat chunks.

2 With a sharp knife, cut down the back of each lobster from head to tail and open it out. Remove and discard the threadlike intestinal canal and the grayish green sac from each lobster.

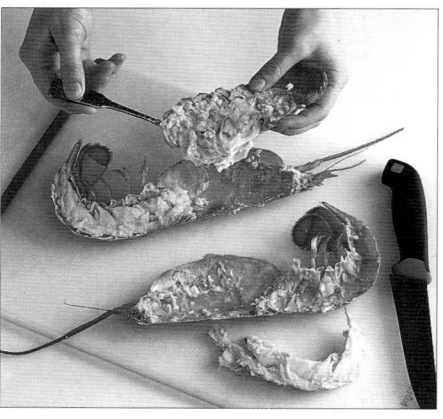

3 Carefully lift the meat from the shells, then cut the lobster meat into thick slices. Wash and dry the shells and set them aside for serving.

4 Melt the butter in a large pan and fry the lobster meat for 3 minutes over medium heat, stirring gently with a wooden spoon.

5 Pour in the Madeira and fish stock or clam juice, then cook slowly until they are almost absorbed. Lower the heat to a bare simmer. Mix the cream, egg yolks and grated nutmeg in a small bowl. Add salt and pepper to taste.

6 Gradually stir the cream mixture into the pan. Cook for 3–4 minutes over low heat, stirring constantly, until the sauce thickens. Taste for seasoning. Be careful not to let the mixture boil, or it will curdle.

7 Spoon the lobster and sauce into the half shells, garnish with chopped parsley, parsley sprigs and lemon wedges, and serve.

VARIATION

Use this delicious sauce with cooked crab, jumbo shrimp or langoustine instead of lobster, if you prefer.

JUMBO SHRIMP *with* NOILLY PRAT

This French vermouth, redolent with herbs, is the perfect accompaniment for Mediterranean flavors.

SERVES 4

20 raw jumbo shrimp (about
  1 pound), heads removed
$^1/_2$ cucumber
2 tablespoons butter
1 tablespoon olive oil
1 small shallot, finely chopped
$^1/_4$ cup drained sun-dried
  tomatoes in oil, chopped
$^1/_4$ cup vegetable stock
2 tablespoons Noilly Prat or
  other dry white vermouth
$^2/_3$ cup heavy cream
1 tablespoon chopped fennel
  leaves
3 tablespoons golden salmon roe
salt and white pepper
fennel leaves, to garnish

COOK'S TIPS
*Try using sun-dried peppers instead
of the tomatoes. The salmon roe
adds a delicious flavor, but isn't essential—omit it if you prefer.*

1 Peel the shrimp, leaving the tail
section on. Cut each shrimp down the
back and remove the black intestine.
Rinse, then dry with paper towels.

2 Peel the cucumber, cut it in half
lengthwise and then scoop out the
seeds. Slice the cucumber thickly
into crescents.

3 Heat the butter and oil in a large
frying pan or wok, add the chopped
shallot and fry until softened.

4 Add the sun-dried tomatoes, vegetable
stock, Noilly Prat and shrimp. Cook
over low heat for 8–10 minutes.

5 Cook the cucumber crescents in a
small pan of boiling salted water for
3 minutes, then drain.

6 Stir the cream and chopped fennel
leaves into the shrimp and cook until
the sauce thickens. Season to taste with
salt and pepper and stir in the cooked
cucumber and the salmon roe. Reheat
and serve, garnished with fennel leaves.

CRAB *and* SHRIMP FILO TART *with* PASTIS

Pastis and shellfish are good companions and make a perfectly delicious filo tart.

SERVES 4–6

2 eggs, beaten
²/₃ cup milk
2 tablespoons pastis
7 ounces crabmeat
7 ounces cooked shrimp, peeled
  and deveined
1 cup ricotta cheese
2 cups mushrooms, chopped
10 filo pastry sheets
¹/₄ cup butter, melted
salt and pepper
²/₃ cup Parmesan cheese
  shavings, to garnish

COOK'S TIP

Work quickly with filo pastry, as it soon becomes dry and brittle. Cover any filo not actually being used with a damp, clean dish towel.

1 Preheat the oven to 375°F. Grease a deep 7-inch tart pan. Mix together the eggs, milk, pastis, crabmeat, shrimp, ricotta cheese and mushrooms in a bowl. Season to taste with salt and pepper.

2 Line the tart pan with filo pastry, placing the sheets at alternate angles and brushing each one with a little of the melted butter. Leave the excess pastry hanging over the sides of the pan.

3 Spoon the filling into the filo-lined pan. Fold the excess pastry over, crumpling it slightly to make a decorative edge. Brush with melted butter. Bake the tart for 35–40 minutes. Scatter the Parmesan cheese on top. Cut into wedges to serve.

SARDINES *with* APPLE RINGS *and* CIDER BRANDY

Fast-fried sardines and apple rings in a sweet-and-sour sauce.

SERVES 4

a few fresh tarragon sprigs
2 pounds large fresh sardines or
  smelts, cleaned and heads
  removed
1 egg white
2 tablespoons cold water
scant ¹/₂ cup cornmeal
oil, for frying
2 apples, cored and sliced in rings
2 tablespoons light brown sugar
pinch of ground cloves
1 tablespoon balsamic vinegar
3 tablespoons cider brandy or
  applejack
²/₃ cup vegetable stock
salt and pepper

COOK'S TIP
Finely crushed taco shells, water-cracker crumbs or oatmeal all make tasty coatings for oily fish.

---

1 Tuck a small piece of tarragon inside each sardine. Set a few tarragon sprigs aside for the garnish.

2 In a small bowl, lightly whisk the egg white with the cold water. Dip each sardine in turn in the egg white, then coat with the cornmeal.

3 Heat the oil in a large frying pan and fry the sardines until crisp and golden on both sides. Lift them out of the pan and keep hot.

4 Add more oil to the pan if necessary and fry the apple slices until crisp and golden. Remove with a slotted spoon and keep hot.

5 Stir the brown sugar, cloves, balsamic vinegar, cider brandy or applejack and stock into the pan. Bring to a boil and simmer for 2 minutes, then season to taste with salt and pepper. Add the sardines and apple rings, spoon the sauce over them and serve immediately, garnished with the reserved tarragon.

TUNA *with* OLIVES, CILANTRO *and* NOILLY PRAT

Rather like a hot tuna salad with a pungent vermouth-flavored sauce.

SERVES 4

3 tablespoons Noilly Prat or
  other dry white vermouth
3 drained canned anchovy fillets
2 tablespoons lemon juice
8 tablespoons (1 stick) butter
1 garlic clove, coarsely chopped
1¹/₂ cups pitted black olives
4 tuna steaks, 4–6 ounces each
oil, for shallow frying
12 ounces red cherry tomatoes,
  halved
3 zucchini, diagonally sliced
olive oil, for brushing
3 tablespoons chopped fresh
  cilantro
dressed mixed greens, to serve

1 Pour the Noilly Prat into a blender or food processor. Add the anchovies, lemon juice, butter, garlic and half the black olives. Process to a rough purée.

2 Sear the tuna in hot oil over high heat for 1 minute on each side. Keep hot.

3 Brush the cherry tomatoes and zucchini slices with a little olive oil. Spread out in a broiler pan and broil until golden, turning occasionally.

4 Meanwhile, pour the olive purée into the frying pan. Bring to a boil and cook for 2 minutes, stirring constantly. Add the chopped cilantro and the remaining olives. Serve the tuna steaks with the sauce poured on top, accompanied by the vegetables and mixed greens.

COOK'S TIP
Tuna is cooked very quickly so that it browns on the outside, yet is still moist and rare inside.

THAI MUSSELS *with* DRY SHERRY

Superb, spiced seafood—East meets West in the fiery, sherry-flavored coconut sauce.

SERVES 4

3–3½ pounds fresh mussels
3 tablespoons dry sherry
3 tablespoons fish stock
1⅔ cups coconut milk, fresh
  or canned
⅔ cup water
2 tablespoons olive oil
1 onion, chopped
2 garlic cloves, crushed
1 piece lemongrass (3 inches),
  sliced
2 tablespoons tomato paste
2 teaspoons Thai curry paste
1 tablespoon grated fresh ginger
1 fresh red chili, seeded
  and sliced
1 tablespoon cornstarch
salt and pepper
¼ cup chopped fresh
  cilantro, to garnish
French bread, to serve

1 Wash and scrub the mussels. Pull off the beards. Discard any open shells that do not close when tapped.

2 Put the mussels into a large, deep pan. Pour in the sherry, fish stock, coconut milk and water. Bring to a boil, cover tightly and cook for 5 minutes or until the shells have opened.

3 Using a slotted spoon, transfer the cooked mussels to a large bowl, discarding any that remain closed. Keep the mussels hot. Strain the cooking juices into a bowl and set them aside.

4 Heat the oil in another pan and fry the onion and garlic for 5 minutes, stirring occasionally, until softened.

COOK'S TIP
If the lemongrass is dry and woody, then leave it whole and bruise it lightly. Remove the bruised stalk from the sauce before serving.

5 Stir in the lemongrass, tomato paste, curry paste, ginger and chili. Pour in the reserved cooking juices and season with pepper. Bring to a boil, lower the heat and simmer for 5 minutes.

6 Blend the cornstarch to a smooth paste with a little water and stir into the pan. Bring to a boil, stirring constantly, then season to taste. Pour the sauce over the cooked mussels. Sprinkle with the chopped cilantro and serve with sliced French bread.

PAN-FRIED SQUID *with* OUZO

Ouzo gives the flavors of anise and herbs to this rustic dish.

SERVES 4

1¼ pounds prepared squid
2 tablespoons olive oil
2 tablespoons sesame seeds
1 tablespoon green peppercorns
2 garlic cloves, crushed
6 scallions, sliced
½ can drained canned anchovy
  fillets (about 6), chopped
1 piece lemongrass, sliced
1 tablespoon chopped fresh parsley
1 tablespoon chopped fresh basil
⅔ cup fish stock or clam juice
2 teaspoons lemon juice
2 teaspoons ouzo
¾ cup snowpeas
salt
fresh basil sprigs, to garnish
4 cooked poppadoms, to serve

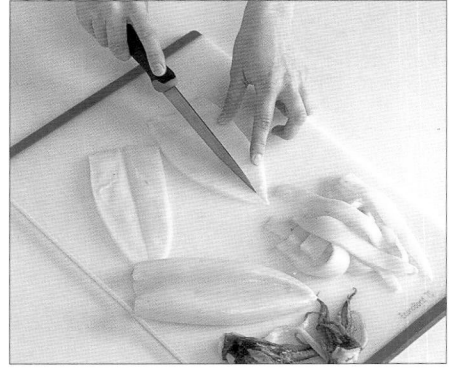

1 Cut the squid into strips, rinse under cold water and dry with paper towels.

2 Heat the oil in a pan and toast the sesame seeds with the green peppercorns for a few seconds.

3 Add the garlic, scallions and squid. Toss to coat in the sesame mix.

4 Stir in the anchovies, lemongrass, chopped parsley and basil. Pour in the stock or clam juice, lemon juice and ouzo and simmer for about 12 minutes. Add the snowpeas and cook for 2 minutes more. Season to taste with salt and spoon onto the cooked poppadoms. Garnish with basil sprigs.

COOK'S TIP
If you find the flavor of the anchovies a little strong, soak them in cold milk to cover for 30 minutes, then drain and use.

MONKFISH BROCHETTES *with* BOURBON MARINADE

The bourbon marinade adds moisture and flavor to this firm fish, making it ideal for a barbecue.

SERVES 4

1¼ pounds monkfish, cubed
2 large green bell peppers,
  halved and seeded
olive oil, for brushing
3 tomatoes, peeled, seeded
  and chopped
2 tablespoons chopped fresh
  basil, plus basil sprigs,
  to garnish
salt and pepper
FOR THE MARINADE
2 tablespoons white wine vinegar
2 tablespoons bourbon
1 tablespoon olive oil
3 tablespoons chopped fresh dill
1 tablespoon mustard seeds
1 tablespoon honey

1 Mix the ingredients for the marinade in a shallow dish large enough to hold all the monkfish cubes in a single layer. Add the fish and stir to coat. Cover and chill for at least 1 hour.

2 Lift the fish out of the marinade and thread onto metal skewers. Set aside half the marinade for basting and pour the rest into a small pan.

3 Place the fish brochettes and pepper halves on a rack over a broiler pan, or on the barbecue grill. Brush the brochettes with marinade and the peppers with olive oil. Broil or grill until the fish is golden and the peppers have browned, basting occasionally.

4 Meanwhile, add the chopped tomatoes and chopped basil to the marinade in the pan. Bring to a boil. Cook for 2 minutes and season to taste with salt and pepper. Spoon into the pepper halves and serve with the brochettes, garnished with basil sprigs.

ROASTED COD *in an* ALMOND CRUST *with* ANISETTE

An anise and lime French dressing is delicious with cod.

SERVES 4

2 tablespoons all-purpose flour
4 cod fillets, 4–6 ounces each
1 cup whole-wheat bread crumbs
½ cup grated Cheddar cheese
½ cup sliced almonds, coarsely
  chopped
2 eggs, beaten
pared lime rind, to garnish
salt and pepper
FOR THE DRESSING
¼ cup olive oil
1 tablespoon anisette
1 teaspoon fresh lime juice

1 Preheat the oven to 400°F. Grease a baking sheet. Put the flour into a plastic bag and season with salt and pepper. Add each cod fillet in turn and shake until evenly coated.

2 Mix the bread crumbs, cheese and almonds in a shallow dish. Add a little salt and pepper. Pour the eggs into a similar dish. Coat the floured fish in egg and then the bread crumb mixture. Repeat the process.

3 Arrange the fish on the greased baking sheet and bake for 20 minutes, until golden.

4 Meanwhile, make the dressing. Put the oil, anisette and lime juice in a screw-top jar. Add salt and pepper to taste, close the jar tightly and shake to mix. Garnish the fish with curls of finely pared lime rind and serve with the dressing.

COOK'S TIP
The cheese, almond and crumb mixture can also be used as a stuffing.

RED SNAPPER *with* CHILI, GIN *and* GINGER SAUCE

Gin and ginger add piquancy and spice to a fine fish dish that tastes every bit as good as it looks.

SERVES 4

1 red snapper (3–3¹/₂ pounds),
  cleaned
2 tablespoons sunflower oil
1 onion, chopped
2 garlic cloves, crushed
¹/₂ cup button mushrooms, sliced
1 teaspoon ground coriander
1 tablespoon chopped fresh
  parsley
2 tablespoons grated fresh ginger
2 fresh red chilies, seeded
  and sliced
1 tablespoon cornstarch
3 tablespoons gin
1¹/₄ cups chicken or vegetable
  stock
salt and pepper
FOR THE GARNISH
1 tablespoon sunflower oil
6 garlic cloves, sliced
1 lettuce heart, finely shredded
1 bunch cilantro, tied with
  red raffia, to serve

1 Preheat the oven to 375°F. Grease a flameproof dish large enough to hold the fish. Make several diagonal cuts on one side of the fish.

2 Heat the oil in a frying pan and fry the onion, garlic and mushrooms for 2–3 minutes. Stir in the ground coriander and chopped parsley. Season with salt and pepper.

3 Spoon the filling into the cavity, then lift the snapper into the dish. Pour in enough cold water to cover the bottom of the dish. Sprinkle the ginger and chilies on top, then cover and bake for 30–40 minutes, basting from time to time. Remove the cover for the last 10 minutes.

4 Carefully lift the snapper onto a serving dish and keep hot. Pour the cooking juices into a pan.

5 Blend the cornstarch and gin in a cup and stir into the cooking juices. Pour in the stock. Bring to a boil and cook gently for 3–4 minutes or until thickened, stirring all the time. Taste for seasoning, then pour into a sauceboat.

6 Make the garnish. Heat the oil in a small pan and stir-fry the sliced garlic and shredded lettuce over high heat until crisp. Spoon alongside the snapper. Place the cilantro bouquet on the other side. Serve with the sauce.

TROUT *and* SOLE PACKAGES *with* VERMOUTH

Contrasting fish, sandwiched with a peppery watercress filling, are served with a simple sauce spiked with vermouth.

SERVES 4

1 bunch watercress
1 zucchini, grated
1 teaspoon Tabasco sauce
grated rind and juice of 1 lemon
4 trout fillets (about 4 ounces
  each), skinned
4 sole fillets, (about 4 ounces
  each), skinned
1/4 cup butter
2/3 cup fish stock
1/2 cup dry white vermouth
salt and pepper
fresh watercress sprigs,
  to garnish

1 Preheat the oven to 400°F. Strip the watercress leaves from the thick stalks and finely chop them. Place them in a bowl with the grated zucchini, Tabasco sauce, lemon rind and juice. Season to taste with salt and pepper.

2 Season the trout and sole fillets on both sides. Cover each sole fillet in turn with the watercress mixture. Top with the trout fillets.

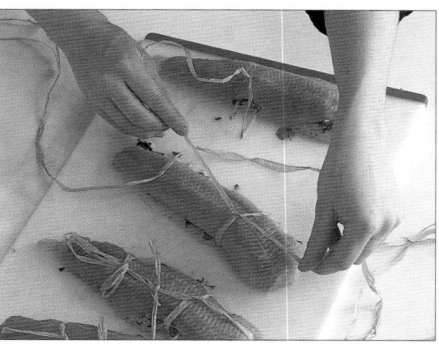

3 Tie the fish "sandwiches" into neat parcels. Put the fish into a shallow flameproof dish and dot with the butter.

COOK'S TIP
If the fish fillets are uneven sizes, trim the larger piece. Finely chop the trimmings and add to the stuffing.

4 Pour the stock and vermouth over the fish, cover and bake for 20 minutes, until tender. Carefully lift the fish parcels onto a serving platter and keep them hot.

5 Transfer the flameproof dish to the stovetop and cook the stock mixture until it has reduced by half. Pour the sauce over the fish, garnish with watercress and serve.

SCALLOPS SAUTÉED *with* GREEN CHARTREUSE

One of the oldest French liqueurs, green Chartreuse gives the flavors of brandy and herbs to this creamy shellfish dish.

SERVES 4

6 tablespoons (³/₄ stick) butter
1 leek, white part only, julienned
1 carrot, julienned
2 tablespoons green Chartreuse
¹/₄ cup light cream or half-and-half
20 scallops
salt and pepper
fresh chervil sprigs, to garnish

1 Heat 2 tablespoons of the butter in a pan, add the julienned leek and carrot and season to taste with salt and pepper. Cook over low heat for about 12 minutes, until soft but not colored.

2 Remove the pan from the heat, add the green Chartreuse and stir. Flambé if you wish.

VARIATION
Use the delicious creamy base with crab, lobster or salmon fillets.

3 Stir in the cream and cook gently until the sauce has reduced a little. Taste and adjust the seasoning if necessary.

4 Meanwhile, heat the remaining butter and, when foaming, add the scallops. Sauté for a few minutes, until just cooked. To serve, put the vegetable and cream mixture onto plates, top with the scallops and garnish with chervil.

HADDOCK RIBBONS *en* PAPILLOTE *with* WHISKEY

Open these parchment parcels to release the heady aroma of warm whiskey.

SERVES 4

4 tablespoons (¹/₂ stick) butter, melted
1¹/₄ pounds haddock fillet, skinned
3 scallions, thinly sliced
2 garlic cloves, crushed
1 tablespoon drained bottled capers
4 ounces drained canned palm hearts, sliced
2 large tomatoes, seeded and sliced
2 tablespoons whiskey
1 tablespoon white wine vinegar
1 tablespoon chopped parsley
salt and pepper
char-broiled bell peppers, onions and snowpeas, to serve

1 Preheat the oven to 425°F. Cut four 11-inch-square sheets of parchment paper. Brush each sheet with a little of the melted butter. Cut the haddock into thin ribbon strips and put some in the middle of each paper square.

2 Top each square with a quarter of the scallions, garlic, capers, palm hearts and tomatoes.

3 Mix the whiskey, wine vinegar and parsley in a small bowl. Add salt and pepper to taste. Whisk well, then spoon over the fish.

VARIATION
Use shellfish, cod or trout instead of the haddock, and artichoke hearts instead of palm hearts.

4 Fold the paper over the fish, making a pleat in the top, then twist the ends to seal. Put the paper cases on a baking sheet and bake for 10–12 minutes, until the paper has turned brown and the cases have puffed up. Transfer to plates and serve at once, with the peppers, onions and snowpeas.

FRENCH FISH STEW *with* MARC DE BOURGOGNE

A traditional recipe using freshwater fish and Marc de Bourgogne.

SERVES 6

*3 pounds mixed freshwater fish,
    such as carp and trout*
3 tablespoons all-purpose flour
4 tablespoons (¹/₂ stick) butter
*8 ounces smoked bacon, cut
    into small strips*
4 shallots, very finely chopped
8 ounces small onions
3 cups mushrooms, chopped
¹/₂ cup Marc de Bourgogne
4 cups red wine
1¹/₄ cups veal or chicken stock
1 garlic clove, crushed
1 bouquet garni
salt and pepper
chopped fresh parsley, to garnish
garlic bread, to serve

1 Clean the fish, remove the heads and fins, fillet the flesh (or ask your fishmonger to do this) and cut into slices.

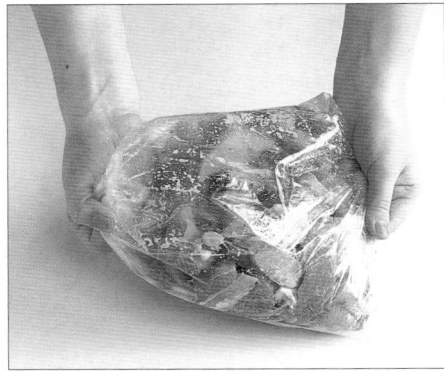

2 Put half of the flour in a plastic bag, season with salt and pepper, add the fish pieces and shake to coat.

3 In a large pan, melt the butter over medium-high heat and brown the fish pieces on both sides. Remove from the pan and set aside.

4 Add the bacon strips, shallots and onions to the pan and cook over low heat for another 10 minutes, until golden. Stir in the chopped mushrooms and cook for another 5 minutes.

COOK'S TIPS

Marc de Bourgogne is a marc brandy from Burgundy. If it is not available, use another brandy. If carp is not available, use extra trout, or substitute another fish, such as gray mullet, porgy or butterfish.

5 Pour in the Marc de Bourgogne, stir and flambé (optional). Add the red wine and simmer for a few minutes.

6 Stir in the stock, garlic and bouquet garni, bring to a boil and simmer for 5 minutes. Add the fish and simmer until cooked.

7 With a slotted spoon, remove the fish and keep hot. In a small bowl, blend the remaining flour with a little cold water and stir into the pan. Bring to a boil and cook for 5 minutes, then return the fish to the pan. Serve garnished with chopped parsley and accompanied by garlic bread.

COD STEAKS *with a* CREAMY SHERRY SAUCE

A molasses marinade gives these cod steaks a dusky color that contrasts well with the creamy sherry sauce studded with pink and green peppercorns.

SERVES 4

2 tablespoons molasses
1 teaspoon salt
2 tablespoons chopped fresh dill
2 tablespoons lemon juice
4 cod steaks, about 6 ounces each
4 tablespoons (½ stick) butter
2 tablespoons olive oil
3 shallots, chopped
⅔ cup fish stock
3 tablespoons dry sherry
1 teaspoon pink peppercorns,
 lightly crushed
1 teaspoon green peppercorns,
 lightly crushed
3 potatoes, sliced
1¼ cups crème fraîche
oil, for frying
3 carrots, thinly sliced
1 zucchini, thinly sliced
1 small parsnip, thinly sliced
salt and pepper
lime wedges and fresh dill sprigs,
 to garnish

1 Mix the molasses, salt, chopped dill and lemon juice in a small bowl. Spread this mixture over both sides of the cod steaks. Put the fish in a shallow dish, cover and chill for 2 hours.

2 Heat the butter and olive oil in a frying pan. Add the shallots and cook until soft. Stir in the stock, sherry and both types of peppercorns. Cook for 2 minutes more.

3 Add the cod steaks to the pan and cook them for 10–12 minutes, turning once. Meanwhile, cook the potato slices in a saucepan of lightly salted boiling water for 5 minutes. Drain and set aside.

COOK'S TIP
Pink peppercorns are readily available from delicatessens. Use them with caution, however, as they can provoke an allergic reaction in susceptible individuals.

4 Lift the cooked fish out of the pan and keep hot. Stir the crème fraîche into the pan, season to taste with salt and pepper and reheat gently.

5 Deepfry the potato slices in hot oil until golden. In a separate pan, stir-fry the carrots, zucchini and parsnip in 2 tablespoons hot oil for 1–2 minutes, until crisp.

6 Divide the potatoes among four plates, add the stir-fried vegetables and top with the cod and sauce. Garnish with lime wedges and fresh dill sprigs.

HERB-STUFFED LEMON SOLE
with a SORREL and VERMOUTH SAUCE

Lemon sole tastes superb when served with a classic, light fluffy egg sauce delicately flavored with vermouth.

SERVES 4

8 tablespoons (1 stick) butter
1 small onion, chopped
1 cup mushrooms, chopped
1 cup whole-wheat bread crumbs
2 tablespoons chopped fresh
  lemon balm
4 lemon sole or flounder fillets
  (about 6 ounces each)
²/₃ cup milk
¹/₄ cup dry white vermouth
2 teaspoons lemon juice
2 egg yolks
handful of sorrel leaves, finely
  chopped
salt and pepper
whole sorrel leaves, to garnish

1 Preheat the oven to 375°F. Melt 2 tablespoons of the butter in a frying pan. Fry the onion and mushrooms until the onion is golden and the mushrooms have absorbed the liquid. Add the bread crumbs and lemon balm and stir in salt and pepper to taste.

2 Place the pieces of sole skinned side up on a board and spread some of the filling on each. Roll up the fish pieces carefully from head to tail and pack them tightly in a shallow casserole.

3 Pour the milk over the fish, cover and bake for 15 minutes.

4 Bring a saucepan of water to simmering point. In a separate pan, heat the vermouth until it has reduced by half.

COOK'S TIP

If the sauce separates, whisk in another egg yolk.

5 Pour the vermouth into a heatproof bowl, set it over the pan of water, add the lemon juice and egg yolks and whisk until fluffy.

6 Remove from the heat and continue to whisk while adding the remaining butter, a piece at a time. Stir in the chopped sorrel, season to taste with salt and pepper and spoon over the fish. Garnish with whole sorrel leaves.

MEAT, POULTRY AND GAME

Alcohol is a traditional accompaniment to meat, poultry and game. A rich Madeira sauce makes a perfect match for ham, while an Armagnac-based sauce is served with lamb. The rich tastes of pheasant with juniper and port make heartwarming fare. Classic or contemporary, all these dishes will make for elegant entertaining.

PEPPER STEAK *with* CHIVE BUTTER *and* BRANDY

A classic dish that never disappoints.

SERVES 4

4 beef tenderloin or beef sirloin
  steaks, 4–6 ounces each
3 tablespoons olive oil
1 tablespoon black and white
  peppercorns, coarsely crushed
1 garlic clove, halved
4 tablespoons (¹/₂ stick) butter
2 tablespoons brandy
1 cup beef stock
salt and pepper
tied chive bundles, to garnish
FOR THE CHIVE BUTTER
¹/₄ cup butter
3 tablespoons chopped fresh
  chives

1 Make the chive butter. Beat the butter until soft, add the chives and season with salt and pepper. Beat until well mixed, then shape into a roll, wrap in foil and chill.

2 Brush the steaks with a little olive oil and press crushed peppercorns onto both sides.

3 Rub the cut surface of the garlic over a frying pan. Melt the butter in the remaining oil. When hot, add the steaks and fry quickly, allowing 3¹/₂–4 minutes on each side for medium-rare. Lift out with tongs and keep hot.

4 Add the brandy and stock to the pan, boil rapidly until reduced by half, then season with salt and pepper to taste. Slice the chive butter and put a piece on top of each steak. Garnish each steak with a chive bundle and serve with a simple vegetable accompaniment, such as boiled new potatoes.

> **COOK'S TIP**
> *Flavored butters freeze well.*

HAM *with* MADEIRA SAUCE

A rich bacon, celery and tomato sauce flavored with Madeira is a perfect match for ham.

SERVES 4

2 tablespoons sunflower oil
2 ham steaks (4–6 ounces each),
  fat scored to prevent curling
1 onion, sliced
1¹/₂ cups button mushrooms
2 small beets (about 6 ounces),
  peeled and julienned
salt and pepper
chopped fresh parsley, to garnish
FOR THE SAUCE
2 tablespoons butter
1 large onion, chopped
1 lean bacon strip, chopped
1 celery stalk, diced
2 teaspoons all-purpose flour
2 tomatoes, peeled and diced
1 tablespoon tomato paste
1¹/₄ cups beef stock
1 tablespoon chopped fresh
  parsley
2 tablespoons Madeira

1 Make the sauce. Heat the butter and fry the onion, bacon and celery for 5–7 minutes, until golden. Stir in the flour and cook until browned, then add the tomatoes, tomato paste, stock and parsley. Bring to a boil, then simmer for 15 minutes.

2 Strain the sauce into a bowl, stir in the Madeira and season to taste with salt and pepper.

3 Heat the oil in a frying pan and fry the ham steaks with the onion for about 10 minutes. Turn the steaks over, add the mushrooms and fry for about 10 minutes more, or until the steaks are fully cooked.

4 Meanwhile, cook the julienned beet in a pan of lightly salted boiling water for 5 minutes or until tender. Drain. Reheat the sauce, pour it over the steaks and serve with the onion, mushrooms and beets. Garnish with the parsley.

> **COOK'S TIP**
> *Straining the sauce through cheesecloth or a very fine mesh will give a shiny, glossy finish.*

FIG-STUFFED PORK *with* BRANDY

Pork stuffed with dried fruit and spiked with brandy makes an ideal dinner-party dish.

SERVES 4

*1 large pork fillet, about
  1¹⁄₄ pounds, trimmed*
3 tablespoons brandy
*2 tablespoons chopped fresh
  herbs, such as parsley, dill or
  chives*
8 dried figs, halved
oil, for brushing
1 tablespoon all-purpose flour
1¹⁄₄ cups chicken stock
salt and pepper
fresh parsley sprigs, to garnish

1 Preheat the oven to 375°F. Cut a deep slit along the length of the pork fillet; do not cut all the way through. Open out the pork. Brush with 1 tablespoon of the brandy, sprinkle with the herbs and season with salt and pepper. Arrange the dried fig halves in a row on top.

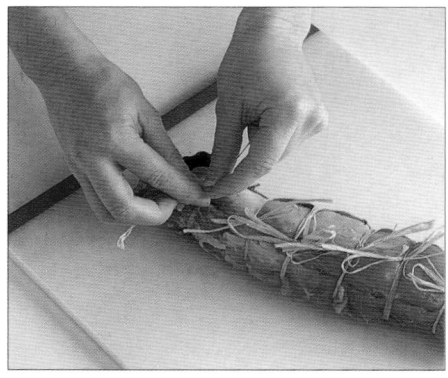

2 Fold the meat over the filling and tie with raffia or string. Put the pork in a roasting pan, brush with oil, season with pepper and roast for 35 minutes.

3 Lift the meat from the roasting pan and keep it hot. Spoon off the excess fat, leaving the sediment and about 1 tablespoon of the fat in the bottom of the pan. Place the pan on the stove over medium heat.

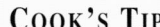

COOK'S TIP
This recipe also works very well with dry sherry, Noilly Prat or Madeira.

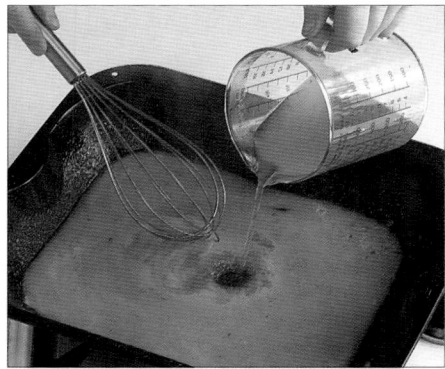

4 Stir in the flour and cook for 1 minute, then whisk in the stock and remaining brandy. Cook until thickened, then boil for 2 minutes, whisking frequently. Season with salt and pepper to taste.

5 Slice the meat, garnish with parsley sprigs and serve with the gravy. Roasted or sautéed potatoes and peas braised with lettuce would be ideal accompaniments.

PORK *with* SHERRY *and* COUSCOUS

A lightly spiced dish with a good balance of flavors between the pork and sherry.

SERVES 4

2 tablespoons all-purpose flour
1¼ pounds boneless pork, diced
3 tablespoons olive oil
1 large onion, chopped
2 garlic cloves, crushed
3 tablespoons tomato paste
1 cup chopped tomatoes
2 tablespoons lemon juice
2½ cups chicken stock
1 cup cooked chickpeas
2 tablespoons dry sherry
3 tablespoons raisins
1½ cups couscous
4 tablespoons (½ stick) butter
3 tablespoons chopped fresh
  parsley
salt and pepper

1 Put the flour in a plastic bag and season with salt and pepper. Add the pork and toss to coat. Heat the oil in a flameproof casserole and fry the onion until soft. Add the pork and cook, stirring occasionally, until golden.

COOK'S TIP
Moistened couscous can be heated in a pan or put in a covered ovenproof dish and baked for 20 minutes. Flavor with herbs, nuts or chopped dried fruits, such as apricots.

2 Stir in the garlic, tomato paste, tomatoes, lemon juice and stock. Season with salt and pepper. Bring to a boil, lower the heat, cover and simmer for 45 minutes.

3 Stir in the chickpeas, sherry and raisins. Cook for 15 minutes more.

4 Line a steamer with scalded cheese-cloth and sprinkle in the couscous. Put the steamer over the stew, cover and cook for 30 minutes. Turn the cooked couscous into a bowl, stir in the melted butter and parsley and fluff up with a fork. Serve with the stew.

GRILLED LAMB ESPAGNOLE *with* SHERRY

Espagnole is a traditional brown sauce, rich in flavor. Given the name, sherry is an obvious addition.

SERVES 4

2 large carrots, chopped
2 parsnips, chopped
4 tablespoons (¹/₂ stick) butter
1 tablespoon chopped fresh
 parsley
8 lamb cutlets
2 tablespoons sunflower oil
1 large onion, sliced into rings
salt and pepper
fresh parsley sprigs, to garnish
FOR THE SAUCE
4 tablespoons (¹/₂ stick) butter
1 small onion, chopped
2 lean bacon strips, chopped
1 celery stalk, sliced
1 small carrot, sliced
¹/₂ cup all-purpose flour
2¹/₂ cups beef stock
2 tablespoons tomato paste
1 bouquet garni
¹/₄ cup dry sherry

1 Make the sauce. Melt the butter in a saucepan and fry the onion and bacon over medium heat for 5 minutes. Add the celery and carrot and cook for about 10 minutes, until browned.

COOK'S TIP
This sauce freezes very well.

2 Stir in the flour. When it starts to brown, stir in the stock and tomato paste. Add the bouquet garni. Bring to a boil, lower the heat and simmer for 25 minutes. Press through a sieve into a bowl. Stir in the sherry, with salt and pepper to taste. Keep warm.

3 Cook the carrots and parsnips in a saucepan of boiling salted water until tender. Drain, mash, stir in the butter and parsley and season to taste. Keep warm.

4 Brush the lamb cutlets lightly with a little of the oil and season with pepper. Cook under a hot broiler for 2–3 minutes on each side.

5 Meanwhile, heat the remaining oil and fry the onion rings until crisp and golden. Spoon a portion of mashed carrots and parsnips onto each plate, place two cutlets on top and add some crisp onion rings. Pour some of the sauce on top and garnish with parsley sprigs.

NOISETTES OF LAMB *with* TARRAGON *and* ARMAGNAC

A generous splash of Armagnac brings out the best in this simple meat dish.

SERVES 4

1 tablespoon vegetable oil
2 tablespoons butter
12 noisettes of lamb
3 tablespoons Armagnac
3 tablespoons dry white wine
1¼ cups lamb stock
2 teaspoons chopped fresh
 tarragon
salt and pepper
fresh tarragon sprigs, to garnish

VARIATION
Untie the noisettes before cooking,
stuff with chopped fresh herbs, smoked
oysters or olive paste, then retie.

1 Heat the oil and half the butter in a frying pan. Season the noisettes of lamb with salt and pepper and fry over high heat until cooked and browned on both sides. Remove the noisettes from the pan and keep warm.

2 Remove the pan from the heat, pour off the excess oil, add the Armagnac and flambé (optional). Add the white wine and heat until reduced by three-quarters of its original volume.

3 Stir in the lamb stock and chopped tarragon. Bring to a boil and simmer for 3–4 minutes. Stir in the remaining butter and season if necessary. Serve the noisettes with the sauce and garnish with tarragon sprigs.

PAUPIETTES *of* VEAL *with* ARMAGNAC

Ham-stuffed veal packages are partnered with a mouthwatering Armagnac sauce.

SERVES 6

6 veal scallops, flattened
4 tablespoons (¹/₂ stick) butter
8 ounces pearl onions, peeled
8 ounces button mushrooms
2 teaspoons tomato paste
3 large tomatoes, quartered
  and seeded
3 tablespoons Armagnac
²/₃ cup dry white wine
1²/₃ cups veal stock
2 garlic cloves, crushed
1 bouquet garni
salt and pepper

FOR THE STUFFING

1 tablespoon butter
1 shallot, finely chopped
1¹/₂ cups mushrooms, finely
  chopped
3 tablespoons Armagnac
2 tablespoons crème fraîche
²/₃ cup finely chopped cooked ham
6 ounces bulk sausage

1 To make the stuffing, melt the butter in a pan, add the shallot and mushrooms and cook for 4–5 minutes. Pour in the Armagnac and simmer for 3–4 minutes. Stir in the crème fraîche, bring to a boil, then remove the pan from the heat and allow to cool. When cool, add the ham and bulk sausage and season with salt and pepper.

2 Lay the veal scallops out on a clean surface and top with some of the stuffing. Fold and roll the scallops over the filling to give a rectangular shape and tie with string or strong thread.

3 In a pan, melt the butter and brown the paupiettes on all sides, then remove and keep warm. Add the onions to the pan and brown, stir in the mushrooms and cook for another 2–3 minutes.

4 Stir in the tomato paste and the tomato quarters, pour in the Armagnac and flambé (optional). Add the white wine, stock, garlic cloves, bouquet garni and veal paupiettes. Bring to a boil, cover and simmer for 45 minutes.

5 Remove the paupiettes, untie them and keep warm. Strain the liquid into a clean pan and, if necessary, boil to reduce, then season to taste. Serve the paupiettes of veal with the sauce.

VARIATION
Turkey or large chicken fillets could be substituted successfully for the veal.

VEAL SCALLOPS *en* PAPILLOTE *with* KÜMMEL

Delicate mushroom-topped veal slices are enhanced with caraway-flavored-Kümmel.

SERVES 4

¹/₄ cup butter
4 veal scallops, flattened
1 tablespoon Kümmel
salt and pepper
cooked asparagus spears, to
* serve*

FOR THE STUFFING

2 tablespoons butter
1 shallot, finely chopped
3 cups mushrooms, chopped
1 tablespoon mixed chopped
* herbs*
1 tablespoon crème fraîche
¹/₄ teaspoon caraway seeds

1 To make the stuffing, heat the butter in a frying pan, add the shallot and cook for 5 minutes. Stir in the chopped mushrooms and herbs, season to taste with salt and pepper and cook for another 5 minutes or until all the juices have evaporated.

2 Stir in the crème fraîche and caraway seeds and set aside to cool.

3 Preheat the oven to 425°F. Cut four pieces of parchment paper, each the size of a dinner plate. Melt the butter and fry the veal scallops until browned, then remove the pan from the heat.

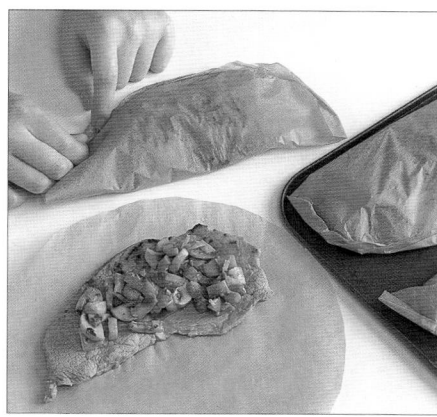

5 Fold the parchment paper over the filling and seal the edges to form a package. Lift them onto a baking sheet and bake 10–15 minutes. Serve immediately with lightly cooked asparagus.

COOK'S TIP

To flatten the scallops, place between sheets of parchment paper and beat gently with the end of a wooden rolling pin.

4 Place a veal scallop on each piece of parchment paper, cover with some of the stuffing and add a splash of Kümmel.

WHISKEY CHICKEN *with* ONION MARMALADE

A whiskey, honey and sesame seed paste enhances the flavor of chicken.

SERVES 4

4 tablespoons sesame seeds,
  crushed
2 garlic cloves, crushed
pinch of paprika
2 tablespoons oil
2 tablespoons whiskey
2 tablespoons honey
4 chicken legs
salt and pepper
FOR THE MARMALADE
2 tablespoons oil
2 large onions, thinly sliced
1 green bell pepper, seeded
  and sliced
²/₃ cup vegetable stock

1 Preheat the oven to 375°F. In a small bowl, make a paste with the sesame seeds, garlic, paprika, oil, whiskey and honey. Season with salt and pepper. Add a little water if the paste is too thick.

2 Make several cuts in the chicken portions and arrange them in an oven-proof dish. Spread with the paste. Roast for 40 minutes or until cooked.

3 Meanwhile, make the marmalade. Heat the oil in a frying pan and fry the onion slices over medium-high heat for 15 minutes. Add the green bell pepper and fry for 5 minutes more. Stir in the stock, season with salt pepper and cook gently, stirring occasionally, for about 20 minutes. Serve warm with the cooked chicken.

VARIATION
Instead of making cuts in the chicken portions, ease the skin away from the flesh and push the paste underneath. This keeps the flesh wonderfully moist.

CHICKEN *with* WILD MUSHROOMS *and* VERMOUTH

Tender chicken slices are folded into a rich sour cream sauce spiked with vermouth.

SERVES 4

2 tablespoons oil
1 leek, finely chopped
4 chicken breast halves, sliced
2 cups wild mushrooms,
  sliced if large
1 tablespoon brandy
pinch of grated nutmeg
¹/₄ teaspoon chopped fresh thyme
²/₃ cup dry white vermouth
²/₃ cup chicken stock
6 green olives, pitted and
  quartered
²/₃ cup sour cream
salt and pepper
fresh thyme sprigs and croutons,
  to garnish

1 Heat the oil and fry the chopped leek until softened but not browned. Add the chicken slices and mushrooms. Fry, stirring occasionally, until just beginning to brown.

COOK'S TIP
Chinese dried mushrooms work well in this dish. Soak them for an hour in cold water before use.

2 Pour in the brandy and ignite. When the flames have died down, stir in the nutmeg, thyme, vermouth and stock, with salt and pepper to taste.

3 Bring to a boil, lower the heat and simmer for 5 minutes. Stir in the olives and most of the sour cream. Reheat gently, but do not let the mixture boil. Garnish with the remaining sour cream, the thyme sprigs and croutons.

TURKEY-STUFFED GRAPE LEAVES *with* NOILLY PRAT

Pretty grape-leaf packages conceal a delicious wild rice and pine nut stuffing flavored with Noilly Prat.

SERVES 4

4 ounces drained grape leaves
  in brine
4 turkey scallops, 4–6 ounces
  each
1¹/₄ cups chicken stock
salt and pepper
FOR THE STUFFING
2 tablespoons sunflower oil
3 shallots, chopped
³/₄ cup cooked wild rice
4 tomatoes, peeled and chopped
3 tablespoons Noilly Prat or
  other dry white vermouth
¹/₃ cup pine nuts, chopped

1 Preheat the oven to 375°F. Rinse the grape leaves a few times in cold water and drain.

2 Make the stuffing. Heat the oil in a frying pan. Fry the chopped shallots until soft. Remove the pan from the heat and stir in the cooked rice, tomatoes, Noilly Prat and pine nuts. Season with salt and pepper to taste.

4 Spread out the meat and top each scallop with a quarter of the stuffing. Roll the meat over the filling.

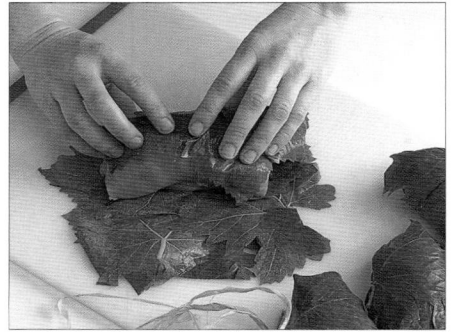

5 Overlap a quarter of the grape leaves to make a rectangle. Center a turkey roll on top, roll up neatly and tie with raffia or string. Repeat with the remaining leaves and turkey rolls.

6 Pack the rolls snugly in an oven-proof dish, pour the stock over them and bake for 40 minutes. Skim any surface fat from the stock and serve with the packages.

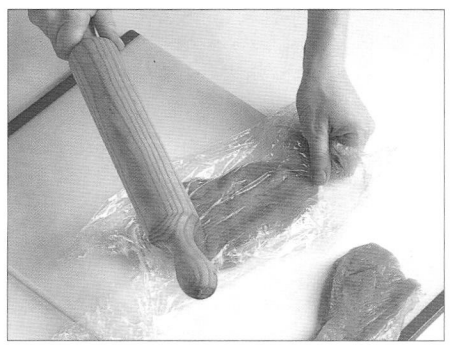

3 Put the scallops between sheets of plastic wrap and flatten with a rolling pin.

COOK'S TIP
Use fresh young grape leaves if you are lucky enough to find them. Trim the stalks, then plunge them into boiling salted water for 20–30 seconds, until they have just wilted. Refresh in cold water and pat dry on paper towels.

DUCK BREASTS *with* CALVADOS

A plum and calvados purée is the perfect accompaniment for glazed duck breasts with endives.

SERVES 4

1 tablespoon lemon juice
4 Belgian endives
4 duck breasts, 4–6 ounces each
1 tablespoon honey
1 teaspoon sunflower oil
salt and pepper
FOR THE PURÉE
1 apple, peeled, cored and sliced
6 ounces plums, halved
 and pitted
1 tablespoon light brown sugar
$^2/_3$ *cup vegetable stock*
3 tablespoons calvados
2 teaspoons sherry vinegar

1 Preheat the oven to 425°F. Make the purée. Put the apple, plums, sugar and stock in a saucepan. Bring to a boil, lower the heat and simmer for 10 minutes, until the fruit is very soft. Press the fruit through a strainer into a bowl. Set aside.

2 Stir the lemon juice into a saucepan of lightly salted water and bring to a boil. Cut the heads of endive length-wise into quarters and add to the pan. Cook for 3 minutes, then drain and set aside.

3 Score the duck breasts, brush with honey and sprinkle with a little salt. Transfer to a baking sheet and bake for 6–9 minutes, depending on weight.

COOK'S TIP

Adding lemon juice to the water used for cooking the endives helps to prevent discoloration.

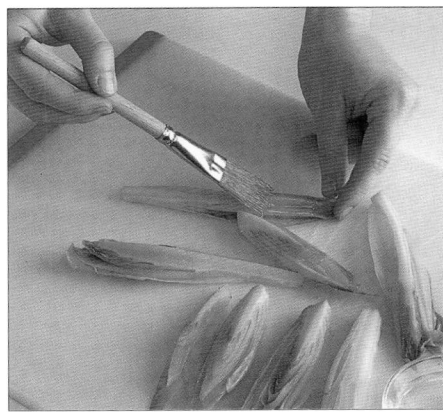

4 Brush the endive pieces with oil and place them alongside the duck. Bake for 6 minutes more.

5 Stir the calvados and vinegar into the purée and season with salt and pepper. Arrange the endive pieces on a platter. Slice the duck breasts and fan them out on top of the endives. Spoon the purée over the duck and serve immediately.

WOOD PIGEON *and* CHESTNUT CASSEROLE *with* PORT

Relish the flavors of the fall in this delicious casserole.

SERVES 4

2 tablespoons oil

4 pigeons or Cornish game hens,
 halved

1 onion, chopped

6 lean bacon strips, chopped

2 tablespoons all-purpose flour

1²/₃ cups game or chicken stock

²/₃ cup orange juice

2 tablespoons port

2 cups shelled chestnuts

2 tablespoons butter

2 oranges, sliced

salt and pepper

watercress sprigs, to garnish

1 Preheat the oven to 350°F. Heat the oil in a shallow flameproof casserole and sauté the pigeons or game hens until browned. Using a slotted spoon, transfer them to a bowl.

2 Add the chopped onion and bacon to the pan and sauté until golden. Stir in the flour and cook for 1 minute, until it begins to brown. Pour in the stock, orange juice and port, with salt and pepper to taste. Bring to a boil, stirring constantly, then return the pigeons or game hens to the casserole. Cover, place in the oven and cook for 30 minutes.

3 Stir in the chestnuts, return the casserole to the oven and cook for 30 minutes more.

COOK'S TIP
To shell fresh chestnuts, make a cross with a sharp knife on each nut. Cook in a hot oven for 15 minutes, until the shells crack, then peel.

4 Just before serving, melt the butter in a frying pan. Fry the orange slices until golden on both sides. Garnish the pigeon casserole with the orange slices and watercress sprigs. Serve at once.

POUSSINS *with* BULGUR *and* VERMOUTH

Vermouth is a valuable asset in the kitchen. It appears twice in this recipe, first flavoring the bulgur stuffing and then in the glaze for the poussins.

SERVES 4

$^1\!/_3$ cup bulgur
$^2\!/_3$ cup dry white vermouth
4 tablespoons olive oil
1 large onion, finely chopped
2 carrots, finely chopped
1 cup pine nuts, chopped
1 teaspoon celery seeds
4 poussins
3 red onions, quartered
4 baby eggplants, halved
4 pattypan squashes
12 baby carrots
3 tablespoons corn syrup
salt and ground black pepper

1 Preheat the oven to 400°F. Put the bulgur in a heatproof bowl, pour in half the vermouth and cover with boiling water. Set aside.

2 Heat half the oil in a large, shallow frying pan. Fry the onion and carrots for 10 minutes, then remove the pan from the heat and stir in the pine nuts, celery seeds and well-drained bulgur.

3 Stuff the poussins with the bulgur mixture. Place them in a roasting pan, brush with oil and sprinkle with salt and pepper. Roast for 45–55 minutes, until cooked.

COOK'S TIP

A poussin is a very small chicken weighing no more than 1½ pounds. It is sometimes sold under the name squab chicken.

---

4 Meanwhile, spread out the red onions, eggplants, pattypans and baby carrots in a single layer on a baking sheet.

5 Mix the corn syrup with the remaining vermouth and oil in a small bowl. Season with salt and pepper. Brush the corn syrup mixture over the vegetables and roast for 35–45 minutes, until golden. Cut each poussin in half and serve with the roasted vegetables.

GAME PIE *with* PORT

A good game pie is one of the triumphs of traditional British cooking, and this is one of the best. Cut the hot-water crust to reveal a rich filling, flavored with port and juniper berries.

SERVES 8–10

4 cups all-purpose flour
2 teaspoons salt
³/₄ cup solid vegetable shortening
³/₄ cup milk or milk and water
beaten egg, for glazing
2 teaspoons powdered gelatin
2 tablespoons cold water
salt and pepper
green salad, to serve

FOR THE FILLING

1¹/₂ pounds lean boneless game,
* such as pheasant, grouse,*
* partridge and rabbit, diced*
4 ounces lean bacon strips,
* chopped*
4 ounces ground pork
2 tablespoons port
2 teaspoons grated orange rind
2 juniper berries, crushed
¹/₂ teaspoon dried sage

1 Preheat the oven to 400°F. Grease an 8-inch springform cake pan. Sift the flour and salt into a bowl and make a well in the center.

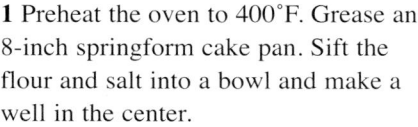

2 In a saucepan, melt the vegetable shortening in the milk or milk and water. Bring to a boil, pour into the well in the flour, and mix with a wooden spoon until cool enough to handle. Knead until smooth, then wrap in plastic wrap and allow to cool.

3 Make the filling. Mix the game, bacon and pork in a bowl. Add the port, orange rind, juniper berries and sage. Season with plenty of salt and pepper.

4 Roll out two-thirds of the dough and fit it into the pan, taking care not to stretch it. Do not trim the edge.

5 Fill the pastry shell with the meat mixture and smooth the surface. Brush the edge of the pastry with beaten egg. Roll the remaining pastry into a round to fit the top of the pie. Make a hole in the middle to allow steam to escape. Fit the lid in place and seal, trim and crimp the edge.

6 Decorate the lid with pastry shapes cut from the trimmings. Brush the lid with beaten egg, add the shapes and brush again.

7 Bake the pie for 30 minutes, then lower the oven temperature to 350°F and bake for 1¹/₄ more hours, covering the pie with foil if the pastry starts to over-brown. About 20 minutes before the end of the cooking time, remove the sides of the pan. Quickly brush the sides of the pie with beaten egg and return it to the oven.

8 Sprinkle the gelatin over the water in a heatproof bowl. When spongy, stir over simmering water until dissolved. Pour through a funnel into the pie and allow to cool. Serve the pie in generous slices, with green salad.

COOK'S TIP

If you are short of time, piecrust pastry can be used instead of the hot-water crust pastry.

PHEASANT *with* JUNIPER *and* PORT

A warming winter casserole, flavored with juniper and thyme, that brings together the rich tastes of game and port.

SERVES 4

2 pheasants
8 smoked bacon strips
2 tablespoons sunflower oil
2 celery stalks, sliced
12 pearl onions
3 carrots, sliced
8 bay leaves
8 fresh thyme sprigs
$^1/_2$ teaspoon juniper berries
$^1/_4$ cup port
$2^1/_2$ cups game stock
1 tablespoons cornstarch mixed
  to a paste with water
2 tablespoons red currant jelly
salt and pepper

1 Preheat the oven to 375°F. Cut each pheasant into four pieces. Wrap each portion in a strip of smoked bacon and tie it on neatly with strong thread.

COOK'S TIP

Pheasant is a very lean meat. Wrapping it with strips of bacon before cooking helps to keep it moist and prevents it from drying out.

2 Heat the oil in a shallow flameproof casserole and fry the pheasant portions until browned. Lift out with tongs onto a plate. Add the celery, onions and carrots to the casserole, with more oil if needed, and cook for 5–7 minutes, until golden, stirring occasionally.

3 Push a bay leaf and a sprig of thyme under the thread on each pheasant portion and arrange the pheasants on top of the vegetables.

4 Add the juniper berries to the casserole, pour in the port and stock and season the pheasant portions to taste with salt and pepper.

5 Cover the casserole and place in the oven. Cook for 1 hour, then remove the casserole from the oven and stir in the cornstarch paste and red currant jelly. Return the covered casserole to the oven and cook for about 15 minutes more or until the pheasant is tender and the sauce has thickened slightly. Serve from the casserole.

VEGETABLES AND VEGETARIAN DISHES

Crisp and refreshing or full-flavored and satisfying, vegetable dishes are never, or certainly never should be, dull. Serve these dishes as an accompaniment or in a larger portion as a main course. Calvados gives some French finesse to spiced cabbage, and Pernod adds a delicate anise flavor to a tomato and dill sauce for spring vegetables.

CARAMELIZED ONIONS *with* MADEIRA SAUCE

Like other fortified wines, Madeira gives a smooth rich flavor to sauces, and is particularly good with onions.

SERVES 4

1 pound pearl onions
²/₃ cup chicken stock
2 tablespoons light brown sugar
4 tablespoons (¹/₂ stick) butter
salt and pepper
fresh herbs, to garnish
FOR THE SAUCE
1 tablespoon butter
1 tablespoon all-purpose flour
1 cup vegetable or chicken stock
2 tablespoons Madeira
2 tablespoons light cream or
* half-and-half*

1 Place the onions in a single layer in a large pan. Pour in the stock—it should just cover. Bring to a boil, lower the heat and simmer for 15 minutes, until the onions are just tender, adding extra stock or water if necessary. Remove the pan from the heat and add the sugar and butter. Mix well, season with salt and pepper, then return the pan to the heat and cook until the onions are a rich golden color.

2 Meanwhile, make the sauce. Melt the butter in a saucepan, stir in the flour and cook for 2 minutes. Gradually add the stock, stirring until the sauce boils and thickens.

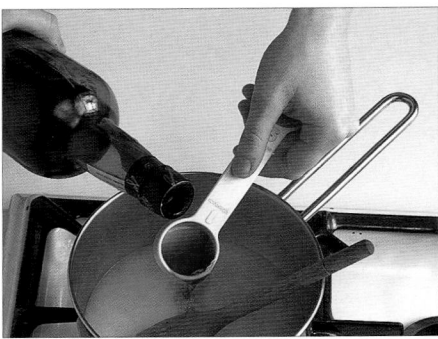

3 Add the Madeira and simmer for 5 minutes. Stir in the cream and reheat gently. Add salt and pepper to taste. Serve the onions with the sauce, garnished with fresh herbs.

ASPARAGUS *with* VERMOUTH SAUCE

Coating grilled young asparagus spears with a vermouth and parsley sauce creates a sensational side dish or appetizer.

SERVES 4

20 asparagus spears
1 teaspoon olive oil
²/₃ cup grated Parmesan cheese
salt and pepper
FOR THE SAUCE
3 tablespoons dry white vermouth
1 cup chicken stock
1 tablespoon chopped fresh
* parsley*
2 tablespoons cold butter, cubed

1 Brush the asparagus spears with olive oil and season to taste with salt and pepper. Place on a broiler rack, sprinkle with the Parmesan and broil slowly until the asparagus is cooked.

2 Meanwhile, pour the vermouth and stock into a saucepan. Boil over high heat until reduced by half. Stir in the parsley and season with salt and pepper.

3 Lower the heat and stir in the chilled butter cubes, two at a time. Continue to stir over gentle heat until all the butter has melted and the sauce has thickened. Arrange the asparagus spears in a serving dish, pour the sauce over them and serve at once.

COOK'S TIP

A Noilly Prat or dry sherry sauce is also good with asparagus.

PEPPER *and* ZUCCHINI RISOTTO *with* VERMOUTH

All it takes is time and patience to create this superb risotto, flavored with vermouth and Parmesan.

SERVES 4

2 tablespoons olive oil
1 onion, chopped
2 garlic cloves, crushed
4 cups chicken or vegetable stock
9 ounces Arborio rice
2 zucchini, chopped
1 green bell pepper, seeded and
  chopped
¼ cup grated Parmesan cheese
2 tablespoons dry white vermouth
salt and pepper
Parmesan shavings, to serve

1 Heat the oil in a large frying pan. Fry the onion until soft, then add the garlic and cook for 1 minute more.

2 Pour the stock into a saucepan. Bring it to a boil over a high heat, then lower the heat slightly, until the stock is barely simmering.

3 Stir the rice into the onion mixture. Add salt and pepper to taste and cook for 2 minutes. Ladle in about ⅔ cup of the hot stock and stir over low to medium heat until the rice has absorbed it.

COOK'S TIP
Use a nonstick pan for this dish. Don't try to hurry the process: It is vital that each batch of stock is absorbed before the next is added.

4 Add the zucchini and bell pepper to the pan, add the same amount of stock and once again cook until it has been absorbed. Stir frequently. Repeat this process until the rice has absorbed all the stock and the risotto is creamy. The process should take about 20 minutes.

5 Stir in the cheese and vermouth, reheat briefly and serve, topped with Parmesan shavings.

PUFF PASTRY BOXES *filled with* SPRING VEGETABLES *in* PERNOD SAUCE

Pernod is the perfect companion for the tender taste of early vegetables in crisp shells.

SERVES 4

8 ounces puff pastry, thawed if
 frozen
1 tablespoon grated Parmesan
 cheese
1 tablespoon fresh parsley
beaten egg, for glazing
6 ounces shelled fava beans
4 ounces baby carrots, peeled
4 baby leeks, cleaned
generous ¹/₂ cup peas, thawed
 if frozen
2 ounces snowpeas, trimmed
salt and pepper
fresh dill sprigs, to garnish
FOR THE SAUCE
1 cup chopped tomatoes
2 tablespoons (¹/₄ stick) butter
2 tablespoons all-purpose flour
pinch of sugar
3 tablespoons chopped fresh dill
1¹/₄ cups water
1 tablespoon Pernod

1 Preheat the oven to 425°F. Lightly grease a baking sheet. Roll out the pastry very thinly. Sprinkle the cheese and parsley on top, fold and roll once more and cut out four 4-inch squares.

2 Lift the rectangles onto the baking sheet. With a sharp knife, cut an inner rectangle about ¹/₂ inch from the edge of the pastry, cutting halfway through. Score crisscross lines on top of the inner rectangle, brush with egg and bake for 12–15 minutes, until golden.

3 Meanwhile, make the sauce. Press the tomatoes through a sieve into a pan, add the remaining ingredients and bring to a boil, stirring constantly. Lower the heat and simmer until needed. Season to taste with salt and pepper.

4 Cook the fava beans in a pan of lightly salted boiling water for about 8 minutes. Add the carrots, leeks and peas, cook another 5 minutes, then add the snowpeas. Cook for 1 minute. Drain all the vegetables very well.

5 Using a knife, remove the notched squares from the pastry boxes. Set them aside to use as lids. Spoon the vegetables into the pastry shells, pour the sauce over them, put the pastry lids on top and serve garnished with dill.

COOK'S TIP

*If there is time, chill the pastry shapes
for 20 minutes before baking.*

MIXED GREEN *and* PARMESAN SALAD *with* SHERRY

Croutons flavored with sherry and oil add crunch to this salad.

SERVES 4

4 eggs
2 garlic cloves, crushed
6 tablespoons olive oil
4 thick slices white bread,
  crusts removed
1 tablespoon lemon juice
1 tablespoon dry sherry
6 tablespoons mayonnaise
6 ounces mixed salad greens
³/₄ cup coarsely grated Parmesan
  cheese
salt and pepper

COOK'S TIP

To make a more substantial main-course salad, add some cooked smoked chicken or fish.

---

1 Hard-cook the eggs and remove the shells. When cool, cut them into quarters. Mix the crushed garlic with 3 tablespoons of the olive oil in a bowl.

2 Make the croutons. Cut the bread into cubes. Quickly toss the bread in the garlic oil, then turn into a hot frying pan. Fry until golden, then drain thoroughly on paper towels.

3 Combine the remaining oil, lemon juice, sherry and mayonnaise in a small bowl. Season with salt and pepper and mix well.

4 Place the salad greens in the bottom of a bowl. Arrange the eggs, croutons and Parmesan on top, then pour the dressing over all. Serve as soon as possible, while the croutons are still crisp.

ROASTED FENNEL *with* PERNOD *and* WALNUT SALAD

Pernod enhances the anise flavor of fennel, and makes an excellent warm salad dressing.

SERVES 4

butter, for greasing pan
4 fennel bulbs, trimmed
¹/₄ cup Pernod
2 tablespoons olive oil
2 teaspoons light brown sugar
salt and pepper
FOR THE SALAD
2 tablespoons olive oil
¹/₂ cup walnut halves, broken
¹/₂ teaspoon mustard seeds
1 tablespoon Pernod
3 handfuls mixed salad greens
1 bunch radishes, with small
  greens left on

VARIATION

This recipe is also very good with celery or Belgian endive.

---

1 Preheat the oven to 375°F. Use the butter to grease a large, shallow casserole. Cook the fennel bulbs in a saucepan of lightly salted boiling water until tender and drain.

2 Cut each fennel bulb lengthwise in quarters. Arrange them in a single layer in the prepared casserole. Pour the Pernod and oil over them, sprinkle with sugar and season with salt and pepper. Cover and bake for about 30 minutes, basting from time to time.

3 To make the salad, warm the oil in a small pan. Remove from the heat and stir in the walnuts and mustard seeds. Return the pan to the heat, cover and heat until the mustard seeds start to pop. Mix in the Pernod.

4 Arrange the salad greens and radishes (some whole, some sliced) on a platter. Pour the warm dressing on top. Top with the roasted fennel and serve immediately.

DRUNKEN MUSHROOMS *with* BRANDY

Mixed mushrooms in a creamy brandy sauce, served on a bed of portobello mushrooms, make a delicious treat.

SERVES 4

1¼ cups heavy cream
1 garlic clove, crushed
2 tablespoons mustard seeds
1 tablespoon drained green
 peppercorns in brine
1 teaspoon Worcestershire sauce
4 cups mixed mushrooms, such as
 button, oyster, chanterelle, shi-
 itake or crimini, sliced or
 halved if large
2 tablespoons coarse-grain
 mustard
2 tablespoons brandy
12 small portobello mushrooms
1 tablespoon olive oil
salt and pepper
Italian parsley, to garnish

1 Combine the cream, crushed garlic, mustard seeds, green peppercorns and Worcestershire sauce in a saucepan. Bring to a boil.

2 Stir in the mixed mushrooms. Cook for 10 minutes, or until the mushrooms are tender and the sauce has thickened.

COOK'S TIP
Use whiskey, gin or vermouth instead of the brandy in the sauce.

3 Stir the mustard and brandy into the sauce. Season to taste. Keep warm over very low heat.

4 Brush the portobello mushrooms with oil, then cook in a hot frying pan, turning once, until browned. Divide among four plates and spoon the creamy mushrooms and their sauce on top. Garnish with Italian parsley and serve.

SWEET POTATOES *with* SHERRY *and* CITRUS TOMATO SALSA

Treat vegetarian guests to a dish that is as delicious as it is different. Sweet potatoes in a spicy sherry dressing are served with a fresh-tasting citrus salsa.

SERVES 4

1¼ pounds sweet potatoes, diced
3 tablespoons olive oil
1 teaspoon mustard seeds
1 teaspoon cumin seeds
¼ teaspoon fennel seeds
2 tablespoons dry sherry
4 small radicchio leaves
salt and ground black pepper
fresh basil sprigs, to garnish

FOR THE SALSA

2 oranges
1–2 tomatoes
1 scallion
handful of fresh basil leaves
2 tablespoons olive oil
pinch of sugar

1 Cook the sweet potatoes in a saucepan of lightly salted boiling water for 6 minutes. Drain and set aside.

2 Heat the olive oil in a large frying pan. Add the mustard, cumin and fennel seeds and cook for 3–4 seconds, until they pop. Stir in the sherry.

3 Add the sweet potatoes, turning to coat them thoroughly, then fry for 10–15 minutes, stirring frequently. Season to taste with salt and pepper.

4 To make the salsa, peel the oranges with a sharp knife, then segment and chop them. Peel, seed and chop the tomatoes, and slice the scallion. Shred the basil leaves.

5 Mix the salsa ingredients in a bowl, season with salt and pepper, spoon onto the radicchio leaves and serve with the potatoes. Garnish with basil.

COOK'S TIP
If you prefer, boil the sweet potatoes with the skins on, then peel and dice.

VEGETABLE RÖSTI *with* WHISKEY

*Based on Swiss potato rösti, but with extra vegetables and a cheese and mushroom filling,
this has a hint of whiskey.*

SERVES 4

3 medium carrots, grated
1 celery root (about 10 ounces),
 grated
1 large potato, grated
2 medium parsnips, grated
3 tablespoons chopped parsley
1¹/₂ cups mushrooms, chopped
¹/₂ cup grated Cheddar cheese
2 tablespoons whiskey
4 tablespoons (¹/₂ stick) butter
2 tablespoons olive oil
salt and pepper
fresh parsley and cherry
 tomatoes, to garnish

1 Mix the grated vegetables with the chopped parsley in a large bowl. Season with salt and pepper. In another bowl, combine the mushrooms, grated cheese and whiskey.

2 Heat the butter and most of the oil in a large nonstick frying pan that can safely be used under the broiler. Add half the grated vegetables and press down in an even layer. Cover with the cheese mixture and top with the remaining grated vegetables. Press down firmly.

3 Cook over high heat for 5 minutes, then cover, lower the heat and cook for about 10 minutes more, or until the vegetables are soft. Brush the top with the remaining oil and cook under a hot broiler until golden. Serve in generous wedges, garnished with the parsley and cherry tomatoes.

COOK'S TIPS

Instead of cooking the rösti on top of the stove, press the mixture into an ovenproof dish and cook in a hot oven for 40 minutes. If you like, make individual röstis to serve with roast meats or fish.

SESAME SEED TOFU *with* EGGPLANT *and* BRANDY

*Tofu is a marvelously versatile ingredient. With little taste of its own, it readily absorbs other flavors.
Marinated and fried, it makes a fine topping for eggplants.*

SERVES 4

¹/₄ teaspoon Chinese five-spice
 powder
1 garlic clove, crushed
2 tablespoons sesame seeds
2 teaspoons soy sauce
12 ounces firm tofu, cut into
 large cubes
2 eggplants, halved lengthwise
oil, for shallow frying
1 carrot, julienned
2 scallions, sliced
2 tablespoons brandy
salt and ground black pepper
chopped fresh cilantro,
 to garnish

1 Combine the five-spice powder, garlic, sesame seeds and soy sauce in a bowl. Add the cubed tofu. Stir until thoroughly coated, then cover and chill for 2 hours.

2 Brush the eggplants with a little oil and set under a hot broiler until cooked and golden.

3 Meanwhile, heat the oil in a frying pan and cook the tofu until crisp and golden. Transfer to a plate. Add more oil to the pan if necessary and stir-fry the carrot strips and scallions for 2 minutes.

4 Add the brandy and seasoning, bring to a boil and return the tofu cubes to the pan. Toss until heated through. Place half a grilled eggplant on each plate and pile the tofu mixture on top. Garnish with cilantro and serve.

VEGETABLE TERRINE *with* BRANDY

A feast for the eye and the palate—that's this luscious layer of brandy-flavored custard and colorful vegetables.

SERVES 4

1 red bell pepper, seeded and quartered
1 green bell pepper, seeded and quartered
½ cup fresh or frozen peas
6 fresh green asparagus spears
2 carrots, cut into thin sticks
⅔ cup milk
⅔ cup heavy cream
6 eggs, beaten
1 tablespoon brandy
¾ cup ricotta cheese
1 tablespoon chopped fresh parsley
salt and ground black pepper
salad greens, cucumber slices and tomato halves, to serve

1 Preheat the oven to 350°F. Grease and line the bottom of a 2-pound loaf pan. Cook the vegetables separately in a pan of lightly salted boiling water until tender, drain and dry on paper towels. Peel the pepper quarters.

2 In a bowl, combine the milk, cream, eggs, brandy, ricotta cheese and parsley. Mix well and season.

3 Arrange some of the vegetables in the bottom of the loaf pan, trimming them to fit if necessary. Spoon some of the cheese mixture on top. Continue layering the vegetables and the cheese mixture, ending with a layer of peppers.

COOK'S TIP
This is a very soft mixture, so it must be cool before you try to turn it out. It also makes a good filling for a deep pastry shell.

4 Cover the pan with foil and stand it in a roasting pan. Pour in boiling water to come halfway up the sides of the pan.

5 Bake for 45 minutes or until the custard is just firm. Leave the terrine in the pan until cool, then remove it from the roasting pan and invert onto a plate. Lift off the lining paper and cut the terrine into neat slices. Serve with the salad greens, cucumber slices and halved tomatoes.

POLENTA TRIANGLES *with* SPICED RED CABBAGE

Smooth and dry, calvados is widely used in French cookery, especially in its native Normandy. It is particularly good with apples and red cabbage.

SERVES 4

2 tablespoons butter
1 tablespoon olive oil
1 onion, sliced
1 garlic clove, crushed
1 red cabbage, shredded (about 5 cups)
1 cup vegetable or chicken stock
3 tablespoons red wine vinegar
3 tablespoons honey
1 tablespoon lemon juice
pinch of ground cloves
2 cooking apples
2 tablespoons calvados
salt and pepper
fresh Italian parsley, to garnish

FOR THE POLENTA

2 cups water
1 teaspoon salt
1 cup polenta
¼ cup butter, diced
2 tablespoons grated Parmesan cheese
3 tablespoons chopped fresh herbs
olive oil, for brushing
¼ cup pine nuts, crushed

1 Start by making the polenta. Bring the water to a boil in a large pan. Add the salt, pour in the polenta and cook for about 8 minutes, stirring constantly with a wooden spoon, until the mixture resembles thick porridge. Do not let it stick to the bottom of the pan.

COOK'S TIPS

Alternatively, you can brush the polenta with oil and broil it, turning once. Spiced red cabbage tastes better the next day, when the flavors have had a chance to develop.

2 Remove the polenta from the heat and stir in the butter, Parmesan cheese and herbs. Spread the polenta about ½-inch thick on a flat plate, cover with foil or plastic wrap and chill.

3 Heat the butter and olive oil in a large frying pan. Fry the onion until golden, then add all the remaining ingredients, except the apples and calvados. Bring to a boil, lower the heat, cover and simmer for 40 minutes. Stir the mixture occasionally and add a little water if it becomes too dry. Preheat the oven to 375°F.

4 Peel, core and chop the apples. Stir them into the red cabbage mixture, then pour in the calvados and add salt and pepper to taste. Simmer for 15 minutes.

5 Grease a baking sheet. Cut the polenta into triangles and arrange on the baking sheet. Brush with oil, sprinkle the nuts on top and bake for 15–20 minutes, until golden brown. Arrange around the rim of a heated serving platter and pile the red cabbage in the center. Garnish with the Italian parsley and serve.

DESSERTS, ICES AND CANDIES

Light and elegant or rich and smooth, desserts, ices and candies are the crowning glory of any meal. Try maraschino crème brûlée with its rich cherry liqueur-soaked fruits covered with a rose water-flavored cream, delight in luscious hot Grand Marnier soufflés with bitter orange iced centers or choose tempting mocha truffles flavored with Café Noir.

CRÊPES SUZETTE *with* COINTREAU *and* COGNAC

Thin pancakes filled with Cointreau-flavored butter and flambéed with cognac may be a classic, but they remain as popular as ever.

SERVES 6

1 cup all-purpose flour
¹/₂ teaspoon salt
2 eggs, beaten
1¹/₄ cups milk
oil, for frying
juice of 2 oranges
3 tablespoons cognac
confectioners' sugar, for dusting
thin strips orange rind,
 to decorate
FOR THE ORANGE BUTTER
12 tablespoons (1¹/₂ sticks) butter
¹/₄ cup sugar
grated rind of 2 oranges
2 tablespoons Cointreau

1 Start by making the orange butter. Cream the butter with the sugar in a bowl. Stir in the orange rind and Cointreau. Set aside while you make the pancake batter.

2 Make the pancakes. Sift the flour and salt into a bowl, make a well in the center and add the eggs. Mix thoroughly. Gradually stir in the milk and beat to a smooth batter. Pour into a pitcher. Heat the oil in a pan, pour in a little batter and make a thin 6-inch pancake. Cook until the underside is golden, turn over and cook the other side. Slide out of the pan. Make at least five more pancakes with the remaining batter.

3 Spread the pancakes with half the orange butter and fold into quarters.

COOK'S TIP
Not traditional, but equally delicious, is to use rum in place of the Cointreau and cognac, and add sliced fresh pineapple and a little toasted coconut.

4 Heat the rest of the orange butter in a frying pan with the orange juice, add the folded pancakes and turn them to heat them through. Push the pancakes to one side of the pan and pour in the cognac. Heat, then carefully set alight. When the flames die down, spoon the sauce over the pancakes. Dust with confectioners' sugar and serve, decorated with strips of orange rind.

HOT SOUFFLÉS *with* GRAND MARNIER ICE CREAM

Grand Marnier contributes the flavors of cognac and bitter oranges to these hot, fluffy soufflés with their surprising iced centers.

SERVES 6

3 tablespoons butter
3 tablespoons all-purpose flour
1 cup milk
3 tablespoons superfine sugar
2 tablespoons Grand Marnier
5 eggs, separated
confectioners' sugar, for dusting
FOR THE ICE CREAM
$^2/_3$ cup heavy cream
2 tablespoons Grand Marnier
2 tablespoons orange juice
2 teaspoons confectioners' sugar

1 Make the ice cream. Mix the cream, Grand Marnier, orange juice and confectioners' sugar in a small bowl. Spoon into a freezer container and freeze for 30 minutes, or until ice crystals begin to form around the edge. Stir well. Freeze.

2 Using two spoons, form the frozen Grand Marnier ice cream into six small ovals. Freeze on a plate until solid.

3 Preheat the oven to 400°F. Lightly grease six individual soufflé dishes. Put the butter, flour and milk in a large pan. Bring to a boil, stirring constantly. Cook for 2 minutes, then remove from the heat. Cool slightly and beat in the sugar, Grand Marnier and egg yolks.

COOK'S TIP
The bowl and whisk used for whisking egg whites must be grease-free.

4 Whisk the egg whites in a large bowl until stiff. Using a metal spoon, fold them into the sauce mixture.

5 Spoon the mixture into the soufflé dishes, stand the dishes on a baking sheet and bake for 25–35 minutes, until the soufflés are risen and browned. Very quickly dust with confectioners' sugar, make a hole in the top of each soufflé and add a spoonful of Grand Marnier ice cream. Serve at once.

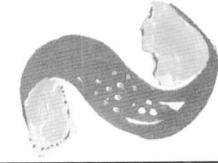

ZABAGLIONE

This gloriously creamy, classic Italian dessert is made with marsala, a Sicilian fortified wine.

SERVES 4

2 ladyfingers, crumbled
6 tablespoons marsala
6 fresh apricots, pitted and
sliced
5 egg yolks
¼ cup superfine sugar

VARIATION
Madeira can be used instead of marsala, and crumbled macaroons instead of ladyfingers.

1 Divide the crumbled ladyfingers among four heatproof dessert glasses. Sprinkle with 1 tablespoon of the marsala. Set aside eight of the apricot slices for decoration and divide the rest among the glasses.

2 Put the egg yolks in a heatproof bowl. Whisk them lightly, then whisk in the sugar and remaining marsala.

3 Put the bowl over a saucepan of barely simmering water and continue to whisk until the mixture is very thick and creamy. When you lift the whisk out of the bowl, the trail should lie on top of the mixture for 2–3 seconds.

4 Pour the zabaglione into the glasses and decorate with the reserved apricot slices. Serve while still warm.

POACHED TANGERINES *with* SHORTBREAD LEAVES

Whole tangerines macerated in a liqueur-flavored syrup make a superb dessert, especially when served with melt-in-the-mouth shortbread cookies.

SERVES 4

generous 1 cup light brown sugar
3 cups water
12 small tangerines or clementines
3 tablespoons Mandarine
Napoléon liqueur
1 tablespoon lemon juice
whipped heavy cream, to serve
FOR THE SHORTBREAD
4 tablespoons (½ stick) butter
⅔ cup all-purpose flour, sifted
2 tablespoons superfine sugar,
plus extra for sprinkling
1 teaspoon finely grated
lemon rind

COOK'S TIP
Store the cookies in an airtight tin. Add a few grains of rice to prevent them from softening.

1 Preheat the oven to 325°F. Grease a baking sheet. Make the shortbread. Put the butter, flour, sugar and lemon rind in a large bowl and knead together until smooth and silky.

2 Roll out on a lightly floured surface to a thickness of ¼ inch. Cut out leaf shapes by hand or with a cookie cutter. Lift onto the baking sheet and bake for 15 minutes. Sprinkle with superfine sugar and allow to cool on the baking sheet for 5 minutes before removing.

3 Mix the brown sugar and water in a large saucepan. Heat until the sugar has dissolved, bring to a boil and simmer until reduced by half. Lower the heat so that the syrup barely simmers.

4 Peel the tangerines and remove any pith. Stir the liqueur and lemon juice into the syrup, add the tangerines, cover and cook gently for 40 minutes. Allow to cool. Serve with the shortbread leaves, and offer whipped heavy cream to those who want it.

SHERRY TRIFLE

There are many versions of sherry trifle, ranging from the everyday to the exquisite.
This one falls into the latter category.

SERVES 6–8

3 ounces macaroons
6 tablespoons raspberry jam
³/₄ cup sherry
1 cup fresh raspberries
2 cups seedless black grapes,
  halved
1¹/₄ cups heavy cream, whipped
candied fruit and confectioners'
  sugar, to decorate

FOR THE CUSTARD
¹/₄ cup cornstarch
2¹/₂ cups milk
3 egg yolks
¹/₂ teaspoon vanilla extract
2 tablespoons superfine sugar

VARIATION
Vary the fruit filling to make the most
of seasonal availability. Match the
fruit to the jam. If preferred, an
appropriate liqueur can be used
instead of sherry.

1 Make the custard. In a heatproof bowl, blend the cornstarch with a little of the milk. Stir in the egg yolks, vanilla extract and sugar. Pour the remaining milk into a saucepan and bring to a boil. Pour the milk onto the cornstarch mixture, stirring constantly.

2 Return to the heat and, continuing to stir, bring to a boil again, then lower the heat and simmer for 3 minutes. Remove from the heat, cover the surface with waxed paper and set aside to cool.

3 Sandwich the macaroons together with the raspberry jam, then arrange them in a deep glass bowl and sprinkle the sherry over them.

4 Spoon on half the custard. Level the surface and arrange the fruit on top. Cover with the remaining custard, making sure that the layers are visible through the side of the bowl. Swirl or pipe the cream on top of the trifle and decorate with pieces of candied fruit. Dust with a little confectioners' sugar just before serving.

GRAPEFRUIT *in* HONEY *and* WHISKEY

A colorful fan of grapefruit segments in a sweet whiskey sauce.

SERVES 4

1 pink grapefruit
1 ruby grapefruit
1 white grapefruit
¼ cup sugar
¼ cup honey
3 tablespoons whiskey
fresh mint leaves, to decorate

1 Peel the grapefruits, removing all the pith, then cut them into segments.

2 Put the sugar and ⅔ cup water in a pan. Bring to a boil, stirring, until the sugar has dissolved, then simmer for 10 minutes.

3 Heat the honey in a pan and boil until it becomes a slightly deeper color or caramelizes. Remove from the heat, add the whiskey, flambé (optional) and pour into the sugar syrup.

4 Bring the syrup to a boil and pour it over the grapefruit segments. Cover and let cool. To serve, put the grapefruit segments onto serving plates, alternating the colors, pour some of the syrup on top and decorate with mint.

VARIATION

The whiskey can be replaced with brandy, Cointreau or Grand Marnier.

FRAMBOISE SABAYON *with* BLUEBERRIES *and* RASPBERRIES

This couldn't be simpler to make, but it tastes superb.

SERVES 4

1 cup fresh blueberries
1 cup fresh raspberries
3 egg yolks
1/4 cup framboise
2 tablespoons superfine sugar
extra sugar, for topping

VARIATION

In the winter, when fresh berries are out of season (and expensive), try this with dried apricots macerated in brandy and topped with plain yogurt.

1 Arrange the fresh blueberries and raspberries in wide flameproof soup bowls or on flameproof dessert plates.

2 Mix the egg yolks, framboise and sugar in a large heatproof bowl. Place the bowl over a pan of barely simmering water and whisk until thick and foamy. Preheat the broiler.

3 Spoon the sauce over the fruits, sprinkle with a little sugar and slide briefly under a hot broiler until the sugar caramelizes and turns golden.

AMARETTO ICE CREAM

Almond-flavored liqueur gives this ice cream a wonderful depth of flavor.

SERVES 4–6

3 cups vanilla ice cream, softened
2 tablespoons amaretto
1 tablespoon orange juice
1/4 teaspoon vanilla extract
thinly pared orange rind,
* to decorate*
FOR THE BRANDY SNAP BASKETS
4 tablespoons (1/2 stick) butter
1/4 cup superfine sugar
1/4 cup light corn syrup
1 teaspoon ground ginger
grated rind and juice of 1 lemon
1/2 cup all-purpose flour

1 Preheat the oven to 350°F. Line three baking sheets with parchment paper.

2 Beat the ice cream until soft and creamy, then beat in the amaretto, orange juice and vanilla extract. Return to the bowl or a similar container for freezing. Freeze until firm.

3 Put the butter, sugar, syrup and ground ginger in a saucepan. Heat gently, stirring constantly until the butter has melted, then turn off the heat and stir in the lemon rind and juice, then the flour.

4 The mixture hardens quickly, so bake only two baskets at a time. Put spoonfuls of the mixture on the baking sheets. Bake for 10-12 minutes, until golden. Cool for a few seconds.

5 Lift each basket in turn with a spatula and drape over a small orange or the outside of an overturned cup. Let cool and harden, then invert onto plates. Add scoops of amaretto ice cream, decorate with the orange rind and serve.

COFFEE *and* KAHLÚA MACADAMIA CREAMS *with* MERINGUE FINGERS

These rich, molded creams have a wonderfully intense flavor, thanks to the coffee liqueur.

SERVES 4–6

2 teaspoons powdered gelatin
3 tablespoons water
1¹/₂ cups heavy cream
²/₃ cup thick plain yogurt
1 tablespoon strong black coffee
¹/₄ cup confectioners' sugar
1 tablespoon Kahlúa
¹/₂ cup macadamia nuts,
 toasted and chopped
toasted macadamia nuts and
 chocolate coffee beans,
 to decorate
FOR THE MERINGUE FINGERS
1 egg white
¹/₄ cup superfine sugar

1 Preheat the oven to 250°F. Cover a baking sheet with parchment paper. Make the meringue fingers. Whisk the egg white in a grease-free bowl until stiff and dry. Whisk in half the sugar until stiff, then fold in the remaining sugar.

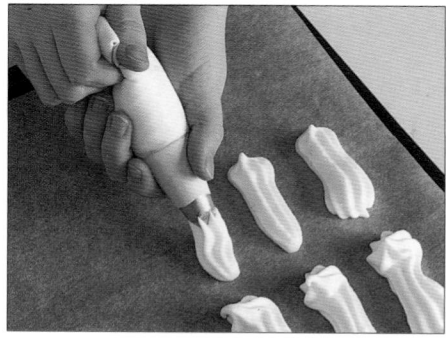

2 Pipe or spoon finger shapes of meringue onto the baking sheet. Bake for 2¹/₂ hours or until crisp.

3 Meanwhile, make the creams. Sprinkle the gelatin over the water in a small heatproof bowl. When spongy, stir over simmering water until dissolved.

4 Combine the cream, yogurt, coffee, confectioners' sugar and Kahlúa in a bowl. Stir in the dissolved gelatin mixture. Chill until on the point of setting, then stir in the nuts and spoon into small molds. Chill until firm, unmold and decorate with nuts and chocolate coffee beans. Serve with the meringue fingers.

MARASCHINO CRÈME BRÛLÉE

Crack the crunchy topping to discover rich cherry liqueur-soaked fruits under a creamy blanket.

SERVES 6

6 eggs, lightly beaten
1¹/₄ cups milk
1¹/₄ cups heavy cream, lightly
 whipped
¹/₄ cup superfine sugar
1 teaspoon rosewater
¹/₂ cup pitted fresh cherries, halved
¹/₂ cup seedless grapes, halved
1 tablespoon maraschino
¹/₂ cup light brown sugar
whole fresh cherries, to serve

1 Mix the eggs and milk in a large heatproof bowl. Place over a saucepan of barely simmering water and heat until the mixture thickens to a light custard.

2 Fold in the cream, sugar and rosewater. Remove the pan from the heat and set aside to cool.

3 Divide the fruit among six flameproof dishes. Sprinkle the maraschino liqueur over the fruit and spoon the custard on top. Preheat the broiler.

4 Sprinkle the sugar evenly over the custard. Place under the broiler until the sugar caramelizes. Serve chilled or at room temperature with whole cherries.

BOURBON BALLS

This southern speciality laces cookie and pecan truffles with bourbon.

MAKES ABOUT 25

6 ounces Nice cookies or
  vanilla wafers
1 cup pecans, chopped
2 tablespoons cocoa powder
³/₄ cup confectioners' sugar, sifted
2 tablespoons honey
¹/₂ cup bourbon

COOK'S TIP

Brandy snaps can be used instead of
cookies or wafers and cognac or
brandy in place of the bourbon.

---

1 Put the cookies in a plastic bag and crush them finely with a rolling pin. Turn the crumbs into a bowl and add the chopped nuts, cocoa powder and half the confectioners' sugar. Add the honey and bourbon. Stir until the mixture forms a stiff paste. Add a little more bourbon if necessary.

2 Shape the mixture into small balls, place on a plate and chill until firm.

3 Roll the balls in the remaining confectioners' sugar, then chill for 15 minutes and roll again in sugar. Serve on a plate or pack into a pretty box as a present.

MOCHA TRUFFLES *with* CAFÉ NOIR

The combination of coffee liqueur and chocolate is irresistible.

MAKES ABOUT 25

6 ounces dark chocolate, broken
  into squares
4 tablespoons (¹/₂ stick) butter
2 teaspoons instant coffee granules
2 tablespoons heavy cream
4 cups pound cake crumbs
¹/₂ cup ground almonds
2 tablespoons Café Noir
cocoa powder, chocolate
  sprinkles or ground almonds,
  for coating

1 Put the chocolate in a heatproof bowl. Add the butter and instant coffee granules. Set the bowl over a saucepan of hot water and heat gently until the chocolate and butter have melted and the coffee granules have dissolved. (Do not let the water boil or let the bottom of the bowl touch the water or the chocolate will overheat.)

3 Chill the mixture until firm. Shape into small balls, roll in cocoa powder, chocolate sprinkles or ground almonds and place in foil petit four holders.

VARIATION

Omit the coffee granules and use
cherry brandy instead of Café Noir.
Hide a maraschino cherry
in each truffle.

2 Remove from the heat and stir in the cream, cake crumbs, ground almonds and Café Noir.

TARTS AND PIES

Crisp, featherlight pastry and a medley of fruits and nuts can be
transformed quite wonderfully into exciting and exotic pies and tarts.
Coffee-flavored pastry is the base for a rich, sticky filling of molasses and
nuts laced with a dusky Highland measure of Drambuie. You will also find
here a mouthwatering meringue pie made with plums and eau-de-vie de
mirabelle, a fruit brandy made from mirabelle plums, and a rich, creamy
custard tart flavored with marsala.

APPLE, RAISIN *and* MAPLE PIES *with* CALVADOS

Calvados accentuates the apple flavor of these individual puff-pastry pies.

SERVES 4

12 ounces puff pastry, thawed if frozen
beaten egg or milk, for glazing
whipped cream, flavored with orange liqueur and sprinkled with grated orange rind, to serve

FOR THE FILLING

$1/2$ cup light brown sugar
2 tablespoons lemon juice
3 tablespoons maple syrup
$2/3$ cup water
3 tablespoons calvados
6 small apples
$1/2$ cup raisins

1 Preheat the oven to 400°F. Make the filling. Combine the sugar, lemon juice, maple syrup and water in a saucepan. Heat gently until the sugar has dissolved, then bring to a boil and cook until reduced by half. Stir in the calvados.

2 Halve and core four of the apples and cut them into eighths. Add the apple wedges to the syrup and simmer for 5–8 minutes, until just tender. Using a slotted spoon, lift the apple wedges out of the syrup and set them aside.

3 Peel, core and chop the remaining apples. Add them to the syrup with the raisins. Simmer until the mixture is very thick, then set aside to cool.

4 Roll out the pastry on a lightly floured surface and stamp out eight 6-inch rounds with a fluted cutter. Use half the pastry rounds to line four 4-inch tart pans. Spoon in the raisin mixture and level the surface.

5 Arrange the apple wedges on top of the raisin mixture. Brush the edge of each pastry shell with egg or milk and cover with a pastry lid. Trim, seal and flute the edges. Cut suitable shapes from pastry trimmings and use to decorate the pies. Brush the tops with beaten egg or milk, then bake for 30–35 minutes. Serve hot, with the flavored cream.

COOK'S TIP

Flavored cream is delicious with pies and tarts. Lightly whip heavy cream, add a spoonful or two of your favorite liqueur and sweeten to taste.

PLUM *and* EAU-DE-VIE DE MIRABELLE MERINGUE PIE

A fruit brandy made from mirabelle plums intensifies the flavor of fresh fruits.

SERVES 6–8

1¹/₂ *cups all-purpose flour*

3 tablespoons cold
  margarine, diced

3 tablespoons solid vegetable
  shortening, diced

3 egg whites

6 tablespoons superfine sugar

FOR THE FILLING

12 ounces plums, pitted and sliced

2 teaspoons sugar

¹/₄ *cup orange juice*

3 egg yolks, beaten

3 tablespoons eau-de-vie de
  mirabelle

1 Make the pastry. Sift the flour into a mixing bowl. Rub in the margarine and shortening until the mixture resembles fine bread crumbs, then stir in enough cold water to give a soft dough. Wrap in plastic wrap and chill for 30 minutes. Preheat the oven to 375°F.

2 Roll out the pastry on a lightly floured surface and line a 7-inch tart pan. Line the pastry shell with foil and fill with baking beans, then bake for 12 minutes. Remove the foil and baking beans and bake for about 5 minutes more, until golden.

3 Make the filling. Mix the plums, sugar and orange juice in a saucepan. Bring to a boil, then lower the heat and simmer until the fruit is cooked and the mixture is thick.

4 Set the plum mixture aside. When it is cool, lightly stir in the egg yolks and eau-de-vie de mirabelle. Spoon the mixture into the tart shell.

VARIATION
This is equally delicious when made with strawberries and framboise or pitted cherries and kirsch.

5 Whisk the egg whites in a clean grease-free bowl until stiff peaks form. Whisk in half the superfine sugar. When the mixture is stiff again, fold in the remaining sugar.

6 Pipe or spread the meringue over the filling and bake for 15–20 minutes, until golden.

ORANGE TARTS *with* COINTREAU

These traditional English tarts combine a creamy filling with a hint of Cointreau.

SERVES 6

1¹/₂ cups all-purpose flour
3 tablespoons cold margarine,
    diced
3 tablespoons vegetable shortening
2 tablespoons superfine sugar
1 large egg yolk
¹/₂ teaspoon ground nutmeg
orange segments and thinly pared
    orange rind, to decorate

FOR THE FILLING

2 tablespoons butter, melted
¹/₄ cup superfine sugar
1 egg
³/₄ cup farmer's cheese
2 tablespoons heavy cream
¹/₄ cup currants
1 tablespoon grated lemon rind
1 tablespoon grated orange rind
1 tablespoon Cointreau

1 Make the pastry. Sift the flour into a large mixing bowl and rub in the margarine and shortening until the mixture resembles fine bread crumbs. Stir in the sugar and egg yolk and add enough cold water to make a firm dough. Wrap the pastry in plastic wrap and chill for 30 minutes. Preheat the oven to 375°F.

> **COOK'S TIP**
>
> *Farmer's cheese is a soft unripened cheese with a milky, tangy flavor. To make a large tart, use the pastry to line a 7-inch tart pan. Spoon in the filling and bake for 45–55 minutes.*

2 Roll out the dough on a lightly floured surface and line six 4-inch fluted tart pans.

3 Make the filling. Combine the melted butter, sugar, egg, cheese, cream, currants, grated rind and Cointreau in a bowl. Mix well. Spoon into the pastry shells, sprinkle the nutmeg on top and bake for 30–35 minutes, until golden. Serve decorated with orange segments and pared rind.

GRAND MARNIER PASSION PIE

Crisp puff pastry is teamed with a wonderfully creamy passion fruit and orange filling enhanced with Grand Marnier to make an unforgettable dessert.

SERVES 4–6

6 ounces puff pastry, thawed
    if frozen
confectioners' sugar, for dusting

FOR THE FILLING

4 tablespoons apricot preserves
6 passion fruits
¹/₂ cup cream cheese
1¹/₄ cups sour cream
2 eggs, beaten
6 tablespoons superfine sugar
grated rind and juice of 1 orange
2 tablespoons Grand Marnier

1 Preheat the oven to 375°F. Roll out the pastry on a lightly floured surface and use it to line a 7-inch tart pan. Prick the pastry base with a fork, then spread with the apricot preserves.

2 Cut the passion fruits in half. Using a teaspoon, scoop out the pulp and press it through a sieve into a bowl. Discard the seeds. Add the cream cheese, sour cream, eggs, superfine sugar, orange rind and juice. Stir in the Grand Marnier.

3 Spoon the filling into the tart shell. Bake for 25–30 minutes, until golden.

4 Heat some metal skewers. Dust the pie with confectioners' sugar. Holding a skewer with oven mitts, press it onto the confectioners' sugar, which will melt and caramelize. Continue to brand the topping, creating a lattice effect.

> **COOK'S TIP**
>
> *If you don't have time to brand the top of the pie, dust it with confectioners' sugar, protect the pastry edge with pieces of foil and put the pie under a hot broiler for a few seconds to caramelize the sugar.*

STICKY NUT PIE *with* DRAMBUIE

Drambuie is a liqueur that combines the flavors of whiskey and heather honey—a delicious combination in this sticky pecan and macadamia nut filling.

SERVES 6–8

2 cups all-purpose flour
8 tablespoons (1 stick) butter
2 tablespoons strong black coffee
³/₄ cup pecan halves
³/₄ cup macadamia nuts, halved
ice cream, to serve

FOR THE FILLING

3 eggs
5 tablespoons molasses
¹/₃ cup dark brown sugar
2 tablespoons honey
2 tablespoons Drambuie
2 tablespoons butter, melted
1 cup pecans, chopped
1 cup macadamia nuts, chopped

1 Sift the flour into a bowl and rub in the butter until the mixture resembles fine bread crumbs. Stir in the coffee and enough cold water to make a soft dough. Wrap in plastic wrap and chill for 30 minutes. Preheat the oven to 400°F.

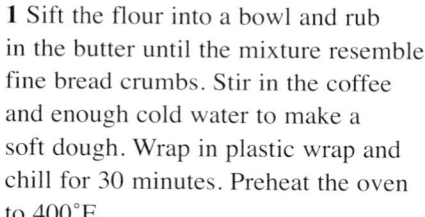

2 Roll out the pastry on a lightly floured surface to a long rectangle, 16 x 6¹/₂ inches. Lap the pastry over the rolling pin and use it to line a 14 x 4¹/₂-inch oblong tart pan.

3 Make the filling by mixing all the ingredients in a bowl. Stir thoroughly, then spoon the filling into the pastry shell. Arrange the pecan and macadamia halves in a pattern on top. Bake for 35–40 minutes, until the pastry is golden. Serve with ice cream.

VARIATION
Use hazelnuts or walnuts instead of the pecans.

APRICOT FRANGIPANE TART *with* KIRSCH

Take a light lime-flavored pastry shell, fill it with almond sponge laced with kirsch and topped with apricots and macaroons, and the result is simply sensational. It is delicious warm or cold, served with yogurt or cream.

SERVES 6

2 cups all-purpose flour
8 tablespoons (1 stick) butter
2 teaspoons finely grated lime
 rind
12 fresh apricots, pitted, some
 halved, some thickly sliced
3 ounces macaroons, crushed
plain yogurt or light cream,
 to serve

FOR THE FILLING

2 tablespoons butter, softened
2 tablespoons light brown sugar
1 tablespoon all-purpose flour
$^1/_2$ cup ground almonds
1 egg, beaten
3 tablespoons kirsch

COOK'S TIP

If you find the pastry difficult to handle, roll it out between sheets of parchment paper or plastic wrap.

1 Sift the flour into a mixing bowl, then rub in the butter until the mixture resembles bread crumbs. Stir in the grated lime rind and add enough cold water to make a soft dough. Wrap in plastic wrap and chill for 30 minutes.

2 Meanwhile, make the filling. Cream the butter with the light brown sugar, then stir in the flour, ground almonds, egg and kirsch. Preheat the oven to 400°F.

3 Roll out the pastry on a lightly floured surface to a 16 x 6$^1/_2$-inch rectangle and use it to line a 14 x 4$^1/_2$-inch rectangular tart pan. Spread the filling in the tart shell and arrange the apricot halves and slices, cut side down, on top. Sprinkle the crushed macaroons on top. Bake for 35–40 minutes, until the pastry is golden. Serve warm or cold, with yogurt or cream.

DEEP APPLE *and* BERRY TART *with* GIN-LACED CRANBERRY SAUCE

Berries abound in this exciting medley of fruit flavors given a special lift with a little gin.

SERVES 6–8

2 cups all-purpose flour
8 tablespoons (1 stick) cold butter
2 teaspoons grated lime rind
egg or milk, for glazing

FOR THE FILLING

8 ounces cooking apples, peeled,
  cored and grated
1¹/₂ cups fresh or frozen cranberries
1 cup fresh or frozen blueberries
¹/₃ cup light brown sugar
grated rind and juice of 1 lime
1 tablespoon gin
²/₃ cup water

FOR THE SAUCE

1¹/₂ cups fresh or frozen cranberries
2 tablespoons honey
2 tablespoons gin
1¹/₄ cups fresh orange juice

2 Make the filling. Put the grated apples, cranberries, blueberries, sugar, lime rind and juice, gin and water in a large saucepan and bring to a boil. Lower the heat and simmer, stirring, until the fruit begins to pulp down and is very thick. Remove the pan from the heat and cool. Preheat the oven to 400°F.

4 Spoon the filling into the pastry shell. Make a lattice top with the pastry strips, brush them with a little egg or milk and attach the flower shapes. Brush the shapes with egg or milk and bake for 30–35 minutes. Remove the tart from the oven and allow to cool in the pan for 15 minutes.

1 Sift the flour into a mixing bowl. Rub in the butter, then stir in the grated lime rind. Add enough cold water to make a soft dough. Wrap the pastry in plastic wrap and chill for 30 minutes.

3 Roll out three-quarters of the pastry on a lightly floured surface to a 10-inch round and use it to line a deep-sided 7-inch tart pan. Roll out the remaining pastry and cut thin strips for a lattice and small flower shapes for the decoration.

5 Meanwhile, make the sauce by mixing the cranberries, honey, gin and orange juice in a small pan. Bring to a boil, then lower the heat and simmer for 10 minutes. Process in a blender or food processor until smooth. Serve hot or cold with slices of the tart.

COOK'S TIP

Give color and flavor to pastry by adding grated citrus rind, ground nuts or spices.

MARSALA CUSTARD TART

The subtle yet unmistakable flavor of marsala transforms a simple custard tart.

SERVES 6–8

1½ *cups all-purpose flour*
3 *tablespoons cold margarine, diced*
3 *tablespoons solid vegetable shortening, diced*

FOR THE FILLING

3 *eggs*
2 *tablespoons light brown sugar*
1 *cup whole milk*
¼ *cup marsala*
freshly grated nutmeg

1 Sift the flour into a mixing bowl. Rub in the margarine and shortening until the mixture resembles fine bread crumbs, then stir in enough cold water to make a soft dough. Wrap the pastry in plastic wrap and chill for 30 minutes. Preheat the oven to 375°F.

2 Roll out the pastry on a lightly floured surface to a 10-inch round and use it to line an 8-inch tart pan. Line with foil and baking beans and bake for 12 minutes.

3 Meanwhile, make the filling. Whisk the eggs and sugar lightly in a bowl. Heat the milk to just below boiling point, stir in the marsala and whisk into the eggs and sugar. Cool slightly, then strain into a pitcher or measuring cup.

4 Remove the foil and baking beans from the tart shell, pour in the marsala custard mixture and grate nutmeg over the surface. Bake for 25–35 minutes, until the custard has set.

COOK'S TIP

For a luxurious variation, use light cream instead of milk.

PRUNE *and* ARMAGNAC TART

Almond-and-apricot-stuffed prunes paired with Armagnac and crisp orange pastry make for a superb tart.

SERVES 4–6

2 cups all-purpose flour
¹/₂ cup cold margarine, diced
2 teaspoons grated orange rind
FOR THE FILLING
3 ounces almond paste
3 dried apricots, finely chopped
12 pitted prunes
2 eggs, beaten
²/₃ cup light cream or half-and-half
1 cup dark brown sugar
3 tablespoons Armagnac

1 Sift the flour into a mixing bowl. Rub in the margarine until the mixture resembles fine bread crumbs, then stir in the grated orange rind. Add enough cold water to make a soft dough. Wrap in plastic wrap and chill for 1 hour.

2 Roll out the pastry on a lightly floured surface. Lap it over the rolling pin and use it to line an 8-inch tart pan. Line with foil and fill with baking beans, then bake for 10 minutes. Set the pastry shell aside. Preheat the oven to 400°F.

3 Make the filling. Knead the almond paste with the chopped apricots on a clean work surface.

4 Press a little of the apricot and almond paste mixture into each pitted prune. When all the prunes have been filled, arrange them in the pastry shell.

5 In a small bowl, combine the eggs and cream with half the sugar. Mix well and stir in the Armagnac. Pour the mixture over the prunes, sprinkle the remaining sugar over the top and bake for 25–30 minutes.

COOK'S TIP

Fill a jar with dried fruits, cover with Armagnac or eau-de-vie and set aside for a few days to make a sauce that tastes superb with ice cream or yogurt.

WHISKEY-LACED MINCE PIES

A little whiskey enhances the fruit-laden filling for these traditional, festive pies.

MAKES 12–15

1 large egg yolk
1 teaspoon grated orange rind
1 tablespoon superfine sugar
2 cups all-purpose flour
10–12 tablespoons cold butter,
 diced
beaten egg or milk, for glazing
confectioners' sugar, for dusting
FOR THE FILLING
1 cup mincemeat
¼ cup candied pineapple, chopped
¼ cup candied cherries, chopped
2 tablespoons whiskey
FOR THE WHISKEY BUTTER
6 tablespoons unsalted
 butter, softened
1½ cups confectioners'
 sugar, sifted
2 tablespoons whiskey
1 teaspoon grated orange rind

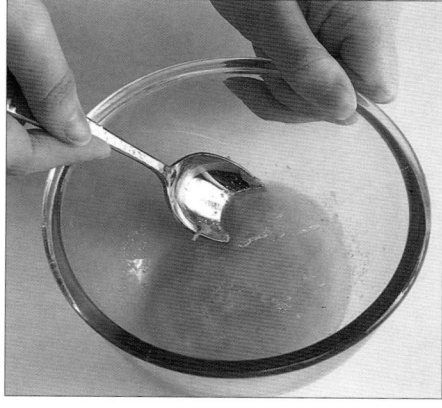

1 Start by making the pastry. In a small bowl, mix the egg yolk with the orange rind, superfine sugar and 2 teaspoons water and set aside.

VARIATIONS

Replace the whiskey in the filling and flavored butter with Cointreau, brandy or an eau-de-vie. Use puff or filo pastry instead of piecrust for a change.

2 Sift the flour into a bowl and rub in the butter until the mixture resembles fine bread crumbs. Stir in the egg mixture and mix to a soft dough. Wrap in plastic wrap and chill for 30 minutes.

3 Make the filling. Mix the mincemeat, candied pineapple and candied cherries in a small bowl. Spoon in the whiskey.

4 Roll out three-quarters of the pastry. Stamp out fluted rounds and line 12–15 tartlet pans. Roll out the remaining pastry and stamp out star shapes.

5 Preheat the oven to 400°F. Spoon a little filling into each pastry shell and top with the star shapes. Brush with a little beaten egg or milk and bake for 20–25 minutes, until golden. Allow to cool.

6 Meanwhile, make the whiskey butter by beating the butter, confectioners' sugar, whiskey and grated orange rind in a small bowl until light and fluffy. Dust the mince pies with confectioners' sugar and serve with the whiskey butter or lift off each pastry star, pipe a whirl of flavored butter on top of the filling beneath, then replace the star.

CAKES

Sumptuous cakes create an impression of luxury, but are not necessarily difficult to prepare. A special cake is an essential feature of any celebration, whether the festivity is a birthday tea or a grand affair. For a striking effect, here is a pineapple and kirsch cake that reveals dramatic spirals of cake and creamy filling. Cakes are for any occasion, of course, and gingerbread brownies with Canton ginger liqueur or Jamaican cupcakes with Malibu are simpler but still tantalizing.

JAMAICAN CUPCAKES *with* MALIBU

This popular rum-and-coconut liqueur makes an unusual and utterly delicious addition to rich sweet yeast-dough cupcakes filled with pineapple, ginger and currants.

MAKES 14–16
4 cups white bread flour
2 teaspoons ground ginger
pinch of salt
4 tablespoons (¹/₂ stick) butter
1 envelope active dry yeast
3 tablespoons dark brown sugar
3 eggs, beaten
²/₃ cup milk
FOR THE FILLING
4 tablespoons (¹/₂ stick) butter,
 melted
1 tablespoon Malibu or rum
¹/₂ cup dark brown sugar
¹/₂ cup candied pineapple,
 chopped
¹/₄ cup currants
2 tablespoons chopped
 preserved ginger
FOR THE TOPPING
2 tablespoons honey
³/₄ cup confectioners' sugar, sifted
2 tablespoons Malibu or rum
2 teaspoons ginger syrup (from
 the jar of preserved ginger)

2 Turn the dough onto a lightly floured surface and knead for 10 minutes, until smooth. Put it back into the bowl, cover with oiled plastic wrap and leave in a warm place for about 1 hour, until doubled in bulk.

3 Grease a baking sheet. Make the filling by mixing half the melted butter with the Malibu or rum, sugar, candied pineapple, currants and preserved ginger in a small bowl.

4 Roll out the risen dough on a lightly floured surface to a 12-inch square. Brush with the remaining melted butter and cover with the fruit mixture.

6 Bake for 15–20 minutes, until well risen and golden brown. As soon as the cakes come out of the oven, brush them with honey.

7 Mix the confectioners' sugar, Malibu or rum and syrup in a bowl. Stir in enough cold water to make a smooth flowing icing. Pour over the cakes and allow to set.

COOK'S TIP
The cakes should just touch, so that as they rise they join together. They can easily be separated for serving.

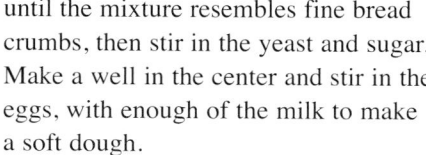

1 Sift the flour, ginger and salt into a large mixing bowl. Rub in the butter until the mixture resembles fine bread crumbs, then stir in the yeast and sugar. Make a well in the center and stir in the eggs, with enough of the milk to make a soft dough.

5 Roll the dough over the filling like a jelly roll and cut into 14–16 slices. Arrange the slices cut side up on the baking sheet, so that they are almost touching. Cover with oiled plastic wrap and allow to rise in a warm place for about 30 minutes. Preheat the oven to 425°F.

BANANA CAKE SQUARES *with* CRÈME *de* BANANE

If you like bananas, you'll love these little cakes, in which the flavor is given a wonderful depth by the addition of banana liqueur.

SERVES 8-10

3 ripe bananas
1 cup dark brown sugar
2 eggs, beaten
2 tablespoons crème de banane
2 tablespoons milk
2 cups self-rising flour
1¹/₂ teaspoons baking powder
pinch of grated nutmeg
12 tablespoons (1¹/₂ sticks) butter
1 cup chopped nuts, to decorate

FOR THE FILLING
2 ripe bananas
1 cup confectioners' sugar, sifted
8 tablespoons (1 stick) butter
2 tablespoons lemon juice

FOR THE ICING
2 cups confectioners' sugar, sifted
2 tablespoons orange juice
1 tablespoon crème de banane

1 Preheat the oven to 325°F. Grease and line an 8-inch square cake pan. Peel the bananas, place them in a bowl and mash with the sugar. Stir in the eggs, liqueur and milk.

2 Sift the flour, baking powder and nutmeg into a mixing bowl. Rub in the butter until the mixture resembles bread crumbs, then thoroughly beat in the banana mixture. Spoon into the cake pan and bake for 50–55 minutes, until cooked. Remove the cake from the pan and allow to cool.

3 Make the filling. Peel and chop the bananas, place them in a pan and add the confectioners' sugar, butter and lemon juice. Beat together over low heat for 5 minutes, then remove from the heat and cool slightly. Slice the cake in half and sandwich back together with the banana filling.

4 Make the icing. Mix the confectioners' sugar, orange juice and liqueur in a bowl and stir with a wooden spoon until smooth. Pour the icing over the top of the cake and decorate at once with chopped nuts. When the icing has set, cut the cake into squares.

GINGER *and* PEACH CAKE *with* PEACH SCHNAPPS

In the center of this moist ginger cake is a luscious layer of peaches and peach-flavored spirit.

SERVES 8

2 cups all-purpose flour
1¹/₂ teaspoons baking powder
2 teaspoons ground ginger
12 tablespoons (1¹/₂ sticks) butter
³/₄ cup superfine sugar
3 eggs, beaten
3 fresh peaches, pitted and sliced
3 tablespoons peach schnapps
FOR THE TOPPING
2 tablespoons butter
¹/₄ cup all-purpose flour
2 tablespoons superfine sugar
¹/₂ cup sliced almonds, crushed

1 Preheat the oven to 350°F. Grease and line an 8-inch springform cake pan. Sift the flour, baking powder and ground ginger into a bowl. In a separate bowl, cream the butter with the sugar until light and fluffy. Beat in the eggs a little at a time.

2 Fold in the flour and spices and mix thoroughly. Spoon half the mixture into the cake pan. Arrange the peach slices in concentric circles on top. Pour the peach schnapps over the peach slices and cover with the cake mixture.

3 Make the topping in a small bowl. Rub the butter into the flour, then stir in the sugar and almonds. Sprinkle the topping over the top of the cake and bake for 1¹/₄–1¹/₂ hours or until cooked.

VARIATION
Use nectarines or plums instead of peaches, or try pitted cherries with kirsch.

HAZELNUT *and* APRICOT MERINGUE ROLL *with* APRICOT BRANDY

A soft, nutty meringue rolled around a creamy apricot filling spiked with apricot brandy.

SERVES 6

5 egg whites
²/₃ cup superfine sugar
1 teaspoon cornstarch
¹/₂ cup toasted hazelnuts, chopped
confectioners' sugar, for dusting
apricot slices and mint sprigs,
 to decorate

FOR THE FILLING
1¹/₄ cups heavy cream
2 tablespoons apricot brandy
¹/₄ cup apricot preserves,
 any large chunks chopped
6 apricots, pitted and thinly
 sliced

1 Preheat the oven to 225°F. Grease a 12 x 8-inch jelly roll pan and line it with parchment paper. Whisk the egg whites in a clean grease-free bowl until stiff but not dry. Whisk in half the sugar and then continue to whisk until the mixture is stiff. Fold in the remaining sugar.

2 Fold in the cornstarch and hazelnuts and spoon the mixture into the pan. Bake for about 45 minutes or until set. Leave the meringue in the pan to cool, uncovered, for 1 hour.

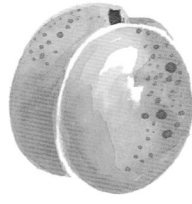

3 Meanwhile, make the filling. Whip the cream lightly in a bowl, then stir in the apricot brandy and preserves. Fold in the apricot slices.

4 Dust a sheet of parchment paper with confectioners' sugar and carefully turn the meringue out onto it. Peel away the lining paper and spread the filling over the top of the meringue.

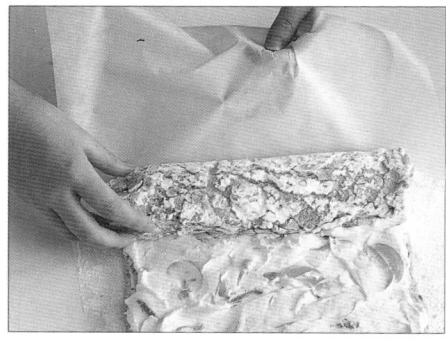

5 With the aid of the paper, and working from a short end, roll the meringue over the filling. Place the roll on a serving plate, dust with more icing sugar and decorate with apricot slices and mint sprigs.

COOK'S TIP
Add extra texture and flavor by turning the baked meringue out onto a sheet of parchment paper dusted with ground hazelnuts.

TIA MARIA CAKE

Whipped cream and Tia Maria make a mouthwatering filling for this light chocolate and walnut cake.

SERVES 6–8

1 1/4 cups self-rising flour
1/4 cup cocoa powder
1 1/2 teaspoons baking powder
3 eggs, beaten
12 tablespoons (1 1/2 sticks) butter,
  softened
3/4 cup superfine sugar
1/2 cup chopped walnuts
walnut brittle, to decorate (see
  Cook's Tip)
FOR THE FILLING AND COATING
2 1/2 cups heavy cream
3 tablespoons Tia Maria
2/3 cup dry, unsweetened coconut,
  toasted

1 Preheat the oven to 325°F. Grease and line two 7-inch layer cake pans. Sift the flour, cocoa powder and baking powder into a large bowl. Add the eggs, butter, sugar and walnuts and mix thoroughly, either with a wooden spoon or with a hand-held electric mixer, until the mixture is light and fluffy.

2 Divide the mixture between the cake pans, level the surface of each and bake for 35–40 minutes, until risen and browned. Turn out the cakes and allow to cool on a wire rack.

3 Make the filling by whisking the cream with the Tia Maria in a bowl until the mixture forms soft peaks.

4 Slice each cake horizontally in half to give four layers. Layer together with some of the flavored cream.

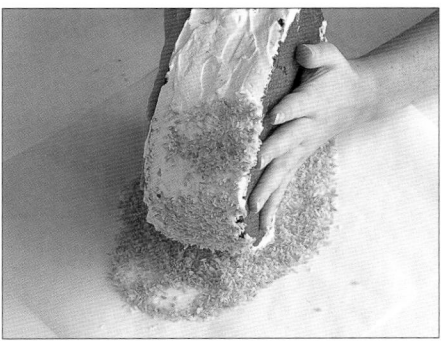

5 Coat the sides of the cake with cream. Spread out the toasted coconut on a sheet of parchment paper. Then, holding the top and bottom of the cake securely, turn it on its side and roll in the coconut until evenly coated. Put the cake on a serving plate, spread more cream over the top and pipe the remainder around the rim. Decorate with walnut brittle.

COOK'S TIP

To make walnut brittle, slowly heat 6 tablespoons superfine sugar in a pan. Then the sugar has dissolved, stir in 1/2 cup whole or broken walnuts. Turn the mixture out onto parchment paper and allow to set. Break the brittle into pieces with a rolling pin.

PINEAPPLE *and* KIRSCH CAKE

A pretty effect is created when this cake, with its creamy cherry-flavored filling,
is sliced to reveal the spiral pattern inside.

SERVES 10–12

12 tablespoons (1½ sticks) butter
½ cup superfine sugar, plus
  extra for sprinkling
2 eggs, lightly beaten
1 cup self-rising flour, sifted
2 teaspoons grated lemon rind
8 ounces gingersnaps, crushed
pineapple wedges and leaves,
  to decorate

FOR THE FILLING AND COATING

3 cups heavy cream, whipped
2 tablespoons kirsch
8 ounces fresh pineapple, finely
  chopped
1⅓ cups dry, unsweetened
  coconut, toasted

2 Meanwhile, melt the remaining butter in a small pan, stir in the crushed gingersnaps and mix thoroughly. Press the crumb mixture evenly over the bottom of the cake pan.

4 Make the filling and coating. Combine half the whipped cream with the kirsch and chopped pineapple. Spread the mixture over the cake and then cut the cake into four long strips.

1 Preheat the oven to 400°F. Grease and line an 11 x 7-inch jelly roll pan. Also grease and line the bottom of an 8-inch springform cake pan. In a bowl, combine 4 tablespoons of the butter with the sugar, eggs, flour and lemon rind. Beat until light and fluffy. Spread the mixture in the jelly roll pan and bake for 10–12 minutes, until firm and golden.

3 When the cake is cooked, turn it out onto a sheet of parchment paper sprinkled with superfine sugar. Remove the lining paper.

COOK'S TIP

Give a marbled effect to the cake
by coloring half the dough mixture with
a few drops of food coloring. Put alter-
nate spoonfuls of plain and tinted bat-
ter in the pan and swirl with a skewer
before baking.

5 Roll the first strip of cake and filling and stand it on one end in the prepared pan, on the crumb base. Wrap the remaining strips around to form an 8-inch cake. Chill for 15 minutes.

6 Remove the cake from the pan and place it on a serving plate. Spoon some of the remaining whipped cream into a pastry bag and spread the rest over the cake. Cover with the toasted coconut. Pipe swirls of cream on top of the cake and decorate with the pineapple wedges and leaves.

CARAMEL MERINGUE CAKE *with* SLOE GIN

Two crisp, flat disks of orange meringue, filled with a refreshing blend of cream, mango, grapes and sloe gin, make a delicious special-occasion dessert.

SERVES 8

4 egg whites
1¹/₃ cups light brown sugar
3 drops white wine vinegar
3 drops pure vanilla extract
2 teaspoons grated orange rind
whipped cream, to decorate
FOR THE FILLING AND
CARAMEL TOPPING
1¹/₄ cups heavy cream
3 tablespoons sloe gin
1 mango, chopped
8 ounces mixed green and black
 seedless grapes, halved
6 tablespoons granulated sugar

1 Preheat the oven to 325°F. Line two 8-inch cake pans. Whisk the egg whites in a large grease-free bowl until stiff. Add half the brown sugar and whisk until the meringue stiffens again. Fold in the remaining sugar, the vinegar, vanilla extract and grated orange rind. Divide the mixture between the pans, spread evenly and bake for 40 minutes. Allow to cool.

2 Make the filling. Whip the cream in a bowl, then fold in the sloe gin, chopped mango and halved grapes.

3 Place one meringue layer on a serving plate. Spread with the cream and fruit mixture, then place the second meringue layer on top and press down firmly but carefully.

4 Line a baking sheet with parchment paper. Put the sugar for the caramel topping into a heavy-bottomed pan. Heat gently until it dissolves. Increase the heat and cook, without stirring, until it becomes a golden caramel color and a spoonful hardens when dropped into cold water. Drizzle some of the caramel onto the paper to make decorative shapes and allow to cool and harden. Drizzle the remaining caramel over the cake. Decorate with whipped cream and the caramel shapes.

COOK'S TIP

For home-made sloe gin, layer sloes and sugar in clean jars and pour in gin to cover. Seal and label, then leave for a few months before filtering.

ORANGE CAKE *with* CURAÇAO

A rich, sweet yeasty cake full of orange flavor boosted with curaçao.

SERVES 8

8 tablespoons (1 stick) butter
1 cup granulated sugar
3 eggs
1³/₄ cups all-purpose white flour
pinch of salt
2 teaspoons active dry yeast
grated rind of 2 oranges
3 slices candied orange, chopped
¹/₄ teaspoon vanilla extract
1 tablespoon orange juice
2 tablespoons curaçao
5 thin orange slices, peel and
 pith removed
1 teaspoon honey

1 Grease and line a 2-pound loaf pan. In a bowl, cream together the butter and sugar until soft and fluffy. Beat in the eggs one at a time.

2 In another bowl, sift together the flour and salt and stir in the active dry yeast.

3 Stir the creamed mixture into the flour, add the orange rind, chopped candied orange, vanilla extract, orange juice and curaçao and mix thoroughly. Spoon the mixture into the prepared pan, then cover and leave in a warm place for 1 hour. Preheat the oven to 375°F.

4 Overlap the orange slices on top of the cake mixture and bake in the middle of the oven for 45–55 minutes or until cooked. When cooked, brush the orange slices with the honey immediately. Allow to cool in the pan for 10 minutes before turning out.

> **COOK'S TIP**
> *This mixture may be baked in a 7-inch cake pan instead of a loaf pan.*

STRAWBERRY *and* KIRSCH CHOUX RING

Kirsch and cream make a wonderful combination with succulent strawberries encased in featherlight pastry.

SERVES 4–6

²/₃ *cup water*

4 tablespoons (¹/₂ stick) butter

9 tablespoons all-purpose flour, sifted

2 eggs, beaten

6 tablespoons granulated sugar, for the caramel

generous 1 cup whole small strawberries

confectioners' sugar, for dusting

whipped cream, to decorate

FOR THE FILLING

²/₃ *cup heavy cream*

2 tablespoons kirsch

2 teaspoons confectioners' sugar, sifted

1 cup strawberries, sliced

2 Beat in the eggs, a small amount at a time, to form a dough. Pipe or spoon the choux pastry in rough balls onto the parchment circle, making a circle on the baking sheet (the balls should just touch).

3 Bake for 15 minutes, then lower the oven temperature to 375°F and cook for 20–25 minutes more. Make one or two slits in the pastry to let the hot air escape and allow to cool.

5 Make the filling. Whip the cream in a bowl until it starts to thicken. Stir in the kirsch and confectioners' sugar and continue whisking until stiff. Fold in the sliced strawberries.

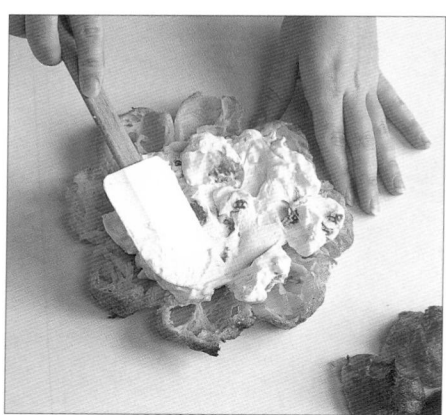

6 Slice the choux ring in half horizontally, spoon in the strawberry cream and replace the top. Dust with confectioners' sugar. Serve in slices, with extra whipped cream and the caramelized strawberries.

1 Preheat the oven to 425°F. Draw a 6-inch circle on a sheet of parchment paper, turn it over and press it onto a greased baking sheet. Put the water and butter in a large saucepan. Heat until the butter has melted, then bring to a boil. Quickly add in all the flour, remove the pan from the heat and beat vigorously with a wooden spoon until the mixture leaves the sides of the pan.

4 Put the sugar into a heavy-bottomed pan, heat gently until it dissolves, then increase the heat and cook the syrup until it becomes a golden caramel color and a spoonful hardens when dropped into cold water. Spear each strawberry in turn on a fork and quickly half-dip them in the caramel. Allow to cool on parchment paper.

VARIATION

To make chocolate choux pastry, replace 1 tablespoon of the flour with cocoa powder.

CARIBBEAN RUM CAKE

This delightfully moist fruit cake is filled with tropical fruits, rum and coconut.

SERVES 10–12

1/3 cup golden raisins
1 cup dried pineapple, chopped
1 cup dried papaya, chopped
1 cup dried mango, chopped
1/4 cup rum
1 cup (2 sticks) butter, softened
1 1/3 cups light brown sugar
4 eggs, beaten
2 cups all-purpose flour, sifted
2 teaspoons pumpkin pie spice

FOR THE TOPPING

1 cup dry, unsweetened coconut
1/3 cup dried papaya, chopped
1/3 cup dried pineapple, chopped

1 Combine the golden raisins with the dried pineapple, papaya and mango in a glass bowl. Spoon the rum over the fruit, cover and set aside for a day or just a few hours.

COOK'S TIP

If the cake mixture separates or curdles when the egg is added, just stir in a little of the flour mixture.

2 Preheat the oven to 350°F. Grease and line an 8-inch round cake pan. Cream the butter with the brown sugar until light and fluffy. Beat in the eggs a little at a time.

3 Fold in the flour and spice mixture, then stir in the soaked fruits. Mix thoroughly, spoon into the pan and level the surface.

4 In a small bowl, mix the coconut, papaya and pineapple together. Sprinkle the mixture over the top of the cake. Bake for 1 1/2–1 3/4 hours or until a skewer inserted in the cake comes out clean. Cover with foil if the top of the cake begins to brown too much. Leave the cake in the pan for 15 minutes before transferring it to a wire rack to cool completely.

WHISKEY-LACED RICH FRUIT CAKE

This classic whiskey-flavored Scottish cake is perfect for afternoon tea.

SERVES 12

1 cup golden raisins
1 cup dark raisins
³/₄ cup currants
scant 1 cup mixed chopped
  citrus peel
3 tablespoons whiskey
1³/₄ cups all-purpose flour
¹/₂ teaspoon baking powder
pinch of salt
2 teaspoons pumpkin pie spice
12 tablespoons (1¹/₂ sticks) butter
³/₄ cup brown sugar
4 eggs, beaten
grated rind of ¹/₂ lemon
¹/₂ cup blanched almonds

1 Put the golden and dark raisins, currants and mixed peel in a bowl. Pour the whiskey over the fruit, then cover and leave overnight or for several hours, stirring occasionally if possible.

2 Preheat the oven to 325°F. Grease and line a 7-inch round cake pan. Sift the flour, baking powder, salt and pumpkin pie spice into a large mixing bowl.

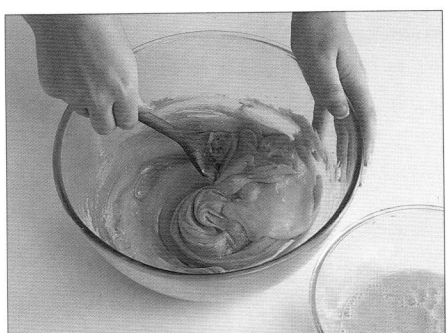

3 In a mixing bowl, cream the butter with the sugar until light and fluffy, then beat in the eggs a little at a time.

4 Fold in the flour and spices, soaked fruit and lemon rind, then stir until thoroughly mixed.

5 Spoon the mixture into the prepared pan and level the surface. Bake for 30 minutes. Remove the pan from the oven and arrange the almonds on top, then return to the oven and bake for 2¹/₄–2¹/₂ hours more, until cooked. Leave the cake to cool in the pan for 15 minutes before turning out onto a wire rack to cool completely.

COOK'S TIP
Cooking times can vary with slowly cooked fruit cakes. To test the cake, push a warmed skewer into the middle. If it comes out clean, the cake is cooked. If not, return to the oven for 10 minutes more, then test again.

YEASTED FRUIT TWIST *with* PORT

This luxurious loaf, packed with dried fruits soaked in port and spiced tea, would make a wonderful gift.

SERVES 6–8

³/₄ cup orange-and-cinnamon
 flavored tea
¹/₃ cup chopped dried figs
¹/₄ cup chopped dried apricots
¹/₃ cup golden raisins
¹/₄ cup granulated sugar
2 tablespoons port
2 cups all-purpose white flour
¹/₄ teaspoon salt
4 tablespoons (¹/₂ stick) butter
2 teaspoons active dry yeast
1 egg
milk
3 tablespoons honey, for glazing

1 Combine the tea, figs, apricots, raisins and sugar in a bowl. Stir in the port, cover and leave for a few hours or overnight if possible.

2 Lightly grease a baking sheet. Sift the flour and salt into a mixing bowl and rub in the butter until the mixture resembles fine bread crumbs. Stir in the active dry yeast.

3 Make a well in the center and add the egg and the soaked fruit with its liquid. Mix until the dough leaves the sides of the bowl, adding a little milk if necessary to make a soft dough.

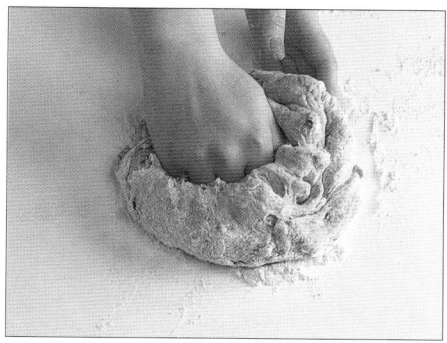

4 Knead the dough on a lightly floured surface for 5 minutes, then return it to the clean bowl, cover with oiled plastic wrap and leave in a warm place for about 1 hour, until doubled in bulk.

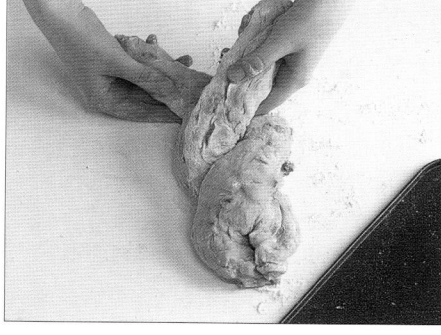

5 Roll out the risen dough on a floured surface to a sausage shape 12 inches long. With a sharp knife, cut the dough in half lengthwise. With each cut side facing up, twist the halves together. Lift the twist onto the baking sheet, cover with oiled plastic wrap and allow to rise for 40 minutes. Preheat the oven to 400°F.

6 Bake for 25–30 minutes, until the loaf is golden. Remove from the oven and brush immediately with the honey. Allow to cool, then serve in slices, with butter if desired.

SAVARIN *with* CHERRY BRANDY

Soaked in cherry brandy syrup and filled with fresh cherries, this savarin is quite sensational.

SERVES 6–8

1¼ cups all-purpose white flour
¼ teaspoon salt
1 tablespoon active dry yeast
2 teaspoons sugar
3 eggs, beaten
6 tablespoons butter,
 melted
5 tablespoons lukewarm milk
4 tablespoons apricot jam
2 tablespoons water
3 cups fresh cherries, with stems
 if possible

FOR THE SYRUP

½ cup superfine sugar
1 cup water
3 tablespoons cherry brandy
1 tablespoon lemon juice

1 Grease an 8-inch savarin mold or ring pan. Sift the flour and salt into a large mixing bowl, then stir in the active dry yeast and sugar. Make a well in the center, pour in the eggs, melted butter and milk and beat to a smooth, thick batter.

COOK'S TIP

The syrup is delicious on its own. Try stirring sliced fresh fruits into it when it has cooled, and serving it with fromage frais or plain yogurt.

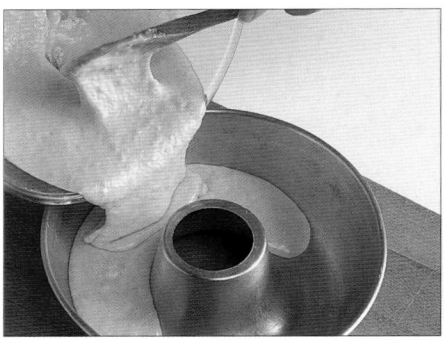

2 Pour the batter into the prepared mold or pan, cover with oiled plastic wrap and set aside in a warm place until the mixture has almost reached the top of the mold or pan. Preheat the oven to 400°F. Bake the cake for 35–40 minutes or until golden brown and firm to the touch.

3 Meanwhile, make the syrup. Mix the sugar and water in a saucepan. Stir over medium heat until the sugar has dissolved, then boil for 6–8 minutes without stirring. Remove from the heat and stir in the cherry brandy and lemon juice.

4 Turn out the warm savarin onto a serving dish and spoon the hot syrup over it so that it will soak in. Put the apricot jam and water in a small pan. Bring to a boil, stirring constantly, then press through a sieve into a bowl. Brush the glaze over the savarin, then fill the center with cherries and serve.

RUM *and* RAISIN CHEESECAKE

Spectacular to look at, and superb to eat, this light cheesecake is studded with rum-flavored raisins and surrounded by diagonal stripes of plain and chocolate cake.

SERVES 8–10

2 eggs
¹/₄ cup superfine sugar
¹/₂ cup all-purpose flour, sifted
1 teaspoon cocoa powder, mixed
 to a paste with 1 tablespoon
 hot water
8 tablespoons (1 stick) unsalted
 butter, melted
8 ounces gingersnaps, crushed
whipped cream and sifted cocoa
 powder, to decorate

FOR THE FILLING

3 tablespoons water
1 envelope powdered gelatin
1¹/₄ cups heavy cream
2 tablespoons milk
¹/₂ cup raisins
¹/₄ cup rum
¹/₂ cup confectioners' sugar, sifted
2 cups farmer's cheese

1 Preheat the oven to 400°F. Grease and line an 11 x 7-inch jelly roll pan. Also line the bottom of an 8-inch loose-bottomed cake pan. Cover a wire rack with a sheet of parchment paper. Mix the eggs and sugar in a heatproof bowl. Place over a saucepan of barely simmering water and whisk until the mixture forms a thick trail. Fold in the sifted flour.

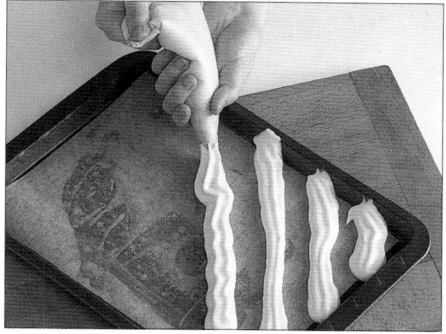

2 Pour half the mixture into a large pastry bag fitted with a 1¹/₂-inch plain nozzle, or use a paper bag and cut the end off. Pipe diagonal stripes of the cake mixture across the jelly roll pan, leaving an equal space between each row.

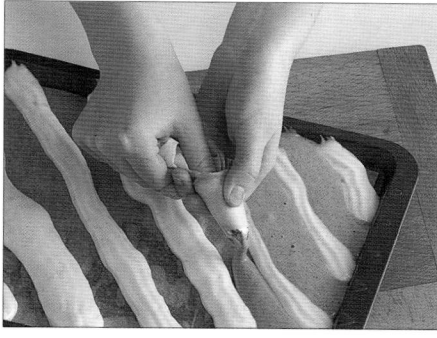

3 Stir the cooled cocoa paste into the remaining cake mixture until evenly mixed. Fill a pastry bag with the mixture and pipe as before to give rows of alternating colors. Bake for 10–12 minutes, then turn out the cake onto the paper-covered wire rack. Peel off the lining paper.

COOK'S TIP

For an instant decoration, pipe whirls of whipped cream onto baking sheets covered with parchment paper and freeze until solid. Store in freezer boxes and use to decorate desserts and cakes.

4 Mix the melted butter and crushed cookies in a bowl. Spread over the bottom of the loose-bottomed cake pan and press down firmly. Cut the cake in half lengthwise and arrange the two strips around the sides of the cake pan. Set the pan aside.

5 Make the filling. Put the water in a small heatproof bowl and sprinkle in the gelatin. When spongy, place the bowl over a pan of barely simmering water and stir until the gelatin has dissolved. Remove from the heat and allow to cool slightly.

6 Whisk the cream with the milk in a bowl. Fold in the raisins, rum, confectioners' sugar and farmer's cheese, then stir in the cooled gelatin. Spoon the filling into the prepared pan and chill until set. To serve, remove the cheesecake from the pan and trim the cake level with the filling. Pipe whirls of cream around the edge and dust with cocoa powder.

INDEX

Absinthe, 64, 91–2
  Absinthe Cocktail, 93
Absolut, 44, 46, 47
Adam, Edouard, 13, 20
Adonis, 119
Advocaat, 62
  Snowball, 62
Agave plant: mescal, 35
  tequila, 42, 43
Alaska, 66
Alexander, 21, 69
Alexander the Great, 80
Almonds: amaretto, 63
  apricot frangipane tart
    with kirsch, 223
  nut liqueurs, 88–9
  roasted cod in an almond
    crust with anisette, 154
Alsace, 27, 33, 34
Amaretto, 63
  amaretto ice cream, 208
  Godfather, 63
  Godmother, 63
Amer Picon, 17
America see United States
  of America
Americano, 17
Angel Face, 83
Angostura Bitters, 16
Anis, 64, 91
Anisette, 64
  pumpkin soup with, 130
  roasted cod in an almond
    crust with, 154
Appetizers, 134–43
Applejack, 25
Apples: apple, raisin and
  maple pies with
    calvados, 218
  calvados, 24–5
  deep apple and berry tart
    with gin-laced cranberry
    sauce, 224
  sardines with apple rings
    and cider brandy, 150
Apricot brandy, 82, 83
  Angel Face, 83
  hazelnut and apricot
    meringue roll with, 238
  Paradise, 82
  Yellow Parrot, 92
Apricots: apricot frangipane
  tart with kirsch, 223
  hazelnut and apricot
    meringue roll with apricot
    brandy, 238
Apry, 82
Aqua vitae, 12, 48
Aquavit, 14
Arak, 15, 97
Argentarium, 65
Armagnac, 18, 20
  noisettes of lamb with
    tarragon and, 171
  paupiettes of veal

with, 172
  prune and Armagnac
    tart, 227
Asparagus: asparagus with
  vermouth sauce, 188
  bourbon pancakes with, 141
Aurum, 65
Australia: liqueur
  muscats, 114

B & B (Bénédictine and
  brandy), 21
Bacardi, 38
  Bacardi Cocktail, 37
Baileys Irish Cream, 68
Balalaika, 47, 67
Ballantine's, 51
Balloon glasses, 18
Bamboo, 123
Banana cake squares with
  crème de banane, 236
Barak Pálinka, 82
Barbara, 47
Batida Banana, 84
Batida de Côco, 84
Beam, Jim, 54
Beef: pepper steak with
  chive butter and
    brandy, 166
Beefeater, 32
Beetroot: ham with Madeira
  sauce, 166
Bell's, 51
Bénédictine, 61, 65
  B & B, 21
Bentley, 123
Berger, 93
Bijou, 66
Bitters, 16–17
Black Cossack, 45
Black Forest, 33
Black Russian, 45, 80, 104
Blackout, 70
Block and Fall, 94
Blueberries, framboise
  sabayon with raspberries
    and, 208
Blunos, Martin, 47
Bols, 62, 69, 73, 82, 83, 90
Bombay Sapphire, 28, 32
Booth's, 32
Borthwick, Master, 77
Bosnia-Herzegovina,
  slivovitz, 41
Boston, 111
Bourbon, 53–4
  Boston, 111
  bourbon balls, 212
  bourbon pancakes with
    asparagus, 141
  Casanova, 113
  monkfish brochettes with
    bourbon marinade, 154
Brandies, liqueur, 82–3
Brandy, 13, 18–23

Alexander, 21, 69
Aurum, 65
B & B (Bénédictine and
  brandy), 21
brandied chicken liver
  pâté, 134
brandied Roquefort
  tarts, 143
brandy blazer, 23
calvados, 24
drunken mushrooms
  with, 194
eaux-de-vie, 26–7
fig-stuffed pork
  with, 168
pepper steak with chive
  butter and brandy, 166
ratafia, 98
sardines with apple rings
  and cider brandy, 150
sesame seed tofu with
  eggplant and, 196
Sidecar, 67
Sundowner, 105
vegetable terrine with, 198
see also Calvados
Bread: croutons, 192
  goat cheese and gin
    crostini with fruit
    salsa, 137
Britain, gin, 29–30
Brizard, Marie, 64, 69,
  82, 96
Brochettes, monkfish, 154
Bronx, 122
Bual, 111
Bulgaria, brandy, 21
Bulgur, with vermouth
  and, 179
Bunny Hug, 93
Burgundy, 34
Bushmills, 56

Cadbury's, 68
Café Noir, mocha truffles
  with, 212
Cakes, 231–50
  banana cake squares

with crème de
  banane, 236
caramel meringue cake with
  sloe gin, 242
  Caribbean rum cake, 246
  ginger and peach cake
    with peach schnapps, 237
  gingerbread brownies with
    ginger liqueur, 232
  hazelnut and apricot
    meringue roll with
    apricot brandy, 238
  Jamaican cupcakes with
    Malibu, 234
  orange cake with
    curaçao, 243
  pineapple and kirsch
    cake, 240
  savarin with cherry
    brandy, 249
  strawberry and kirsch
    choux ring, 244
  Tia Maria cake, 239
  whiskey-laced rich fruit
    cake, 247
  yeasted fruit twist with
    port, 248
California: brandy, 22–3
  grappa, 34
Calvados, 24–5
  Angel Face, 83
  apple, raisin and maple
    pies with, 218
  Bentley, 123
  Depth Charge, 25
  Diki-Diki, 97
  duck and calvados
    terrine, 140
  duck breasts with, 177
  polenta triangles with
    spiced red cabbage, 199
  Wally, 83
Campari, 16, 17
Canada, whiskey, 56–7
Cantaloupe with port, 134
Captain Morgan, 39
Caramel meringue cake
  with sloe gin, 242
Caramelized onions with
  Madeira sauce, 188
Caraway seeds, Kümmel, 81
Caribbean, 36, 84
Caribbean rum cake, 246
Carrots: vegetable rösti with
  whiskey, 196
Carthusians, 66
Casanova, 113
Catarratto grape, 113
Celery root: vegetable rösti
  with whiskey, 196
  venison steaks with
    Drambuie and, 183
Chambers, 114
Chambéryzette, 122
Champagne: Kir Royal, 71

with crème de
  banane, 236
caramel meringue cake with
  sloe gin, 242
  Caribbean rum cake, 246
Marc de Champagne, 34
Stratosphere, 70
Charente, 12, 18
Charlie, Bonnie Prince, 75
Chartreuse, 61, 66
  Alaska, 66
  Bijou, 66
  Golden Slipper, 78
  scallops sautéed with
    green Chartreuse, 158
  Yellow Parrot, 92
Cheese: brandied Roquefort
  tarts, 143
  crab and shrimp filo tart
    with pastis, 149
  French onion soup with
    cognac, 131
  goat cheese and gin
    crostini with fruit salsa,
    137
  mixed green and Parmesan
    salad with sherry, 192
Cheesecake, rum and
  raisin, 250
Cherries: kirsch, 33
  maraschino, 86
Cherry brandy, 60, 82–3
  Pick-Me-Up, 83
  savarin with, 249
  Singapore Sling, 83
Cherry Heering, 83
Chestnuts: to shell, 178
  wood pigeon and chestnut
    casserole with
    port, 178
Chicken: chicken with wild
  mushrooms and
    vermouth, 174
  poussins with bulgur
    and vermouth, 179
  whiskey chicken with
    onion marmalade, 174
  see also Liver
Chile, brandy, 23
Chilies: pumpkin soup with
  anisette, 130
  red snapper with chili, gin
    and ginger sauce, 156
Chive butter, pepper steak
  with brandy and, 166
Chocolate: Cointreau
  chocolate colettes, 214
  mocha truffles with Café
    Noir, 212
Cider, 24
Cider brandy, sardines with
  apple rings and, 150
Cilantro, tuna with olives,
  Noilly Prat and, 150
Cinzano, 122
Coates, 32
Coca-Cola, 125
Coconut: Malibu, 84
Coconut milk: Thai mussels
  with dry sherry, 152

Photographs

All photographs by David
Jordan and Janine
Hosegood (cutouts) except
pictures supplied by Cephas
Picture Library: pp. 6 and 7
Aviemore Photography; pp.
8 and 9 Mick Rock; p. 12
(top left) Nigel Blythe,
(bottom left) Mick Rock
and (right) Stuart Boreham;
p. 13 Stuart Boreham; p. 60
(top) John Heinrich,
(bottom left) Tripelon/Jarry
and (bottom right) Herve
Champollion; pp. 61, 108
and 109 Mick Rock.